AF619325

# GIRLS' EDUCATION AND EMPOWERMENT IN RURAL AREAS

Dr Pamela Dasgupta

Made with ♥ on the Notion Press Platform

www.notionpress.com

*This book is dedicated to my loving Baba*

# CONTENTS


*Acknowledgement* *ix*

*Abbreviations and Acronyms* *xi*

**CHAPTER 1: INTRODUCTION** **1**

1.1 Statement of the Problem 2

1.2 Background 3

1.3 Gender Equality and Empowerment of Girls 5

1.4 Policy Initiatives for Girls' Education 11

1.5 Incentive Schemes for Girls' education in West Bengal 15

1.6 Uttar Dinajpur – The Land and People 16

1.7 Rationale of the Study 21

1.8 Research Questions 23

1.9 Research Objectives 23

1.10 Definition of Key Terms 24

1.11 Limitations of the Study 24

1.12 Educational Implications 25

**CHAPTER 2: REVIEW OF LITERATURE** **26**

2.1 Studies Related to Status of Girls' Education and Exclusion 26

2.2 Studies on Gender Inequalities in Classroom Settings 34

2.3 Studies on Incentive Schemes and its Effectiveness 37

2.4 Decision on School Choice and Subject Choice 40

2.5 Studies on Girls Education, Decision-Making and Empowerment 42

2.6 Gap in literature 47
2.7 Theoretical Framework 47
2.8 Conceptual Framework 56
2.9 Conclusion 58

**CHAPTER 3: RESEARCH METHODOLOGY 59**
3.1 Introduction 59
3.2 Research Design 59
3.3 Population and Sample for the Study 61
3.4 Tools for Data Collection 66
3.5 Reliability and Validity 69
3.6 Pilot Study and Analysis 70
3.7 Procedure for Data Collection 71
3.8 Analysis and Interpretation of Data 73
3.9 Confidentiality 74
3.10 Ethical Dilemma 74

**CHAPTER 4: THE STATE OF WEST BENGAL: UNDERSTANDING GIRLS' EDUCATION 76**
4.1 Introduction 76
4.2 The Present Status 76
4.3 Access and Enrolment Patterns 79
4.4 Repetition, Transition and Dropout 86
4.5 Conclusion 88

**CHAPTER 5: FACTORS DETERMINING GIRLS' EDUCATION AND EMPOWERMENT 90**
5.1 Introduction 90
SECTION I 91
5.2 Profile of Parents, Students and Teachers 91

SECTION II 108

5.3 Decision-Making Process in Education and Family 108

5.4 Household Factors and Other Factors Influencing Education 136

SECTION III 166

5.5 Educational Factors: Are Schools Gender Friendly? 166

5.6 The Role of Teachers' and Principals in Gender Friendly Schools 190

5.7 Parents' Perception on Parent Teacher Meeting 209

5.8 Parent's Perception on Teachers' Home Visits 209

5.9 Parents' Perception on Challenges Which Girls Face in Schools 210

5.10 Conclusion 215

**CHAPTER 6: BEYOND THE SCHOOL: A CASE STUDY ON GIRLS IN UTTAR DINAJPUR 216**

6.1 Introduction 216

6.2 Family Background and Schooling Experiences 217

6.3 Impact of Societal Attitude on Education of Girls 223

6.4 Role of Education and Career in Economic Empowerment 228

6.5 Dominance of Patriarchy 233

6.6 Overall View 234

6.7 Summary 236

**CHAPTER 7: CONCLUSION AND RECOMMENDATION 237**

7.1 Introduction 237

7.2 Major Findings 240

7.3 Role of Family in Education of Girls 256

7.4 Linkages between Education and Empowerment 257

7.5 Policy Recommendations 258

7.6 Policy Implications of the Study 262

7.7 Scope for Further Research 262

*Notes* *265*

*References* *267*

# ACKNOWLEDGEMENT

My study is dedicated to all the girls in school, out of school and girls dreaming for a second chance of education to be an empowered individual. In this endeavour, I wish to extend my sincere thanks to my supervisor Prof. Madhumita Bandyopadhyay for her guidance, support and constructive comments at every stage of my work. Her patience and encouragement are an inspiration in my life.

My heartful thanks to Prof. Shashikala Wanjari, the present Vice Chancellor of NIEPA. I would like to extend my sincere thanks to Prof. J.B.G Tilak, Prof. N.V Varghese and Prof. Sudhanshu Bhushan (Former Vice Chancellors of NIEPA) for their constant support. My sincere thanks to our Registrar, Administrative officer and other administrative staff of NIEPA. My special thanks to Prof. V. Sirohi (Former Chairperson Steering Committee) and Prof Manisha Priyam chairperson steering committee and all the faculty members at NIEPA for their support to pursue my doctoral degree. Special thanks to Ms Rekha and other student cell staff for their support throughout my work. The library staff of NIEPA has been generous and cooperative especially Parshuramji and MS. Puja Singh.

My special thanks to Mr. Prabir Kumar Patra (District Education Officer SMSA) and Mr. Sandeep Lahiri, Mrs Shivani Mishra (Block Development Officers) and their team members for providing me support and better understanding of the geographical terrain to locate the schools and also granting permission to conduct the study. I would also like to extend heartfelt thanks to the head teachers, teachers, parents and students of the schools for their participation in this study. They cordially welcomed me to share their personal experiences, desires, thoughts and agreed to be a part of my study.

I am grateful to all my friends at NIEPA- Meenakshi, Disha, Jyotsna, Sumit, Dipendra, Aparajita, Anupam, Raunak,

Pooja, Anuradha, Vaishali, Sangita, Praveen and Vartika for their valuable suggestions. I would also like to thank my dearest friend Shaifali and Tanu for being with me.

My gratitude towards my father, Late Mr. Parthasarathi Dasgupta who silently waited for me to achieve this goal. You taught me the utmost dedication and sincerity towards work. Many thanks to my loving family especially, my mother for encouraging me and giving her precious time. My special thanks to my elder sister and brother-in law for their constant support. Thanks to my youngest cousin sister for sharing her views and suggestions. I would also like to thank my parent-in laws for supporting me inside and outside household.

My sincere affection for my guru mother (Ms. Romaika Karandikar) for her constant spiritual guidance and support in this path of life. My appreciation for my wonderful daughter Reanna who patiently waited for me, loved me and supported me in my work. Last but not the least my heartfelt thanks to the strength of my life Mr. Rajib Dasgupta (my soulmate) who accompanied me in the field trip and constantly motivated me through this tireless journey. Your comments, insights and endless love helped me in the completion of my work.

# ABBREVIATIONS AND ACRONYMS

ST: Scheduled Tribe

SC: Scheduled Caste

OBC: Other Backward Class

UNICEF: United Nations International Children's Emergency Fund

UNHCHR: United Nations High Commissioner for Human Rights

UNESCO: The United Nations Educational, Scientific and Cultural Organisation

UEE: Universalisation of Elementary Education

RTE: Right to Education

NEP: National Education Policy

KGBV: Kasturba Gandhi Balika Vidyalaya

SSA: Sarv Siksha Abhiyan

NPEGEL: National Programme for Education of Girls at Elementary Level

MS: Mahila Samakhya

DPEP: District Primary Education Programme

DHRD: District Human Report for Development

RMSA: Rashtriya Madhyamika Siksha Abhiyan

SPSS: Statistical Package for the Social Sciences

B.Ed.: Bachelor of Education

MDG: Millennium Development Goals

DISE: District Information System for Education

GER: Gross Enrolment Ratio

NER: Net Enrolment Ratio

GPI: Gender Parity Index

NSSO: National Sample Survey Office

NFHS: National Family Health Survey

U-DISE: Unified District Information System for Education

UNGEI: United Nations Girls' Education Initiative

MHRD: Ministry of Human Resource and Development

NCERT: National Council of Educational Research and Training

# CHAPTER 1
# INTRODUCTION

*"I am not a one to die easily. I have just started living. A life without dignity and choice, a life in which she can be no more than appendage of someone else, is a type of death of her humanity."*

**– Martha C. Nussbaum**

This statement was written in a letter by Mrinal to her husband in one of the stories of Rabindranath Tagore. Nussbaum has illustrated many such rich narratives in her book, of those struggling to live for their identity with respect and human dignity. Right to education and material support should be provided to women so that they are capable of discharging human functions (Nussbaum, 2000). For emancipation of women, the focus must be on increasing their achievements in education, even if education of women, in itself is essential, it is not singly sufficient to promote equalitarianism in conjugal relationships. Efforts at promoting women's education must be accompanied by opportunities for women's employment in order to enable them to be equal and effective partners (Indranidevi, 1987).

Education is one of the important constituent aspects of the social system and being part of the social system, it has multiple roles to play both at the macro and the micro levels- for individuals, groups and the societies. Some of the important roles played by the educational system are related to maintenance of the existing orders as well as to promote development-oriented change. In the light of the emerging needs and requirements of the society. It promotes control and stability in a sustainable manner. Within a broader perspective school education has an important role to play in human development and empowerment.

## 1.1 STATEMENT OF THE PROBLEM

Education is a critical indicator of status. In India raising the status of women must be a goal to be achieved through education on a priority basis (Chanana, 2006). The educational statistics since Independence show that while gender gap has indeed decreased, it is still nowhere near closing. In other words, enrolments of girls have been lower than that of the boys. Also, a majority of the out-of-school children are from the Scheduled Castes and Tribes, minorities and from rural inaccessible areas. But there are enough data to show that girls from a sizeable proportion of these are out-of-school drop-outs, working children, non-enrolled children, children of migrants and the poor, and the disabled children too. It is also true that while caste, tribe, socio-cultural and economic factors keep more girls belonging to specific social groups out of schools than boys. (Chanana 2001). However, there has been a decrease in gender gap. In the recent years the enrolment in the primary schools at national, state and district level are worth noting. 100 percent enrolment has been recorded in the primary schools (U Dise + 2021-22). The recent data (U Dise + 2021-22) indicate that GER has improved significantly above 100 percent for primary level in the states. It is disheartening to see that GER remains low for girls and boys (50.1 in 2019 to 57.5 in 2022) in higher secondary level for the states. In the last three decades there has been improvement in the female literacy rates (65.5 percent in 2011 to 54 percent in 2001). Gender Parity Index in primary school education has improved from 0.53 in 1981, 0.97 in 2011 to 1.02 in 2020, 1.03 in 2022 at the national level. At the national level GPI has improved significantly except in case of secondary and higher secondary level GPI is 1 from 2018-2022. The reason is high transition rate from upper primary to primary and elementary to secondary. It is equally important to note that dropout rate is higher in case of upper primary to elementary. It is more common among the girls belonging from Socially-Economically Disadvantaged Group (SEDG) in rural areas. There are substantial gender gaps in rural areas (16.5) and urban areas (9.4). Thus, difficult areas and socially and economically disadvantaged groups needs attention. The focus also needs to be on the effectiveness of school functioning system (Govinda and Bandyopadhyay 2021& Neeti Dutta 2022). There are nine backward states which account for 60 percent of the illiterate population Uttar Pradesh, Bihar, West Bengal Rajasthan, Madhya Pradesh, Maharashtra and Andhra Pradesh. The regional variations are more evident at the district level. Further the variations are more visible among different social economic groups and households (Govinda & Bandyopadhyay 2021). The story becomes more pronounced when other factors – location, identity, economic status, school type and gender (Ramachandran, V. 2018). It is in this context this research study has been taken up to explore the education and empowerment of girls in rural areas.

## 1.2 BACKGROUND

In the early 1970s the education of girls was an international agenda. The Education for All was adopted in Dakar Framework, 2000 stressed on girls' access to schooling, education quality and gender equality (Falkowska, 2013). The education of girls is a matter of concern and global priority raised in the Fourth world Conference on Women in Beijing, focused on education of girls, training of girls, removal of illiteracy and equality of education (Winthrop and Sperling, 2015).

Women of all ages had struggled to educate themselves. The traditional Indian women were denied access to education except for those belonging to the privileged classes of society. By the early 1920s education of women came to be a public agenda. Nehru wrote that women's movement in India has assumed a huge proportion. There was unrest among the women to bring about a change in social order. The twentieth century saw educated women leaders involved deeply in women's movement. These leaders were Sarojini Naidu, Cornelia Sorabji, Ramabai Ranade, Kasturba Gandhi and Kamala Nehru. There were four major agents who played an important role in women's education Christian Missionaries, Social Reformers of India, British Government and Foreigners interested in women's movement (Chanana, 2001). The Christian missionaries were the first to take initiatives for girl's education. The Bengal Council of Education in 1849 was advised to include female education. The Bethune school was established in Calcutta for girls. This gave impetus to setting up more girls' schools. Few social reformers promoted girls' education in this period. Raja Ram Mohan Roy rose against sati, child marriage and worked for female education. Jotiba Phule, Swami Vivekananda advocated for girl's education. The Arya Samaj, Parathana Samaj and Brahmo Samaj promoted girl's education in various parts of the country. In India, the universalization of elementary education (UEE) became a national goal, since independence. MHRD mentions, UEE promotes 100 percent enrolment and retention of all children. It involves three phases universalisation of provision, universalisation of enrolment and universalisation of retention (Islam, 2022).

In India the central and state government has been working on Universalization of Elementary education. Education has been made a fundamental right in the 86$^{th}$ Constitutional Amendment for the age group of six to fourteen years (Singh, 2018). The major initiatives taken by the central government are direct involvement of the central government with the state government at the ground level. Secondly, decentralization of governance through Panchayati Raj Institutions. Thirdly promoting community mobilization drive. The interventions taken by the central and state governments promotes enrolment, retention and learning achievements to bridge the gender gap (Govinda and Bandyopadhyay, 2011). The Sarva Shiksha Abhiyan flagship programme focusses on interventions to encourage girls to maintain pace with the boys. The special interventions were adopted to include gender equality goals-infrastructure, academic inputs, governance and incentives (Sudarshan, 2018).

The Constitution of India not only grants equality to women but also enjoins upon the state to adopt measures for positive facilitation — positive discrimination — in favour of women for neutralising the cumulative socioeconomic, education and political disadvantages faced by them. According to the 2011 census, women constitute 48.26 per cent of the total population. They thus constitute a valuable human resource of the country for the development of the socioeconomic arena and set pace for sustainable growth for the economy. The principle of gender equality is enshrined in the Constitution — in its Preamble, Fundamental Rights, Fundamental Duties and Directive Principles of State Policy. All said and done, however, the position of girls in India is at present far from being satisfactory overall. In India, in the matter of participation in education, girls lag far behind boys at all levels of education in the earlier years. The low priority with reference to the girl child is embedded in our cultural and religious beliefs that question the usefulness of investing in girls' education, particularly after completion of elementary education.

## 1.3 GENDER EQUALITY AND EMPOWERMENT OF GIRLS

The Millennium Development Goal 3 revealed that advances in the matter of gender equality had remained uneven over the preceding ten years.[1] According to informal estimates, women and children are half of world's population which mostly comprises the poor and the excluded. By 2005, girls accounted for 57 per cent of the world's out-of-school population. Despite the international recognition that education of girls is the most powerful tool for women's empowerment, gender discrimination continues to keep them out of school. In the developing regions, only 95 girls were enrolled in primary schools for every 100 boys in 2007. Equal numbers of boys and girls are enrolled in primary education in 2020. There is a significant increase in enrolment in South Asia and India in particular. The enrolment of girls in primary and secondary level has increased by 180 million. However, gender parity is evident in low- and middle-income countries and in rural areas (Global Education Monitoring Report, 2020).

While gender parity in school education for primary level has increased significantly in most part of the world, girls' participation level has declined at the secondary level in many regions. In India, enrolment of girls at the secondary level has slightly increased from 43 to 48 percent in 1990s. There are regional variations which shows their overall participation in secondary schools is among the lowest in the some of the developing countries of the world and the gender disparities are among the widest (ICRW, 2012). Although girls made equal participation with boys but male completion rates are twice more than the females at senior secondary level (Global Education Monitoring Report, 2020).

While there is a steady growth in enrolment in school education at the national level, India has also witnessed a fall in the enrolment of girls and boys post Covid 19 pandemic in states and district (Chart1.1 and Chart 1.2). It can be noted that girl's enrolment has improved from primary to higher secondary in the states. But considering total enrolment there is a sharp decline from primary to higher secondary level at the states and district. Girl's enrolment declines from primary to higher secondary level in the district, blocks and villages. Overall enrolment has improved in all the levels of school education in the last decade (U Dise + 2022).

**CHART 1.1**

**Gender wise Enrolment Ratio in West Bengal**

**Source UDise+2022**

## CHART 1.2

## Gender wise Enrolment Ratio in Uttar Dinajpur

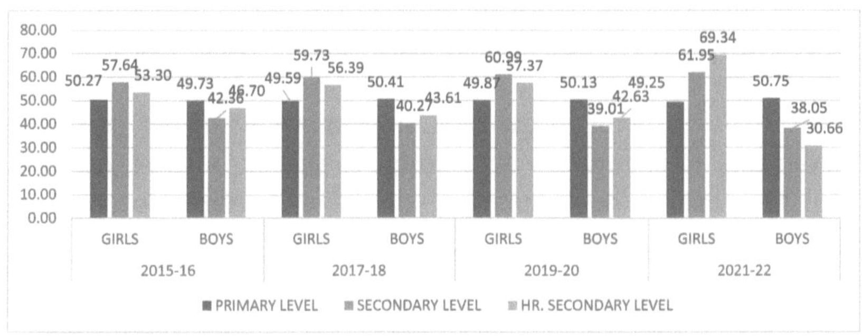


Source UDise+2022

## Table 1.1

## Dropout Rate in West Bengal and Uttar Dinajpur

| State/ District | Levels | 2016-17 | | | 2019-20 | | | 2021-22 | | |
|---|---|---|---|---|---|---|---|---|---|---|
| | | Girls | Boys | Total | Girls | Boys | Total | Girls | Boys | Total |
| West Bengal | Primary Level | 7.80 | 8.20 | 8.05 | 0.33 | 0.93 | 0.63 | 8.15 | 9.07 | 8.62 |
| | Secondary Level | 27.60 | 26.50 | 26.9 | 13.61 | 14.10 | 13.83 | 17.60 | 18.30 | 17.98 |
| Uttar Dinajpur | Primary Level | 13.80 | 14.50 | 14.2 | 0.00 | 2.80 | 1.3 | 4.30 | 5.80 | 5.1 |
| | Secondary Level | 32.80 | 35.90 | 34.19 | 24.02 | 22.40 | 23.4 | 17.60 | 18.30 | 17.9 |

Source UDise+2022

At the national level there is high dropout from primary (1.45) to secondary level (12.61) in 2022. It is observed that the dropout rate (17.9 in 2022) is also high at the secondary level in the state. It is more among the SC and ST category. It is to be noted that SC dropouts are higher at the national, state and district level. In the district dropout is equally high as the state. The table 1.1 shows that dropout rate increases from primary to higher secondary level. The dropout rate of girls is marginally higher than the boys in 2016-17. However, the dropout rate has substantially decreased over the last few years.

Education for All (EFA) assessment of 2000 and 2003 shows low transition rates from primary to upper primary and high school (Ramachandran, 2018). The transition rate is an equally important indicator to find the whether the girls get a chance as the boys to transit to the next level of education. The transition level of girls from primary to upper primary, elementary to secondary are similar to that of boys at the state level. However, it declines from secondary to higher secondary (Chart 1.3 and Chart 1.4).

**CHART 1.3**

**Transition Rate in in West Bengal**

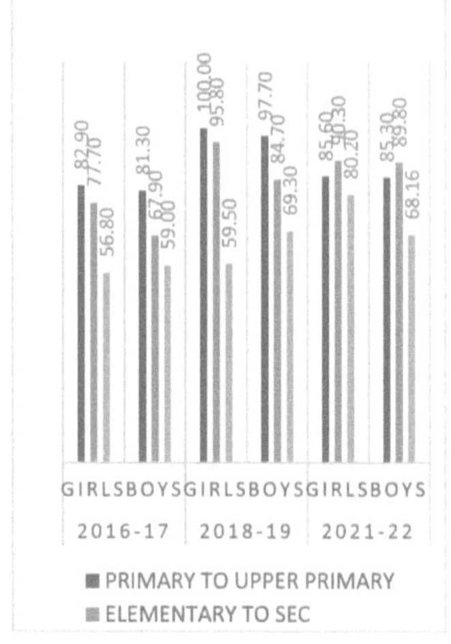


Source UDise+2022

**CHART 1.4**

**Uttar Dinajpur Transition Rate**

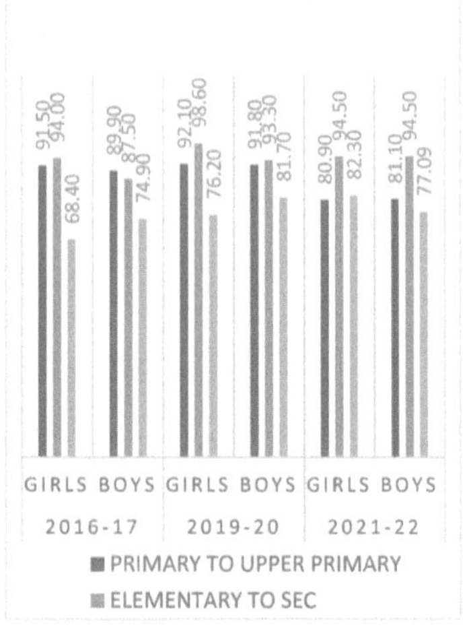


Source UDise+2022

In the district level transition rate remains lows especially for girls. It is to be noted that transition rate declines abruptly from primary to senior secondary. It is found that transition level improves from primary to elementary in the subsequent years but in case of transition from secondary to higher secondary it is negligible at the district level. The transition rate is higher at the state than the district. The transition rate declines from secondary to higher secondary among the ST category (57.7) at the district level (U Dise + 2022). It was found that there is considerable change in the transition rate at the state and district over last few years.

Thus, overall scenario shows that enrolment of girls has improved at the state and district level. But the dropout rate is equally high for girls in the higher secondary level at the state, district and blocks. It indicates that girls from socially and economically disadvantaged groups are unable to complete their schooling due to financial constraints, cost of education, dearth of higher secondary schools as well as integrated schools and preferences of sons over daughter. It shows that gender gap is high in the block level and subsequently in the rural areas.

The gender gap in educational access is wider here due to several challenges - no less because girls experience a 'density of transitions' during their adolescence due to biological changes and societal attitudes. Girls are more likely to marry at an early age and even if they do not marry, they have to bear the burden of domestic responsibilities, - often having to care for siblings and- extended family members or spending time on domestic chores. Other factors which contribute to gender inequality are household wealth, geographical location and few schools at secondary stage.

Gender inequality in access to education is also explained in the perception of the family towards the benefits and costs of education. Parents' perception of the current cost of education and future benefits also determines the size of investment in female education and in their decision about sending their girl to school. The gender gap is, at the same time, much wider among the poor families than the richer ones (ICRW, 2012). In this way household decisions have an important bearing on the education of the girls. There are a range of crucial factors in household decision-making such as who takes decisions, whether decision-making process is inclusive or authoritarian, and who and who are able to influence the household decisions (Sinha & Pankaj, 2008). Studies have shown that many fathers prefer to invest their resources in their sons in comparison to their daughters. However, the process of decision-making in household is less gender biased when mothers participate equally with the fathers, whereby daughters receive preference over their sons.[2] In patriarchal societies, women are constrained by various specific norms, beliefs, customs and values which limit their freedom of choice in every aspect of their life. Wherever in patriarchal societies women have higher bargaining power, they are more likely to participate in the decision-making process — a factor that may be relevant while examining educational decisions made for girls. These can lead to empowerment.

Empowerment is a radical approach which was articulated in the 1980s and 1990s. It emerged as a result of the feminist discontentment in the developing countries which challenged the caste and religion that plays an important role in determining the position and condition of women in India. The term empowerment in the 90's was used with pride for the process of social change, gender and better equality of women (Batliwala, 1994). In the conventional context it is a process of involving people in the decision-making process and making them aware of their own interest and benefits to enable them to influence the decision-making process (Rowland, 1996).

Education is one of the key ingredients of empowerment (Batliwala,1994). Empowerment means the power to bring about changes in a situation of inequality and discrimination. It is a process of challenging the existing power relations and of gaining greater control over the sources of power (Bandkar, 2012). The focus is on women's subjectivity and consciousness as a critical aspect of the process of change. This means the capacity of women to exercise control over and participate in the key aspects of their lives. Scholarly contributions have attached a great deal of significance to the need for women to come together collectively. The process of empowerment was seen as a collective dimension (Kabeer, 2011). Thus, women's access to educational opportunities and employment not only reduces household poverty but also improves the dynamics within and outside the household.

Women's education leads to considerable social development. Educated women engage not only in decision-making of the household but also participate in the civic affairs and attend political meetings. *World Education 1999-2000* has provided technical assistance to organisations in India to meet the needs of women who participate in the microfinance programmes. Thus, the women become active members of independent, self-sustainable savings and credit groups, and move towards making more informed choices about their livelihood activities.

The role of education in facilitating social and economic progress is well accepted. Access to education is critical for benefiting from emerging opportunities that are accompanied by the economic growth. The government of India has been working towards evolving several commissions and committees for the empowerment of the girl child. The reports and researches conducted on women best describe the status of women in India.

## 1.4 POLICY INITIATIVES FOR GIRLS' EDUCATION

The Durgabai Deshmukh Committee, also known as the National Committee on Women's Education (1958-59), made several recommendations for improvement of girls' education. These included appointment of school mothers where there are no woman teachers, schemes for awarding prices to villages with highest proportion of enrolment and average attendance of the girls, prizes to be awarded to the girls for regular attendance, help in cash and kind such as covering the cost of books and stationery, school uniform and other educational equipment to all girls up to the middle level. It also recommended free or subsidised transport facilities to be provided in order to bring middle and secondary school girls, within easy reach for them and with suitable hostel facilities.

The Education Commission (1964-66) emphasised on educating the public and working towards changing their opinion so that they shed their traditional prejudices against girls' education. It recommended appointment of women teachers in the schools, provision of free text books and writing materials and, if needed, clothing as well. One recommendation was for popularising mixed primary schools and opening separate schools for girls at the higher primary stage.

According to the National Perspective Plan for Women (1988-2000), the educational programmes need to be restructured and school curricula need to be modified to eliminate the gender bias. The school timings need to be flexible for the girls and schools need to be within the walking distance. Hence, a substantial increase was required in the number of schools for girls.

The National Policy on Education (1986) emphasised on "Equalisation of Educational Opportunities" for girls. The education of girls should receive emphasis not only on the grounds of social justice but also because it accelerates social transformation. This National Policy on Education was revised in 1992. It marked a shift in the policy perspective towards girls' education. The removal of women's illiteracy and obstacles inhibiting their access to and retention in elementary education were to receive overriding priority, through the provision of special support services, setting time targets and effective monitoring.

The 86th Constitution Amendment Bill made elementary education a fundamental right for children between 6 and 14 years of age. The RTE Act 2009 also provided for free and compulsory education to all children of the 6-14 age group. In pursuance of the above policy framework, the government has taken up various schemes to mainstream the rural girls. The National Programme for Education of Girls at Elementary Level (NPEGEL) is one such scheme which is being implemented at educationally backward blocks of 21 districts. It has additional components such as the development of model of upper primary school for disadvantaged girls at the elementary level. It also provides for incentives and remedial teaching, bridge courses and awards for girls.

The Tenth Five Year Plan (2002 – 2007) recognised the pressing need to enhance the level of girls' participation in education if the country has to achieve universal elementary education in the stipulated time frame. The Government of India also introduced a new scheme called "Kasturba Gandhi Balika Vidyalaya" to reach out to the rural girls. It was also meant to take note of the various socioeconomic, cultural and other factors which compel the girls to discontinue their education. The scheme is being coordinated with the existing schemes like Sarva Sikhsha Abhiyan (SSA), National Programme for Education of Girls at Elementary level (NPEGEL) and Mahila Samakhaya (MS). The scheme provides for reservations of 75 per cent of the seats for girls belonging to the SC, ST, OBC or minority communities; as for the remaining 25 per cent, priority is accorded to girls from the families below poverty line (BPL).

The 11th Five Year Plan (2007 – 2012) focussed on incentive schemes for education of girls in most of the states. The opening of schools exclusively for girls was due to the poor access to schools in rural areas. It also focussed on improving the quality of education and recruiting additional teachers to schools.

The 12th Plan based its strategy on mainstreaming the out of school children, reduce dropouts and improving the learning outcomes of children. It also sought to ensures gender equality in elementary education. Special focus on gender sensitive curricula, pedagogical practices, teacher training and evaluation were to be developed. The plan focussed more on expansion and strengthening of the KGBVs in educationally backward blocks due to the high migration rates in urban and semi-urban areas. The NPEGEL programmes included the opening of bridging centres and developing model schools for gender equity and quality integration. Partnership with the SSA and Mahila Samakhaya was developed to ensure increased investments in girls' education and to strengthen the local service delivery in order to ensure gender equality in basic education.

The RMSA emphasises on universalisation of secondary education. The access to secondary education can be achieved by increasing the enrolment of girls, SC and ST in various streams and by providing secondary schools within a reasonable distance of any habitation. The quality of education should be improved to ensure that no child is deprived due to gender or socioeconomic disability and due to other barriers. Vocationalisation of secondary education would enable students to be employable. The achievement of these goals is also linked with the progress of the common school system. The Central Advisory Board of Education (CABE) also set up a committee on girls' education and common school system that recommended for making good quality education at affordable fees and for more investment in public school systems.

SMSA (Samagra Shaiksha Abhiyan) policy, 2018 identifies the girls and boys from excluded from the marginalized communities to bridge the social and gender gaps. This centrally sponsored scheme identifies special focus zones to address the gender and equity issues in the country. It is an integrated scheme which focuses on quality of education, social inclusion and gender equity.

The National Education Policy (2020) focusses on equitable development for all. Special educational zones will be set up for the disadvantaged groups. It will ensure development in all the and states. It will ensure 100 per cent participation at all levels at close the gender gaps at all levels. This policy seeks to encourage the leadership role for girls. The government would encourage 'Gender Inclusion Fund' in two-stream formula grants — for provision of sanitation and toilets, bicycles and cash transfers and discretionary funds — in order to overcome local barriers faced by girls. Females will be given leadership roles — as teachers, head teachers, health workers and instructors. The policy talks of giving scholarship to outstanding girls in teacher education programmes and employing them after completion of the programme.

To policy talks of providing safety and security to girls within and outside schools, for the sake of a gender friendly environment. This would be mandatory for institutional accreditation. It also has a bicycle access programme in order to ensure safety of transportation. Social workers will play an important role by holding discussions with parents on social issues in order to improve the enrolment and regularise the attendance. The gender sensitisation training is meant to remove the gender stereotypes in society. The policy focusses more on girls from the unreserved category.

## 1.5 INCENTIVE SCHEMES FOR GIRLS' EDUCATION IN WEST BENGAL

The incentive schemes are in fact interventions by the government at the state and central levels to improve the state of education for the girls and to motivate them to continue their schooling from elementary to the secondary stage.

1.5.1 *Incentive Scheme for Girls Students of Classes IX to XII in the State of West Bengal:* As a part of these very processes, the Government of West Bengal launched a new scheme for girl students, especially for those belonging to poor families, in 2008-2009. The scholarship per month is 100 rupees.

1.5.2 *Centrally Sponsored National Scheme of Incentive to Girls for Secondary Education:* There is a centrally sponsored scheme for girl including the SC/ST girls, who pass Class VIII and enrol in Class IX in the government schools, government aided schools or local body schools. It also covers all the girls who pass from the Kasturba Gandhi Balika Vidyalaya, irrespective of caste. The eligibility criteria for the scheme are that a girl should be below 16 years of age and unmarried before enrolling in Class IX. In this scheme a sum of 3000 rupees is deposited in the name of the girl who can withdraw the amount after reaching the age of 18 years.

**1.5.3** *West Bengal Merit-cum-Means Scholarship:* This scheme is essentially for the poor and meritorious students. The total income of a girl's family, for her eligibility, has been fixed up to 80,000 rupees. The students securing 75 per cent marks in secondary examination can enrol for this scheme. The scholarship amount under the scheme is 500 rupees per month. There is no fixed quota for distribution of this scholarship.

1.5.4 *National Means-Cum-Merit Scholarship Scheme:* This scheme is for the meritorious student belonging to the economically weaker sections of the society. The students belonging studying in Class IX to XII are the major beneficiaries of this scheme. Under it, financial assistance is provided to students belonging to the low-income groups. The scheme's aim is to retain the students in school after Class VIII. Scholarship is provided to the students after the completion of the senior secondary level. To get its benefits, general category students have to attain 55 per cent marks and those of other social categories need to attain 50 per cent marks. As much as 50 per cent of the scholarship fund has been earmarked for the girls.

1.5.5 *Kanyashree Prakalpa:* According to the baseline survey conducted by the West Bengal Government, Kanyashree Prakalpa is designed to protect a girl child from the malpractice of child marriage which is still prevalent in the society. This scheme is an intervention by the government to promote the education of girls and prevent dropouts from the school. This scheme has an annual scholarship of 500 rupees and a one-time grant of 25,000 rupees after the concerned girl is 18 years of age. This grant will be given to girls who has family income is up to 1, 20,000 rupees.

## 1.6 UTTAR DINAJPUR – THE LAND AND PEOPLE

The district of Uttar Dinajpur lies between 25° 11' of north and 26° 49' north latitude; its width ranges from 87° 49' east to 90° degrees 00' east longitude. The district is spread over an area of 3140 square kilometres. The headquarters of the district are located at Karnojora, Raiganj. The district of Uttar Dinajpur is surrounded by Panchagarh, Thakurgaon and Dinajpur districts of Bangladesh on the east; Kishanganj, Purnia and Katihar districts of Bihar on the west; Darjeeling and Jalpaiguri districts on the north; and Malda and Dakshin Dinajpur districts on the south. The major rivers flowing through the district are Mahananda, Nagar, Gamari, Srimati, Tangan and Kulik. (District Census Handbook of Uttar Dinajpur, 2011).

**Picture 1.1: Uttar Dinajpur, West Bengal**

This region has flat plains and slopes towards the south. There are no hills. The district is divided into two regions: Islampur-Goalpokhar plain and Sudhani-Mahananda-Gamari plain. The Islampur-Goalpokhar plain forms the northern part of the district. Mahanada River flows through the northwest part of the district. This region is covered with old alluvial soil. This region has tropical forests. The Sudhani-Mahananda-Gamari plain lies in the southern part of the region. This region also has marshes along with the tropical forests (District Census Handbook of Uttar Dinajpur, 2011).

1.6.1 *Administration:* The district of West Dinajpur emerged before India's Independence, in fact on the eve of the Partition of India on the 15th August 1947. The main Dinajpur district of the pre-Independence days was later divided into two parts and one third was included as West Dinajpur in the Indian Union and other half as Dinajpur in East Bengal currently known as Bangladesh. West Dinajpur was further subdivided into Uttar Dinajpur and Dakshin Dinajpur Districts on the 1st April 1992 in order to upscale the level of administration in the mainland. There were two subdivisions of Uttar Dinajpur, namely, Raiganj and Islampur subdivisions having a distance of 110 kilometres from one another (Basak & Roy Mukherjee, 2014). Uttar Dinajpur has nine police stations: Chopra, Islampur, Goalpokhar, Chakalia, Karandighi, Raiganj, Hematabad, Kalaiganj and Itahar. The four municipalities are Raiganj and Kaliaganj in Raiganj subdivision. Dalkhola and Islampur in Islampur subdivision. There are nine development blocks or panchayat samitis, namely, Chopra, Islampur, Goalpokhar 2, Goalpokhar 1, Karandighi, Hemtabad, Raiganj, Kaliyaganj and Itahar. Further, the blocks are subdivided into 98 gram- panchayats and 1,516 villages (Census 2011). The panchayats function in a three-tier system. The panchayat system started in West Bengal in 1978 — the zila parishad at the district level, the panchayat samitis at the CD block level, and the gram panchayat elected from the villages at the lowest level (District Census Handbook of Uttar Dinajpur, 2011). The total number of households existing in Uttar Dinajpur district at the time the present research was conducted was 6,05,674. There were 5,32,383 rural households and 73,291 were the urban households (Cohort Study – Unpublished, Census 2011).

Uttar Dinajpur district had a population of 30,07,134. Rural population had been estimated to be 26,44,906 and the remaining population, aggregating to 3,62,228, resided in the urban areas of the district. Thus, the literacy rate is 60.13 per cent. In this district 87.95 per cent population lived in rural areas. The total number of households found was 92,046, in which 88,456 were the rural and 3,590 the urban households. The sex ratio of Uttar Dinajpur district is 936 females out of 1000 males. The growth rate of the population is 22.90 per cent. The proportions of girl child (0-6) years in Uttar Dinajpur were

16.26 per cent in the Census 2011 and 21.32 per cent in the Census 2001. The male and female literacy in the district were 66.52 per cent and 52.17 per cent (Census 2011).

1.6.2 *Livelihood of People:* Agriculture is the predominant source of livelihood. Migration from the district is high due to landlessness. The work participation rate in Uttar Dianjpur is 38.31 per cent. The female work participation rate is 23.84 per cent (District Human Development Report, Uttar Dinajpur, 2010). The district of Uttar Dinajpur is lives mainly on based on agriculture. The major crops grown are rice (namely, Aus, Aman and Boro), jute, mustard, wheat, potato, oilseeds and sugarcane. Some of the blocks of Uttar Dinajpur have high tracts of wasteland that are not suitable for agricultural purposes. Hence, these areas have been utilised for horticultural activities and tea plantation. The Aman rice is cultivated during the kharif season — from the month of July to November. The season for cultivation of Aman rice is from November to April. Another variant, Aus, is cultivated from March to July. The soil of Uttar Dinajpur is mainly alluvial, but some is of sandy-to-sandy loam type. There is higher content of organic matter in the soil. (Report of Kisan Vikas Kendra; Soil Survey Department Report, 2012)

This district has shown remarkable improvement in agricultural productivity through its strong focus on the irrigation system. These blocks are more focussed on private investments in the irrigation system. This has led to a higher agricultural growth. The fertile lands are irrigated by groundwater-based irrigation technology. This covers 96 per cent of the total cultivable land. The remaining lands have availed the surface irrigation installation facility as an alternate mechanism for irrigation (District Human Development Report, Uttar Dinajpur, 2010).

1.6.3 *Climatic Conditions:* Being situated to the north of the Tropic of Cancer, the district of Uttar Dinajpur witnesses subtropical pre-humid climatic conditions. Higher rainfall (up to 2,087 mm in a year) are witnessed during the months from June to September, often causing floods in certain areas of the district. Humidity rate varies from 64.32 per cent to 98.31 per cent. On the other hand, winters are cold and dry (Kisan Vigyan Kendra Report, Uttar Dinajpur, 2014). The winter season starts from November and continues to the end of January. The summers start from March. May is the hottest month (District Census Handbook of Uttar Dinajpur, 2011).

1.6.4 *Transportation and Communications:* The Northern Frontier Railway and National Highway 34 and 31 are the major means of transportation connectivity, linking the district with other parts of West Bengal and the adjacent areas (Basak & Roy Mukherjee, 2014). Radhikapur Express connects Raiganj, the headquarters of Uttar Dinajpur, with Kolkata, the capital city of the state of West Bengal. The total distance covered is 444

**Picture 1.2 : Raiganj Railway Station**

km. Passengers coming to Uttar Dinajpur by train have to arrive first at Raiganj and then travel to the other parts of the district. Raiganj got connected to Kolkata with the railways from 30th December 2004 via Malda (Minority Concentration District Project Uttar Dinajpur, West Bengal, 2018).

1.6.5 *Raiganj:* The total area of Raiganj is 472.13 square kilometres, of which 466.19 sq km are in rural areas and 5.94 in urban areas. Raiganj block has fourteen-gram panchayats and two census towns. It has a population of 4,30,221. According to the census of 2011, Raiganj has a literacy rate of 63.52 per cent. The dominant religion is Hinduism (97.37 per cent), followed by Islam (2.16 per cent). Raiganj has a distinguished feature — the bird sanctuary — which seasonal migrant birds visit. It is a popular tourist destination in Uttar Dinajpur (District Census Handbook of Uttar Dinajpur, 2011).

## 1.7 RATIONALE OF THE STUDY

Many of the studies mentioned in the review of literature have found that the status of girls' education in India is low, especially that of the rural girls. The girls belonging to rural areas have to face community deprivation as well as negative and suppressive forces. The situation of the rural girls in India is more disheartening as they have to face many disadvantages — because of their very gender, because they belong to villages and to poor family, and because of their caste status. All these adds to their disadvantage. Some household factors are also responsible for the lower participation of rural children, such as the care for siblings and extended family members, early marriage, child bearing, discrimination and spending significant amount of time in the domestic chores (UNESCO, 2012; ICRW 2012).

The schemes proposed for girls' education and the ground realities of implementation of those schemes shows that many children still remain out of school, which means these schemes have failed to cover all the children. Most of the policies designed to promote girls' education, while looking into issues like enrolment, retention and dropout, are conceptualised within a narrow framework. For instance, the scheme called the National Programme for Education of Girls at Elementary level (NPEGEL) looks like a loosely packaged bag of ideas without any overarching vision. Educational opportunity cannot be limited to bringing the girls to school and leaving them there. It involves the removal of mental blocks that bind them to the traditional roles. These mental blocks can be removed through knowledge made available to the girls in the process of schooling (Kumar & Gupta 2008). In other words, the policy makers and providers of education should be able to empower the girls and break the cycle of oppression. Researches from Kenya and Bangladesh indicate that the quality of teaching and gender sensitivity of the school environment influence the demand for education of girls even more than the boys.[3 & 4] However, school level factors are not the only contributors to the learning outcomes. Recent data indicate that both school and household related variables have a bigger effect on the learning outcomes in so far as the empowerment of girls is concerned. (ICRW Report).

The present study aims to explore the situation of the girls' education residing in Uttar Dinajpur district of West Bengal. It is important to investigate the decision-making capacity of girls and how education equips them with the necessary attitudes and skills to negotiate the challenging situations within their own families, within the community, market and work place. Thus, decision-making capacity plays a crucial role in the development of women as empowered adults in future. The study examines whether education influences and changes the gender role within and outside a household. This is the reason the study had to focus on girls who are currently enrolled in schools and have completed ten years of schooling.

The study was conducted in Uttar Dinajpur district of West Bengal for the following reasons: the average literacy rate of Uttar Dinajpur district is only 59.07 per cent (Census, 2011) which is the second lowest literacy in the state. The average male literacy is 65.52 per cent and female literacy 52.17 per cent.

The literacy rate of the scheduled tribe population is 28.68 per cent, out of which female literacy is a meagre 17.63 per cent (Census, 2001), and that of the scheduled caste population is 50.06 per cent, in which female literacy is 35.71 per cent (Census, 2001), which is the lowest in West Bengal. The population composition is much higher in rural areas, i.e., 87.95 per cent of the district, than the urban areas, i.e., only 12.05 per cent (Census, 2011). The average literacy rate in rural areas is much lower, i.e., 55.99 per cent as compared to that of urban areas, i.e., 80.28 per cent. In this district, the female literacy rate in rural area is much lower, i.e., 48.72 per cent than that of urban area, i.e., 76.32 per cent (Census, 2011). Out of 10 least literate blocks in West Bengal, 5 blocks are in Uttar Dinajpur. They are Goalpukur I, Goalpukur II, Karadighi, Chopra and Islampur. This region has been identified as Integrated Special Focus Zone by the government of India for the number of out of school children (Census, 2011, Basak & Mukherjee, 2014).

## 1.8 RESEARCH QUESTIONS

1. What are the factors which determine that girls would continue their education?
2. Are schools' gender-friendly in terms of physical infrastructure and academic facilities?
3. How does education influence and strengthen decision-making, right awareness and aspirations of girls?
4. What is their present status, perceptions on school education and experiences of the passed-out girls? To what extent the educated (secondary level) girls make use of their schooling?

## 1.9 RESEARCH OBJECTIVES

The following objectives were undertaken for the study:

1. To study the factors determining the girl's education;
2. To study the influence of education on different components of empowerment (decision-making, right awareness and aspirations) of girls;

3. To explore how the school education has helped the girls in their lives.

## 1.10 DEFINITION OF KEY TERMS

- *Decision-making*: It can be an act or opinion of choice. It can be regarded as a mental process (cognitive process) resulting in the selection of a particular course of action among many alternative scenarios. In the present study, decision-making has been used for the choice of school, subject and profession.
- *Empowerment*: It is self-governance, self-sufficiency and self-maintenance. It means the development of women's capacity to manage their domestic and economic environment efficiently.

  In the present study the indicators of empowerment are aspirations, decision-making ability and awareness of rights on gender equity. The terms awareness of rights has been used in the context of mobility, freedom of speech, early marriage and right to education. The term aspiration has been linked to higher education, profession and social dignity.
- *Gender*: It is a socially constructed phenomenon as distinct from the biological ones.

## 1.11 LIMITATIONS OF THE STUDY

The main limitation of this study, as it was felt, concerned the time spent in field research. A study which deals with different aspects of human life, particularly a girl's life within a rural community, requires much more acquaintance with the social climate of that place. It could have been more revealing if the researcher had conducted an ethnographic study through a long and continuous stay in the villages. Also, the study did not use a representative sample and was conducted in one district of the state, and hence the results may not be generalisable for the whole population of Uttar Dinajpur.

The study did not focus on the economic factors and the researcher did not collect data on the household incomes and expenditures. As a result, economic data on the expenditures on education in private schools have not been focussed.

Observations of every sampled school as a unit were conducted to know the gender dimension but no direct classroom observations were conducted as they would have produced an artificial result. All the classrooms were observed by the researcher from outside. This enabled the researcher to understand the behaviour of a teacher in class and reflected on the classroom activity. The activities and behaviour patterns of the girls and boys were observed and focussed group discussions were also conducted for a triangulation of the results. The present study focussed on government and private schools and hence madrasa and other management schools were not included.

## 1.12 EDUCATIONAL IMPLICATIONS

The study seeks to develop an understanding of the educational situation of girls and how they are able to sustain in the education system. It may enable us to know the impact of education on their decision-making capacity in the larger society. The study also reflects the parents' motives and choices with respect to the education of their children, both sons and daughters. It may help us to assess the school environment and spread gender sensitisation, resulting in a raising of the enrolment of girl. Listening to the local people an invaluable way of identifying the factors and constraints that affects the girls' education and promotes effective learning. It is expected that the findings will benefit the policy makers to gain insights into the impact of their policies and suggest measures to overcome them.

# CHAPTER 2

# REVIEW OF LITERATURE

The review of literature traces the hurdles faced in the path of girls' education and helps to understand the reasons for low literacy rates among the girls of Uttar Dinajpur in particular. It is evident that educated girls' have a significant position in family and society. Education plays a positive role in improving the status of women (Ramachandran-India Education Report). The review of literature has been categorized under broad themes.

## 2.1 STUDIES RELATED TO STATUS OF GIRLS' EDUCATION AND EXCLUSION

In developing countries girls from disadvantaged groups face various discriminations in society and institutions. Warner et.al (2012) highlights that in most parts of the world education at primary level has increased and girls' participation at secondary level has declined in many regions. Women's education has been a major policy in most of the developing countries over decades. There are persistent gender gaps in the developing countries which leads to low level female education and enrolment (Hill & King, 1993).

There are persistent gaps in female literacy has narrowed down over the years but male literacy is higher (Govinda and Bandyopadhyay, 2021). Globally the enrolment of girls has risen three times in primary and secondary level from 1995 to 2108. In South and Central Asia girls' enrolment has increased 47 percent. There are equal number of boys and girls in primary and secondary level in 2018. Subsequently gender parity has rose in primary and secondary education. However, the intersection of gender with external factors impacts the gender parity such as school attendance, low-income groups and rural areas (Global Education Monitoring Report, 2020). Global Education Monitoring Report identifies various reasons of exclusion of learners from school such as gender, poverty, location and religion. These exclusions can be removed by collecting data from households rather than schools. The school data focuses on enrolled children and children not attending schools. There is a huge chunk of non-enrolled children which is missing from the surveys. The data of non-enrolled children have been collected from household survey post Covid 19 pandemic. These data highlighted the inequities in the education system. It shows that female literacy and overall literacy of the population remains low in poverty stricken and rural areas (Global Education Monitoring Report: Inclusion and Education, 2020).

ANTRIEP Newsletter (2016) focuses on addressing issues related to gender equality in school education. In India the status of girls' education can be better understood through the interplay of social inequalities and gender relations. Although 98 percent of girls have access to schools. The scenario changes when it comes to upper primary to secondary and high school the access goes down as the number of schools are less. The gap increases from 50 percent in primary to 71 percent in secondary (Ramchandra, 2018). NFHS 5 data focuses on non-enrolled girls above 6 years of age is 82.5 percent in urban areas and 66.8 percent in rural areas. NFHS 4 data reflects 80.6 percent in urban and 63 percent in rural areas have non-enrolled girls. Recent data shows only 33.7 percent from rural areas has completed 10 years of schooling. The average women literacy in urban areas is 81.4 percent and in rural areas is 61.5 percent (NFHS5). A recent study on the state of Kerala with highest literacy of 100 percent shows that there is inadequate educational record of the fisherman community. It is found that only 6 percent of the fisherman population has literacy. Female literacy was found to be lower within this community (Ramachandran, 2016). The gender inequality education can be assessed through the number of girls and boys continue their education. In the national level the average dropout rate has increased from 20.1 in 2014 to 22.1 in 2017 at the secondary level (Bandyopadhyay, 2018b). Recent data indicates that overall dropout rates have decreased in India and the states. However, the dropout rate is high at all levels of education in the states and the blocks 1.4 in primary to 12.6 in secondary education. The proportion of dropout is higher among the girls belonging from ST and SC community (U Dise + 2022). A study of Uttar Dinajpur shows that dropout rate is high in the blocks 27.5 percent in Raiganj Municipality. It is more evident among the SC, ST and Muslim community. The reasons behind dropouts of girls are lack of elementary and higher secondary schools, financial constraints, children not interested in studies, unavailability of clean toilets, household work and parents do not spend on education of girls. The government do not provide free education after elementary level also leads to dropout of girls (Paul, 2018). The girls belonging from socially and economically disadvantaged groups in rural areas are more deprived. In West Bengal there is lack of data on the percentage of Muslim women in higher education. In case of school education there are a considerable number of girls enrolled in primary and secondary level in the West Bengal Board. This is because the schools provide meals which are an attraction to the poor families. The parents withdraw girls from school post-secondary level: as government provides free education up to elementary level, lack of schools and financial problems (Siddiqui, 2016). Thus, literacy of population depends on location, gender, poverty, social class and category, number of schools at different levels, infrastructure of schools, cost of education, parents interest, preferences of son's education over the daughter.

In India, the progress of girls' education is existing but not at a good pace according to the surveys conducted by NCERT 1993-94 estimated that 70% of out of school children are girls (NCERT 1998). It also focuses attention on policy makers and effective leadership to ensure sincere implementation of governments policies after fourth world conference of women in Beijing. It also mentions the rural and urban and age- wise differences in enrolment the government needs to take to promote the education of girls (Ramchandran,1998). The access and equity are two important factors in universalization of elementary education (UEE). All the programmes and strategies were adopted for bridging the gender gaps for girls, Scheduled Caste/Scheduled Tribe children, under privileged children, minority groups and children from unreachable areas. The data suggests that girls transition rate of girls are below 60 percent in Bihar, Jammu and Kashmir, Uttar Pradesh and Rajasthan. It is evident from data that gender gaps are present at higher grades in rural and urban areas. The girls attending schools from rural areas are 68 percent and 81 percent of girls are attending schools from urban areas. The gaps become wider when compared with girls of rural areas with boys of urban areas (Bandyopadhyay and Subrahmanian 2008). The states like Bihar, Madhya Pradesh, Orissa, Rajasthan, Uttar Pradesh and West Bengal have highest proportion of never enrolled children. The number of females who have never attended schools are highest (Govinda and Bandyopadhyay 2011). The UNESCO report mentions that gender disparities and inequalities in education increases at the secondary level.

The women constitute half of the total population in the country. But the degree of their participation in different walks of life has either been limited or has been invisible. Education has positively affected different demographic variables pertaining to women. She analysed that the educational policies framed around universal education and non-formal education have a big drawback in the entire approach. The models are generally those of western democracies, which hardly fit the Indian socio-cultural and socio-economic milieu (Chaudhary, P 1995).

In this context N Paul (2008) examined the historical context of the problem of declining status of girl child during the Brahmanical period when several restraints were imposed on them, restricting their mobility and confining them to the domestic spheres. When, towards the end of the 19th century, the need for education of women was realised, the government examined the position of the girls with regard to the discrimination faced by them in getting enrolled and attending schools, while the problems were found rooted in the wider socio-economic and cultural contexts. Therefore, the government evolved several policies to improve the accessibility of education. The researcher asserted that the right to education is the first aspect of the issues of gender equality. The performance of duties as well as obligations by the government, in respect to the rights relating to the attainment of the education, arising within the human framework, must therefore be made mandatory.

Chanana (2006) emphasised that the exclusion of girls from elementary education would continue as long as schools are sites for maintenance of gender identity and inequality with the active support of educational policies and programmes. She argued that all education reproduces the stereotypes, and that the Indian educational policies, supposedly designed to promote education of girls, are not to be accepted to be change agents since they are conceptualised within a narrow framework. The main focus of this paper is on analysing the educational policies, how educational policies are constructed around the traditionally determined social roles of women, even when it overcomes the social roles of women, as was the case of National Policy on Education as the basic frame; in fact, the final text of this document does not circumvent this thinking and, further, there is hardly any policy analysis from a gender perspective. Still further, Chanana describes the persistent gender gap in education which indicates that policies have not been implemented realistically. There is discrimination at the implementation level where girls receive fewer and lesser benefits from various schemes as the education system is not able to reach out to all the children, especially girls.

The girls from Scheduled Caste and Scheduled Tribe category are doubly disadvantaged due to their social status and gender. They also face cultural and physical isolation. The transition from upper primary to elementary is low. The dropout rate of girls scheduled caste girls are 60 percent and scheduled tribe girls are 67 percent. These girls do not prioritize their education for family and social roles (Sedwal, M. and Kamat, S 2011). Poverty is one of the major factors for exclusion of children, poor parents are unable to educate their daughters due to economic constrains (Unterhalter, 2007). There are nearly seventy percent girls out of school which form socially excluded groups. The proportion of out of school girls are higher than the boys (Lockheed, 2010).

It is evident from the research conducted by Dunn, D (1993) on gender inequality and education. The focus of this study is on the situation of women in scheduled caste and scheduled tribes- groups which are referred to "weaker sections of people" and granted special safeguards and concessions under Indian Constitution. Women in these under-privileged groups are disadvantaged as their minority group status interacts with India's patriarchal culture to produce deplorable living conditions. Drawing from both ethnographic and statistical sources, the paper presents a descriptive profile of scheduled caste and tribes women's status in Indian society. Under Indian census data, the study document reveals the extreme degrees of gender inequality among the scheduled groups. This study suggests that socio-economic development serves to reduce the disadvantage of schedule group of women relative to men. Ramachandran (2001) states that the enrolment status of scheduled caste boys and girls are low in Gujrat, Rajasthan, Maharashtra and Bihar. The percentage of girls who were never enrolled in schools are also higher among this group.

In Uttar Dinajpur, the social composition of the blocks determines the levels of human development as it is evident from the different literacy levels of various communities in these regions. Uttar Dinajpur has a high concentration of weaker social communities such as the Scheduled Castes, Scheduled Tribes and Muslims. Raiganj depicts a highly uneven concentration of social communities as the bulk of population belonging to the general communities is much lower than in the other blocks. The literacy attainment of this block is uneven due to the high presence of diverse social communities. The literacy levels are lower among the Muslims and Schedules Tribes. There exist glaring literacy differences between the Scheduled Castes (49.2 per cent) and Scheduled Tribes (39.8 per cent) in the Raiganj block; it is still lower in case of the Scheduled Tribe females (23.3 per cent) compared to the Scheduled Caste females (34.4 per cent) in the rural blocks of Raiganj (DHRD Report 2010).

Ramchandran (1998) emphasises on the issues which influence the education of girls such as systemic issues, content of education, economy, society and cultural issues. These systemic issues include the problems of access, quality of schools and motivation of teachers. The problems of content and process of education are gender stereotyping, perception of gender bias and economical and societal issues are poverty, powerlessness, status of women and domestic chores. G. Sandhya Rani (2010) conducted a similar study on the status of women's education in India and different provisions for improving the situation of women's education. The findings of the research suggested that different international and national initiatives have been made to promote girls' education but social discrimination and economic exploitation, occupation of child in household chores and the absence of female teachers in schools are the main barriers in this regard.

The Indian Sponsor Foundation Report by A. kumar, et.al (2007) focuses on the education of girls in Delhi slums. It is survey carried out to understand and estimate number of children in school and out of school in the under privileged areas of Delhi. It emphasises on gender gap, poverty gap and caste gap with respect to educational attainment. The survey indicates that gender gap exists primarily due to cultural and socio-economic constrains and can be reduced through awareness campaigns, child care centres, direct incentives and hiring of more female teachers etc. Poverty affects whether children enrol in school, stay in school and how much they learn in school. The survey found that poverty was the most important reason for children dropping out of school. Parents cannot bear the direct and indirect costs of schooling. Direct costs include expenses such as cost of text books, private tuitions, transport to school and school uniform etc. indirect costs include child labour and other household responsibilities. Due to these reasons parents do not send their child to school and girls provide domestic help. Therefore, socialization of girls and gender-based division of labour determine whether girls will be sent to school, for how long and why.

A Nuna (2003), in her remarkable study, attempted to bridge the gender gaps in education in general and in higher, technical and professional education in particular. A total of 250 households were surveyed to ascertain the perceptions of parents and girls regarding gender disparities in higher education and the urban-rural disparities that exists in girls' education. The participation of rural girls is comparatively lower than the urban girls in higher education due to poor availability of and accessibility of higher education institutions. Girls in rural areas generally opt for arts stream because of the non-availability of women science teachers. At the graduation level, girls opt for common subjects in which job opportunities are very few. Besides the sociocultural constraints, the non-availability of higher secondary schools too leads to drop out of 65 per cent of girls before completing their 12 years of schooling. Parents find it hard to support girls' education if resources are not available within the village boundary. The Global Monitoring Report (UNESCO 2004) highlights the role of gender in access and participation. The participation depends on various factors such as regularity of school attendance, the teaching and learning process, how much the learn through this process. It also focusses on their retention in schools. The schools should give more importance to creativity and development of skills, knowledge and values to be responsible citizens along with development of cognitive skills. There are various other factors which come to interplay in the context of access and participation.

Dreze and Kingdon (1999), in their study on participation of children in rural India, found that the probability of school participation of both boys and girls increases with an increase in parents' education. The study found that education of mothers largely determines the education of girls. The increase of girls' enrolment depends upon the relative importance that parents attach to the education of girls. Another study by Rena (2007) on the factors affecting the enrolment and retention of children at primary level in a village of Andhra Pradesh found that gender disparity continues to exist in elementary education in entire rural areas of the state. Girls in rural areas continue to be discriminated against by the parents --- first with respect to enrolment in schools and later in providing them higher as well as better education. The study found that girls were forced to take up household responsibilities or economic activities at a younger age when compared to boys. The study recommends providing gender sensitivity to parents and that must be an integral part of the programmes meant for development of poor families. Parents of girl children must be encouraged to enrol their offspring in schools and must be prevented from withdrawing their children from school before completion of their education.

## 2.2 STUDIES ON GENDER INEQUALITIES IN CLASSROOM SETTINGS

There are several studies deals with the number of schools, infrastructure enrolment and pupil teacher ratio however we tend to overlook the actual teaching learning happening in classrooms. Meaningful access is not only to participate and enrolling school system but to engage them in quality education. Right from the time the children enter school. It should provide safe learning environment. It also includes individual support to children by teachers to keep up with the pace and space to express their own feelings, opinion and identity without the fear of discrimination (Ramachandran 2018).

Warner et.al (2012) revealed that attending school does not equate to learning or gaining skills. There is abundant data to show that many children are leaving schools without having acquired the basic knowledge, skills and competencies amounting to global learning crisis. More importance should be given to gendered aspects of school quality, including teachers' attitude towards female students, gender responsive textbooks and materials, supportive and empowering classroom environment.

Similarly, enrolment and completion rates only tell a part of the story of educational attainment. Simply attending a school does not mean learning and gaining skills required to live healthier and more productive lives (ICRW, 2012; UNESCO, 2012). The generally available data tell us very little about the quality of the learning environment and what is being taught or learned in classrooms. The inequalities that influence girls and women's lives in the wider society often get compounded with the learning content, pedagogies, textbooks and learning environment once girls arrive in schools.

The UNGEI Report (2008) suggests that school quality has a stronger impact on girls' education than on boys' education. It was observed in many countries that school learning environment favoured boys over girls --- for such reasons like the lack of female teachers, unfavourable treatment of girls in the class, sexual harassment by male teachers or students, bullying, curricula or textbooks favouring adult role models only for boys. It looks into a number of quality indicators from gender perspective to assess quality.

It becomes more evident from the DPEP reports analysis of the classroom activities in local district schools. The study included 14 districts in eight states. The findings reveal that teachers' cultural backgrounds and traditional mindset often lead to biased attitudes towards children. However, the bias may be unintentional though, when communicated to the class, it strengthens the social indifferences. Lack of openness to the new pedagogy is clearly reflected among the teaching community, especially among the aged and senior teachers. It was reported that most schools lacked basic infrastructure amenities and had only a few classrooms. Toilets and drinking water facilities were absent. The report reveals problems with regard to social equity and gender discrimination:

1) Separate seating arrangement for boys and girls in all the schools,
2) Formation of separate groups during class activities,
3) Biased teachers using a language that creates consciousness of the gender distinctions,
4) Providing opportunity to one group in preference to another,
5) Group leaders from one category only.

Thus, the prevailing social inequality affects all children, especially the poor girls, rather than children from privileged group who can opt to move from government to private schools (Ramchandran,2004).

In a recent study (Srivastava 2022), indicate that boys are given more opportunities of interaction in classroom settings than girls. This gives the boys a dominant position in the classroom provides them with a learning experience fostering their confidence inside the classroom. The girls remain marginalized from the process of participation and teaching learning. It has been observed that boys are more appreciated and girls remain inactive in the process of participation. This low participation leads to invisibility in classrooms. The girls face learning difficulties due to less feedback from the teachers.

This study is further supported by Majumdar, M & Mooji, J (2011) work explores the picture of interactions within the classrooms in the village schools. Classrooms are relational spaces that are fundamentally influenced by the relationship between teacher, students and amongst the students. It was observed in Kurnool that boys and girls of Grade I occupied different places in the classrooms. Boys and girls were given different extra-curricular work from the teachers reinforcing gender-division of labour. The findings from data showed higher enrolment figures of boys than girls. Mostly boys are enrolled in private schools and girls are over represented in minority language schools such as Urdu and Kannada language schools in Andhra Pradesh.

The ideology of equal opportunities has been challenged by Arnot (2002) who reflects on the hidden curriculum frameworks which promotes education as preparing a person for life which is more inclined towards patriarchy. The hidden curriculum defines the world of work is primarily for boys and world of home is primarily for women. The working women should consider their work as secondary and more focus be on domestic life. Thus, provision of schooling mainly focussed on domesticity.

The context of women's education was related to the social context in the pre-independence era. The curriculum was framed to traditional role of women in society. It was discussed that girls mostly did not take up a job after completing schooling their job would be confined to play the role of mothers and housewives after completing their education. Thus, there was a desire for change in curriculum in the pre independence era. The feminine subjects were home science, needle work, hygiene and music and physics chemistry and mathematics became masculine subjects (Chanana, 2001). The hidden curriculum of government schools is the poor infrastructure facilities which the teachers endorse (Sedwal & Kamat 2011).

## 2.3 STUDIES ON INCENTIVE SCHEMES AND ITS EFFECTIVENESS

Many studies indicate the multiple strategies for girls' access and participation. Several incentive schemes have been promoted by the government of India. Such schemes are for the empowerment of girls. A centrally sponsored scheme is Beti Bachao and Beti Padhao. This scheme enabled girls to be educated and nourished without any discrimination (Paul, 2018). Another centrally sponsored scheme was Sabla for empowerment of women through education, life skills, nutrition and health (Paul, 2018).

Similarly other schemes like Kanyashree Prakalpa were aimed to improve the condition of school going girls. This scheme provides financial support to the socially and economically disadvantaged girls by giving annual scholarship and one time grant to the unmarried girls after enrolling in a university (Ghara & Roy, 2017). The KGBV scheme was launched for rural and socially and economically disadvantaged girls. The scheme included textbooks, scholarship for girls and residential facilities (Bandyopadhyay, 2018). One of the major reasons for enrolment of tribal children was that they get admission in schools and hostels easily and the delays in getting incentives such as clothes, scholarships and textbooks, etc., do not seem to bother them much. The delay in the supply of facilities and incentives has been very well documented in a study by Sujatha (1987): "The incentives provided by the Welfare Department do not reach the secondary school students in time." However, it was found that there were difficulties in implementation of such schemes. The functions of Kasturba Gandhi Balika Vidyalaya (KGBV), focussed on the problems impeding the overall development of girls. In this regard the scheme needs to be given a second chance for mainstreaming rural girls belonging to social and deprived backgrounds (Kumar & Gupta, 2008). The policy scheme for the purpose of implementation was examined in three KGBV schools located in the rural villages of UP, India. The observations and interviews with the teachers to analyse the educational opportunities and increase participation of educationally disadvantages girls. The major concerns were the lack of female teachers, lack of educational provisions after elementary level and inadequate budget for medical treatment. In spite of all these constraints, the scheme is beneficial for the girls and provides them education (Watanabe, 2009).

A study was conducted which focussed on the functioning and effectiveness of scholarships and incentives intended for girls and children of the disadvantaged communities. It uncovered issues such as monitoring and implementation of the schemes and incentives. The scholarships did reach the needy population, but the study also complained that they did not cover all the needy children. In most cases, incentives in the form of food were more effective in increasing the girls' enrolment and attendance (Acharya, 2006). Similar study was conducted on the conditionalities and procedures of registration under these schemes. There was a lack of field monitoring of the schemes in some states and a lack of coordination between different states. It adversely affected the implementation of programmes regarding health, education and social welfare. The implementing officers complained that they were not receiving the required support, and this was resulting in delays and difficulties. In most of the schemes, the involvement of the local panchayat, NGOs and women's groups was limited (Sekhar, 2010).

Another study conducted by the CERID, a research centre for educational innovation and development, aimed at identifying the gaps in the programmes designed for girls and educationally backward children. It also suggested measures for improvement in enrolment and retention as well as future strategies for the education of girls and disadvantaged groups. A major finding of this research was that the participation of girls and disadvantaged children was low because parents wanted their daughter to get married rather than sending them to school. The incentive schemes did not cover all the girls because the incentives were distributed on the basis of a survey list. The names of many of the girls were missing from the survey list, and all the disadvantaged girls did not receive incentives because only the school going ones were taken as eligible for incentives.

These incentive schemes had very less payment and it could not meet the income lost through school attendance for a child who had been previously employed. The parents responded to the economic incentives for enrolling their children, but these responses varied by gender. It seems that the more effective programmes focussed on girls were needed in order to close the gender gap (Arends, 2007).

## 2.4 DECISION ON SCHOOL CHOICE AND SUBJECT CHOICE

The choice of school and subject is an important factor that impacts their decisions regarding further educational possibility. The choice of school depends largely on who has access to what kind of schools. Research study from West Bengal have shown that government schools cater children from poor socio-economic background and girls. The study discusses the access to private school is more for girls and boys from privileged background. This has led to great demand for flourishing of private sector schools and lack of facilities in government schools. Aggarwal (2000) emphasised that children from privileged background especially boys enrol in private schools and a huge proportion of girls and socially disadvantaged groups goes to government schools. Many studies have been found on gender and school choice. It has been found the middle- and rich-income groups prefer to send their children to girls' school. This is due to the fact that education and environment in government schools have declined. It is by law that government school appoint qualified teachers and private schools appoint unqualified teachers. The demand for private school is more due to two reasons firstly, poor infrastructure in government schools and secondly, medium of instruction is regional language and English is introduced in later grades (Sedwal and Kamat, 2011, Kingdon, 1996).

Majority of parents prefer sending their sons to private schools over their daughters. (Dreze, J. and Kingdon, G. 1999) describes the schooling situation of girls in rural India. It discusses the availability of private schools are less and children from socially weak background are excluded. Parental interest in sending their sons to school is more than daughters and they mostly complain about low teaching levels in government schools. Another study discusses says parents do not invest in daughter's education as they get married and prefer to invest on their sons who will stay for lifelong with them. They also perceived that enrolling girl to school is a negative investment (Hunte, 2005). Parents invest less on girls' education. There are diverse reasons for not investing in education the under value of female labour, they are primarily associated with domestic work and the idea that female education brings low returns. The gender gap in schooling is less at the primary level and more at secondary and higher secondary level (Bandyopadhyay & Subrahmanian, 2008).

Studies have shown in educational choices of girls and boys social environment plays an important role in the choice of discipline. Girls tend to choose non science and boys science and mathematics discipline in senior secondary level not only for higher education but choice of career which is guided by the traditional gender roles. It was found in the article that boys made subject choices based on occupation and higher education. Girls are household makers and their choice of subjects are more feminine (Vleuten et.al. 2016). According to Arnot (2002), the academic disciplines has been questioned in order to understand their gender. Few subjects in school appear to be feminine and masculine. The answer to the question is based on the employment of men and women in labour market. He ascertains how the child learns division of labour with family. This concept is further strengthened in school where the curriculum stresses on gender codes introduced by Bernstein theory- categorise of masculine and feminine and power relations between them. In the bourgeoise culture the mental labour is related to males and physical labour to females. These were the gender codes followed in the school system. In case of working-class physical labour was equivalent to wage labour or unpaid domestic work and it was reinforced as a part of family culture. The profession of male and female were on the basis of school education. The school system has failed to recontextualize the occupational destiny and diffusion of class discontent.

It has been found from researches that boys and girls make different choice of subjects depending on their social environment, peers, parents, teachers and schools. Adolescents internalizes gender role expectations in their ideology and it plays an important role in choice of subject. However, girls selected subjects that are masculine such as science but for boys it was difficult to enter feminine domain. Traditional discourses shows that majority of secondary school students select gender-stereotypical subjects. It was claimed that both the sexes were good at both the subjects. The paper seeks to discover the subject preferences among gender and the reasons for the selection of subjects are based on ability or anything else (Francis, B., 2000). Similar study shows that girls suffer gender inequalities in choice of subjects. The boys are not allowed to take Home Science as a subject. The girls are preferred to select social sciences as it is assumed they are not good in mathematics. There is an immense burden on girls and boys to practise and carry forward the social norms (Srivastava, 2022). In the earlier years in India the structure and content were similar for boys and girls. In 1882 a reform in curriculum was introduced to include feminine subjects-hygiene, home science and music for girls and mathematics, physics, chemistry for boys. Thus, curriculum was designed to perform different role in society (Chanana, 2001).

## 2.5 STUDIES ON GIRLS EDUCATION, DECISION-MAKING AND EMPOWERMENT

There are several studies revolving around education and decision-making power which impacts the empowerment of girls. It is evident from the studies that that education has gradually shifted from 'human capital' theories of development economics to other domains such as equality, rights and social justice. The rate of return of women's education is not only confined to the labour markets but also applies within the household. She found that the impact of women's education on fertility behaviour, children's education and child survival have been impressive (Kabeer, 2011). It was found that the percentage of women having an effective or highly effective say in different decision-making areas is quite small, except in some areas such as social and religious ceremonies, agriculture and cattle rearing. They have little or no say in areas which are thought to be an exclusively male domain — like investment, savings and purchase of goods (M. Rani and M. M. Goel, 2008) in their article titled "Women Empowerment in Haryana: A Study of Decision-Making in Household Economy,"

Sinha and Pankaj (2008) emphasised that there are several crucial aspects in household decision-making, which have an important bearing on the empowerment of girls. The range of factors influencing household decisions are schooling, distribution of food and nutrition, social mobility, etc. Adolescent girls are far behind boys despite the fact that the average age at the time of first enrolment is not much different. The case of dropout is high as the level of education goes up. The decisions about the dropout of girls are largely guided by parents, guardians and husbands. This is mainly because of two reasons. Firstly, adolescents drop out from school primarily due to the high opportunity costs. Secondly, parents clearly see the costs involved and withhold the girls at home by taking one-sided decisions. Adolescent girls are also found to hand over their entire earnings to their parents — in some cases voluntarily but mostly because of force. This evidence shows that employment alone is not enough for empowerment. There exists a gap at the household level which needs to be filled up before actual empowerment is ensured.

The cost of schooling for example uniforms, books and transport which restricts schooling for girls and boys. When the resources are limited and it is economically not affordable by the families, parents choose schooling of boys over the girls. The cost of schooling is lesser than girls as their clothing are cheaper and transportation is not needed (Unterhalter, 2007). Similar studies show that household preferences determine education and life of girls and boys. In most of the state's parents make choices of boy's education over girls' education. Thus, in patriarchal societies girls' education and retention is a concern (Bandyopadhyay, et.al, 2022)

The levels of education and income also determine whether fathers or mothers have the greater decision-making power. Household decisions are primarily taken by fathers. For the fathers have more education and earn more money than the mothers. An increase in the participation of fathers in the household decision-making positively ensures the dropout of girls. The household decisions reflect the preferences for sons over daughters. The reason to build up the sons' resource capital is that sons are expected to continue the family lineage as well as generate income for the family in future. The benefit of a girl's earnings goes to her husband and not to her parents. In Bangladesh, too, household decisions are made by fathers who discourage the girls from attaining education. Consequently, the rate of female enrolment is lower than that of male enrolment, especially at the secondary level (Shahidul, 2013).

In patriarchal societies the household decisions are mostly made by husbands. Women are mostly constrained by the norms, culture and values which limit their freedom of choice in every aspect of their lives. When mothers participate with their partners in making the household decisions, they have less of the gender bias or daughters receive as much preference as the sons, if not more. It was found that mothers are less apt to differentiate with respect to gender (Sarker, 2013)

N. Kabeer (1994), in her book *Reversed Realities: Gender Hierarchies in Development Thought*, highlights the dynamics of household decision-making. She considers two different approaches to the households: that which treats household as a unit of 'altrustic' decision-making (as a benevolent dictator) and that which considers it as a sight of bargaining and conflict. She suggests that in Northern India, Pakistan and Bangladesh, men own and control most of the household assets. In such a system, women are socially constructed as passive and vulnerable, and are dependent on male provision and protection for their survival. Women's wellbeing is tied to the prosperity of the household collectively and their long-term interests are best served by subordinating their own needs to those of male family members.

The ICRW (2012) report traces the implications of girls' educational attainments and positive outcomes for development. It suggests that education enhances individual resources and individual agencies which are essential components for empowerment. There are multiple ways in which school going can delay and improve the transition to adulthood. School going girls tends to be incompatible with marriage or pregnancy because social norms and mores make it difficult for a girl to go to school and become a wife at the same time. When girls are exposed to quality education, they can acquire information and skills which would enable them to secure high paid jobs and compete in the labour market. Quality education also enhances their aspirations, autonomy and decision-making ability, all of which contribute to their ability to plan their future.

M. S. Alam (2011) opines that, within families, men and women neither have equal access to resources, both material and non-material, nor do they experience equal life chances, with these differences leading to differential outcomes. A family is a site of various forms of gender inequalities at various stages of a woman's life cycle. The degree to which women have control over their lives, decide things for themselves, are able to negotiate with their male partners and participate in the decision-making process on usual family matters is reflective of their empowerment as it reflects their choices, behaviour and various positive outcomes. This study reflects that education for women may serve as a liberating force as it enables them to assert their rights and privileges in the family, and provides them financial independence, which in turn frees them from patriarchal constraints and traditional values. Women in western and southern regions are better placed in terms of educational attainment than in the other regions of India. In the southern region, a family values daughter, both socially and economically. As a result, they are more likely to survive, be educated and exposed to work outside home.

The emerging changes in the role of performance and decision-making as a result of education and employment of women in Hindu families. The impact of education can be gauged by the fact that husbands dominate in only 7 out of 20 decision areas in case their wives are employed. Employment has furthered the process of change, leaving solitary areas like the purchase of a car/scooter to the final decision of the husband. Another significant fact that emerged from the study is that wives' contribution to family resources is a crucial determinant to facilitate the change process in the direction of equality between the spouses (Indiradevi,1987).

Similarly, women empowerment can be seen through community participation. The emergence of a new power group in villages which would take charge of the panchayats in an increasing way. The quote for women in Gram Sabhas has been increased to 50 per cent. Women's NGOs play a significant role in training and preparing women for their new role. The number of women elected in Bihar, in 2001, was much more than the number reserved in 2000, showing the role women would play in panchayats. This is because development initiative is becoming a concern for women-folks who bear the brunt of poverty and feel more concerned to improve the health and education of their children than their male partners. It is reflected in a tremendous growth of female self-help groups in villages in spite of the paltry wages and meagre jobs offered by the government in the last five years (Sinha and Pankaj,2008).

The Department of International Development (2005) suggests that women leaders have been effective in supporting girls' education. Countries such as Ethiopia has benefitted from the long-standing involvement of the Minister of Education, a woman, who has also been chair of the Forum for African Women Educationists (FAWE). The success in Ethiopia indicates the importance of local leadership which can also be seen in Yemen, Mexico, India and Egypt. The demand for change should be initiated from the grassroots level for the development of girls' education.

A study in West Bengal and Mizoram titled "Women's Empowerment and Education: Panchayat and Women's

Self-Help Groups in India." The Government of India has reserved 33 per cent seats for women in the Panchayati Raj institutions for empowering women. The said study aimed to explore the impact of the reservations and self-help group movement on women's life. It was found that a majority of women do not take decisions independently and are dependent on male members of the family and panchayat. Party members and male members of the family take decisions regarding the panchayats while women party members are formal representatives (rubber stamps) with no power. Women members join a panchayat mostly under the pressure of male members of the family (Ghosh, et.al, 2015)

## 2.6 GAP IN LITERATURE

There are several studies on status of girls and their exclusion from education. Studies on education quality and school infrastructure are also available. However, there are few studies on household decision and women empowerment. There is a paucity of research on choice of subject and safe learning environment of girls and support they get from teachers. There are very few empirical studies that have narratives and experiences of school going girls at secondary level. There is also a dearth of studies connecting girls' education to empowerment. In this context this study has been undertaken to share the experiences of girls within and outside school.

## 2.7 THEORETICAL FRAMEWORK

The theoretical framework for the study concentrates on the links between girls' education and empowerment in a global context. The findings of the study are based on three main theories — N. Stromquist's theory on different dimensions of empowerment, Moser's theory on gender planning in the third world and human capital approach by Martha C. Nussbaum. These theories, especially the human capital approaches, are based on the philosophical voices of the women and their struggles for power in society. The theories of Stromquist and

Moser are based on gender and development approaches, and they focus on the gender power relations existing in society. This framework focusses on marginalisation and discrimination of women in society which other framework overlooks (Falkowska, 2013).

Moser (1989) demonstrated that men and women in third world countries have different roles to play and often have different needs. The rationale of gender planning focusses on the triple role of women and distinction between practical and strategic gender needs. According to Moser, women have to balance triple roles: productive (income-earning activities), reproductive (child care and domestic labour) and community management. The author argues that women have to continuously balance these roles which mostly get ignored. The author draws a distinction between the *practical* gender needs and the *strategic* gender needs. Practical gender needs focus on the daily living conditions, the gender roles of women and men and basic welfare requirements. Gender disparities are met by addressing the gender needs. Strategic gender needs are related to the power structures. It involves increasing the consciousness of women, and improving their opportunities and social positions.

Stromquist's theory highlights different dimensions of empowerment and various factors that leads to empowerment. Stromquist's article, titled "Women's Empowerment and Education: Linking Knowledge to Transformative Action," explains the concept of empowerment as a theory of social emancipation and discusses the realities of women in the developing and industrialised countries. The article defines various forms of empowerment — economic empowerment, political empowerment, knowledge empowerment and psychological empowerment. A holistic theory of women's empowerment has been proposed based on feminist researches and women's movements. She has placed women's empowerment among other components of social change. It has been seen that empowerment and schooling are the over-estimated pillars of social change. It is not just resources such as education leads to empowerment. There are other dimensions too.

Empowerment has been defined as a set of knowledge and skills that women possess in order to understand the world and act upon it. Women's empowerment has four interlocking dimensions—economic dimensions or some measure of financial autonomy, political dimensions or the ability to represent oneself at the decision-making venue, knowledge dimensions or awareness of one's reality which includes various possibilities and obstacles to women's equality, and psychological dimensions orb the ability to analyse their own value and the fairness or otherwise of their existence. There is a need for transformation from awareness to action, not only for individuals but also for agencies to engage in various forms of support and mobilisation. The organisations working on various gender issues must play a major role in women's empowerment.

Another major dimension is the role of individual and agency in bring the process of social change. In the theory proposed by Stromquist education plays a vital role in bringing empowerment but it also needs to be linked with economic, political and psychological dimensions.[5] The term empowerment started from the women's movements and not from any feminist approach and it is known as the inductive theory of change. Since the concept of empowerment is complex and diverse, it cannot be reduced to a few quantitative indicators; instead, it has to be grouped into various dimensions which support each other.

### *Economic Empowerment*

In relation to economic empowerment, both macro and micro levels of empowerment must be considered. A strong correlation exists between women's economic development and women's legal rights such as the right to hold property, access to bank loans, protection from violence, and abortion decisions. The ownership and control of property eliminates the gender gap and improves the women's economic wellbeing and social status, thus helping in her empowerment. Economic empowerment at the micro or household level is through women's income and it helps women to be the independent members and take their own decisions. The household work gets unnoticed as there is no wages and the market focusses on economic gains through exchanges. The burden of work is double among the employed women who get very little chance to move to the upper levels of employment.

### *Political Empowerment*

An elected women representative at the macro level helps women to gain voice that can be used in development of gender relations in society. At the micro or household level, there exists a division of labour between men and women. Women are engaged in more household chores than men. This leads to an imbalance which emerges and increases in the lives of the girls as they grow older. At the micro level, imbalances in household work are considered as a major target of social change. This is because of many reasons — male dominance through physical violence, women's work which is not remunerated at home, etc. These create financial and psychological barriers for women and make them dependent on male partners. Time constraints lessen the scope for self-development and enlightenment and mobilisation, thereby preventing women from negotiating their freedom.

### *Knowledge Empowerment*

Knowledge broadens the mental horizon of a person, enabling them to see the larger pictures and details of various social phenomena. The knowledge needed to understand the oppression of women depends on the conditions of women's subordination, and their experiences, and they have to explore how such conditions can be contested. Knowledge can be acquired and transmitted through channels of formal education and/or non-formal education.

Formal education or schooling helps women to improve their economic conditions through better paid jobs and enjoy their social mobility. It is seen that schools are unable to dispense gender related knowledge. The school curriculum focusses more on science and technology than on social skills. There is a need of gender sensitive curriculum which has rooms for discussion on various issues such as sex education, men and women's responsibilities regarding the management of a household and childcare, understanding of the patriarchal norms and gender ideologies that shape everyday life. Thus, modification of curriculum and the gender sensitive in-service training of teachers and school administrators may help remove the gender stereotypes from books and elsewhere. Education provides knowledge which impacts the psychological dimensions of empowerment by increasing the self-esteem, efficacy and future aspirations. Data and empirical evidences show that educated women may make better decisions than men. The formal knowledge of gender related aspects remains abstract for girls as they are unaware of the political and economic dimensions of women's lives. It is only when they move to the university level that they gain experiences of gender identity and feel the structural constrains. The Millennium Development Goals focus on the years of schooling as one of the key indicators of women's empowerment. The other two factors related to empowerment are the share of women in wage employment in non-agricultural sector and the proportion of seats held by women in the parliamentary institutions.

In this regard, non-formal education is provided through gender awareness programmes which are meant for all women. These programmes have empowering outcomes for women, provide a comfortable place for healthy discussions and encourage them to think critically about gender related aspects (Warner & Malhotra, 2014). These interactions help in building knowledge and lead to changes in behaviour patterns and attituded.

Empowerment has been defined as a process of supporting people to become aware of the power relationships and to understand how the balances of power contribute to more rewarding relationships. It has been found that discussions in groups and use of the native languages have positive outcomes on women's experiences, thereby contributing to their empowerment (Eldred, 2013).

### *Psychological Dimensions*

Women's empowerment needs active participation of organisations that lead to collective action and may result in emancipation of women. The involvement of different organisations helps to provide institutional change and support in everyday life and personal conduct. Psychological empowerment requires specific consideration as it helps women to attain positive attributes. Women participate in various public spheres and develop self-confidence, self-esteem, self- assertiveness. The participation in group activities and sharing them with individuals helps to build their will power to challenge the existing gender relations. Thus, connection between psychological empowerment and the local spaces seems to be critical.

Empowerment is a concept that is based on the theory of social change and has various dimensions that interact with each other, resulting in synergistic outcomes. Empowerment depends upon self-discovery, self-assertiveness and critical learning about one's own world. The knowledge dimension prepares women for labour market as well as builds an understanding about the social world. There are various factors that narrow the scope of formal education, like the age of the students; their academic achievement which is hardly linked to life skills, and gender sensitive teaching and learning.

### *The Human Capital Approach*

In her book *Women and Development: The Capabilities Approach*, Martha Nussbaum highlights the lives of women in developing countries. The concept of the capability approach is based on systemisation and theorisation of thoughts on women, how they can improve their life, and what policies the government should frame to secure their rights. Thus, capabilities are equivalent to empowerment of women's thinking and exploring more opportunities and choices.

Nussbaum emphasised how Amartya Sen had made major contributions to the theory of social justice and gender justice. His ideas highlight how capabilities are relevant when justice related issues are concerned. Inequalities between men and women and the achievement of gender justice in society have been his central concerns. The theory of inequalities is based on sex and different elements such as health, education, mobility and political participation. Nussbaum argued that feminist philosophy focusses on the needs and interest of women in the developing countries. The author proclaims that the problems related to poor working-class women and middle-class women should be highlighted and given the utmost priority. Gender inequality and poverty leads to failure of human capabilities.

Like Sen, Nussbaum too stressed on the capability approach which focusses on "what people are able to do and to be;" these are their central concerns. This theory determines the social minimum standards that are required so that that life is worth living with dignity. The author has argued that a person's capability is based on a person's end. "Women have been treated as the supporters of the ends, rather than as ends in their own rights. Thus, this principle has particular force with regard to women's lives" (Nussbaum, 2000: 5-6). The author's primary concern are women who suffer from various kinds of deprivation and lack of capabilities. These women mostly belong to the developing world. They do not give preference to the education and healthcare of girls. Women's right to property, freedom and political aspects have always been unequal to men. Nussbaum developed a list of central human capabilities based on the idea of basic social minimum that should be universally respected and implemented in various fields.

The list of core human capabilities, which was developed by Nussbaum, is not based on the theory of justice. The list has evolved from Aristotelian conception of choice based on the meaning of good life and moral conception. The list of the central functional capabilities includes the following:

1. Life: A person should be able to live to the normal length. It should not be reduced to be a non-worthy life.
2. Bodily Health: A person should lead a healthy life and have proper nourishment with a shelter to live in.
3. Bodily Integrity: A person should be able to move from one place to another freely, to protect oneself against any kind of harassment, assault and domestic violence. A person should have the rights and take decisions in reproductive matters.
4. Sense, Imagination and Thought: One to be able to logically reason out things and reflect on the ideas through culmination of education. A person should be able to connect his thoughts and ideas with own experience, self-sufficiency, and freedom of expression. It helps one to search the meaning of life.
5. Emotions: A person should be able to help others, love and care for us.
6. Practical Reason: A person should be able to form critical reflection on one's own life.
7. Affiliation: One should be able to live and show concern for others and engage in various forms of social interaction, to show self-respect for others and be treated equally. One should have protection against the discriminations or injustices based on race, sex, religion and caste.
8. Other Species: One should show concern for animals, plants and nature.
9. Play: One should be able to love, laugh and enjoy his life.
10. Control over One's Environment: A person should have the right to participate politically. This in turn gives the person freedom of speech and enables them to make

decisions in their life, leading to employment. Secondly, one should have real property rights; there should be equality of property between the male and female; they should have equal employment rights.

The capability approach provides a framework for measurement of the quality of life, and it can be used for a comparison between nations. The capability and human development framework represent a right based approach. Education is a powerful tool to widen their capabilities through earning, increasing bargaining power and extending control over their own environment. This theory highlights the intrinsic value of education as it is a constituent of human freedom and capability. In this study, Sen's role of education plays a pivotal role in enhancing the wellbeing, agency and empowerment of women through capability building.

As a part of this approach, the author highlights three different types of capabilities. First, the basic capabilities include the innate, inherent qualities of an individual for development. Second, there are internal capabilities that develop over a period of time. These capabilities develop with the help of the environment. These are freedom of speech, freedom to play with others, freedom to make choices, and the like. Third, there is a huge probability that internal capabilities are influenced by the external conditions. Thus, a person may have the internal capability for employment and political participation, but is highly dependent on the combined capability. These capabilities are related to human equality. Discrimination on the basis of race, sex, caste and religion is considered as a degradation and collapse of the capability.

Therefore, in education, evaluations should not only focus on such aspects as the number of teachers, number of classes, learning materials or output such as earnings from education. It should also focus on other dimensions such as how for girls the opportunity to receive education is constrained by the lack of resources, by social norms concerning the gender division of labour and decision-making within family (Falkowska, 2013).

## 2.8 CONCEPTUAL FRAMEWORK

The conceptual framework guiding this study has been derived from the literature review and depicts the lines of enquiry of this research. It revolves around the rural girls' lives and opportunities of schooling. The researches on girls' education in India focusses on systematic and structural issues of schooling at primary level and based on this background there are very few empirical studies that discusses the experiences and narratives of school girls in the educational system at the secondary level (Shah, 2015 &Nambissan, 2005). This group needs more attention as the dropout rates are higher among the secondary girls. The proportion of girls being out of school is significantly higher among the other children. The girls at the age group of 11-16 years (secondary stage) are more vulnerable to drop out. The lack of schooling facilities and poor learning achievement compel student to drop out (Bandyopadhyay, 2018, Rajagopal,2009). The girls in this study are at a crucial stage where they have to make a major decision to continue their education or leave the school and end their education (Shah, 2015). This group of girls were suitable for the study as they are exposed to the school culture-empowerment oriented for a longer period of time. These girls are marginalized and suffer from the socio-cultural practices where women are subservient to men. Additionally, the lack of the interest of the parent to send them to school, financial constraints lead them to silent exclusion. Chanana, K. (2006) emphasized that the exclusion of girls from elementary education will continue as long as schools are sites for maintenance of gender identity and inequality. Silent exclusion is a process in which the children get excluded from the educational system. As education is an essential resource, denial of utilization of this resource can lead to silent exclusion. Silent exclusion is a cause of social exclusion which is linked to educational exclusion. The reasons for the exclusion are school, family and community. Hence there is a need to capture the events and experiences that surrounds the life of the girls to understand the exclusion of the girls (Govinda and Bandyopadhyay 2008, Shah 2015). The study analyses how education influences decision making capacity within and outside a household. It is concerned more with the empowering outcomes of education and changing the balance of power within households. This is in terms of women gaining a voice, participation in household decisions, awareness of rights, self-esteem and financial independence. Empowerment can be measured through a choice of subject, choice of school, participation in classroom activities, voicing their opinion aspirations regarding higher education, jobs, earning and spending. The other indicators for measuring empowerment are autonomy in decision making and gender gap in classroom. When girls are exposed to quality education, they can acquire information and skills which would enable them to secure high paid jobs and compete in labour market. The schools also provide a safe learning environment for girls where they can voice their opinion and learn to cultivate the various dimension of empowerment. Quality of education also enhances their aspirations, autonomy and decision-making ability, all of which contribute to their planning their future (ICRW, 2012). The quality of education remains a major cause of concern. There are range of factors influencing 'gender-friendly' education at school level. It depends mainly of school culture, policies and practices such as teacher's cultural background, social and cultural attitudes, lack of openness to new pedagogy, infrastructural facility, teaching methods. The school quality has a stronger impact on girls' education than boys' education such as a lack of female teachers, unfavourable treatment of girls in class, sexual harassment my male teachers or students, bullying, curriculum or textbooks favouring adult role models only for boys (UNGEI, 2008). Arnot and Reay (2007) and Shah (2015) opines that it is important to know how girls conceptualize and contextualize empowerment and the whole process must be analysed in a large context of family and school environment.

**Figure 2.1: Conceptual Framework**

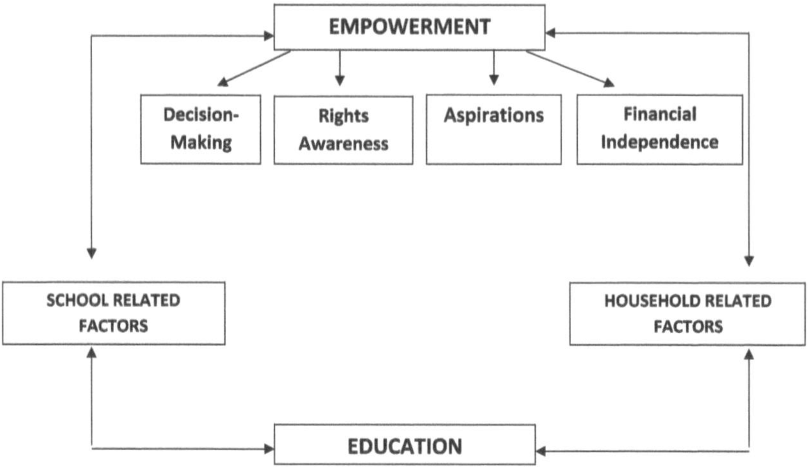

Source: Made by researcher

## 2.9 CONCLUSION

In this backdrop, the study has been designed to provide an insight of the rural marginalized girls who are school going to understand their perspectives and experiences in the light of empowerment. To maintain a link between school-household-empowerment the theoretical conceptualization has been drawn from Stormquist, Moser and Nussbaum. The discourses links schools with the various dimensions of empowerment. The class environment and curriculum with cognitive dimensions and behavioural aspects like self-confidence and self assertation with psychological dimensions, career, job and choice of subject to economic dimensions of empowerment (Shah 2015). Nussbaum highlights the opportunities of women's right to freedom, education and political rights. Education provided in schools can improve their positions in society through bargaining power (voicing opinion) which is otherwise very limited. Moser focuses on balancing the triple roles- productive, reproductive and community management in society.

CHAPTER 3

# RESEARCH METHODOLOGY

## 3.1 INTRODUCTION

This chapter describes the methodology of data collection for the present study. The details include research design, population and sample, sources of data collection and the tools used for data collection.

## 3.2 RESEARCH DESIGN

Research design refers to the logical and systematic manner in which data are collected and analysed. The need for a design stem from the desire to obtain results that are not subject to alternative interpretations and to avoid unnecessary ambiguity (Borg and Gall, 1984-86). The purpose of the study was to explore the impact of secondary education on girl's lives in rural areas of Uttar Dinajpur district of West Bengal. The study is descriptive in nature, based on a qualitative approach and aimed to understand the impact of higher secondary level of schooling on girls' lives. This approach is seen as an appropriate research method as it helps to discover the empowerment of women through personal views and social attitudes surrounding girls' education. This descriptive research design is suitable in collection of in-depth information, something which other approaches lacks. This approach tries to collect information widely on all the aspects and variations of the studied phenomenon as captured in the sample (Elliot & Timulak 2005). In order to seek answers to the research questions, the researcher used a qualitative approach so as to understand the lives of the girls in rural areas and how (secondary) education encourages or inhibits them in making decision within and outside households, enlightens them about their self-esteem, creates the rights awareness and leads to their financial independence. The answers to research questions required direct interactions with the target group within their own settings.

Mixed methodology research has been used for primary survey. It involves collecting and analyzing both qualitative and quantitative data. A quantitative approach has also been used in the study, though the qualitative approach has been given priority over the quantitative one in the study. The combination of both the approaches helped the researcher to look at the population from different perspectives. The quantitative data includes close ended questions and qualitative data includes open ended questions for the purpose of interview (Chaudhary, P, 2022).

Mixed methodology focuses on real contextual problems, narratives, pragmatic perspectives and rigorous quantitative research used for assessing the frequency and percentages (Johnson, Onwuegbuzie, & Turner, 2007). A pragmatic perspective focuses on diverse approaches giving importance to objective and subjective knowledge (Morgan, 2007).

The present chapter discusses the sources from which data were collected. The researcher used both primary and secondary sources for data collection. Primary data were collected from (1) students (boys and girls) enrolled at the secondary and higher secondary levels, (2) students who have passed the secondary level schooling (girls), (3) students who have not passed the secondary or higher secondary level of schooling, (4) teachers and principals, (5) and parents of students studying at the secondary and higher secondary schools of Uttar Dinajpur district in West Bengal. The primary data sources included school information schedules, interviews with students, parents and teachers, and in-depth interviews with students who have passed the higher secondary level, focus group discussion with secondary and higher secondary students, and observation to understand the views and experiences of the respondents. The interview schedules were prepared separately for students, teachers, students who have passed the higher secondary level of schooling, and those who have not passed this level of schooling. Interview schedules were of two kinds — structured and semi-structured.

The secondary data collected were on the enrolment of the students, gender parity index, availability of teachers, pupil teacher ratio and infrastructure facilities available at the state, district and block levels. These were collected from the U-Dise, NHFS reports and Human Development reports of Uttar Dinajpur. Various other books, articles and reports on girls' education were also used for secondary data.

## 3.3 POPULATION AND SAMPLE FOR THE STUDY

The population for the present study includes the secondary and higher secondary level students enrolled in schools; girls who have completed higher secondary schooling at least two years ago; girls who have not completed the secondary or higher secondary level of schooling belonging to the same age group; parents of the enrolled students, principals and teachers of the school.

Purposive sampling was adopted for the study. It was appropriate to select purposive sampling as the data was majorly qualitative. Purposive sampling was used to select schools, students and parents. Cohen and Manion (2007) observe that purposive sampling is a technique which enables the researcher to pick the cases to be included in the sample on the possession of particular characteristics being sought. Qualitative samples tend to be purposive rather than random. Samples in qualitative studies evolve once field work begins. The initial choices of participants lead you to similar and different ones. This is conceptually driven sequential sampling (Miles, Huberman & Saldana, 2014).

The sample was drawn from Raiganj block in Uttar Dinajpur district of West Bengal. This block was selected purposively on the basis of these assumptions. First, the block is a part of an administrative division in Raiganj subdivision of Uttar Dinajpur. The average female literacy in rural areas is lower than in urban areas. The female literacy in this block is 43 per cent

(Census 2011) which is lower than in urban areas. As this block has both urban and rural areas, sizeable ones, it gives a glimpse of the rural-urban diversity. It would be helpful to find the impact of education upon girls and their level of empowerment. Secondly, this block has both government and private schools with different managements. Several other blocks did not have higher secondary government and private schools. It was expected that the participation of girls and schooling experience would be varying in the schools under different managements. This was expected to provide a comparative perspective. Thirdly, the selection of this block was done with the intention to track and identify students going for higher education within the district. There are a number of higher educational institutions — Netaji Subhas Chandra Bose Teachers Training College, Raiganj; B. Ed. College, Raiganj; Polytechnic College; and Raiganj University in Raiganj. Fourth, Raiganj block is well connected with railways and roadways. It was difficult to reach out to some other blocks as the transport facility was poor; only private vehicles plied to those areas. In some areas, there were no pucca roads, petrol pumps and service stations. Educational officials insisted that we should not choose those areas as there is no communication and nobody could reach in case of emergency. Educational officials themselves go to those areas in teams to collect data once or twice a year.

The schools were identified purposively to find different management schools (private and government) in the study area. Other reasons were that the units of the study such as school's location in view of the district. Integrated government and private schools were selected. The choice of one school led to the choice of another school.

Here is something about the higher secondary schools located in Raiganj block, which we visited. There are 27 higher secondary schools (25 government and 2 private) here. On the basis of purposive sampling, a total of 4 schools (2 government and 2 private schools) were selected. Since there were only two private schools here, both were included in the study. The two sampled government schools were located near the private schools which were taken for the study. Thus, an equal number of government and private schools was taken for the sake of a comparative study.

Similarly, the girl respondents at higher secondary were selected from each department equally based on their availability and enrollment. In private schools' enrollment of girls were lower compared to government schools. Purposive sampling was used to identify the girls from different social category, different economic background and the subjects selected at the senior secondary level. It was also used to select and interview the girls who completed and those who did not complete secondary education and parents of the enrolled students in the same manner.

**FIGURE 3.1: SAMPLING FRAME OF THE STUDY**

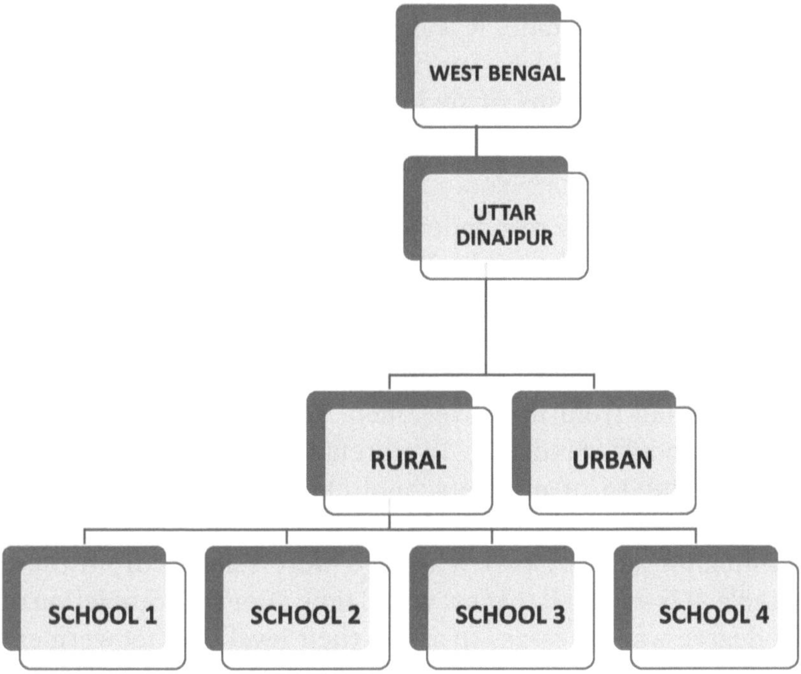

WEST BENGAL

UTTAR DINAJPUR

RURAL

URBAN

SCHOOL 1

SCHOOL 2

SCHOOL 3

SCHOOL 4

Source: Made by researcher

The purposive sampling technique is suitable for selecting participants in a case study. It involves selection of participants in a special situation. There are three reasons for selecting purposive sampling in case study. First, the researcher thought it prudent to select unique and informative cases; second, the cases were from difficult and different places; and third, when the researcher found out some different cases and listed them for an in-depth investigation. The purpose of the sampling was thus to gain an insight into a situation and not to draw a generalisation, and hence the sample could well be non-random (Ishak & Bakar, 2014).

3.3.1 *Sample:* The sample was selected from 4 higher secondary co-educational schools. Only the higher secondary and secondary students were considered for the study. The number of girls were selected purposively from each grade on the basis of availability. An equal number of boys and girls was taken from every grade. It was assumed that the responses of girls and boys would be varying and sometimes boys indeed depicted the problems of society in a better way. Other than this, a comparative perspective of girls' and boys' opinions on similar matters was used.

As many as 252 respondents from 5 sub-respondent groups were selected for the study. Put of a total of 174 students, 87 were girls and 87 boys. As many as 110 students were from the government schools, in which 55 are girls. Of the 64 students from private schools, 32 were girls. A total of 22 teachers were selected from the government schools and 16 from the private schools. Similarly, 16 parents of government school children and 16 of private school children were selected for the study. Seven girls who had completed the higher secondary examination at least two years ago were selected from these schools. It is assumed that six years' time after the completion of the degree was necessary to assess their level of empowerment through education. One girl who had not completed her higher secondary education was selected for the study. Two girls from private schools and 6 girls from government schools, who had completed higher secondary education, were selected through purposive sampling. These included one dropout while there were no dropouts from private schools. The school principals helped to get the contacts of the girls who had completed or dropped out of the school. Out of the selected students, eight parents from each school were interviewed. The researcher included the principals in this category of teachers.

**TABLE 3.1**

**Sampling Frame: Number and Category of Respondents**

| S. No | Category of Respondents | Number of Respondents |
|---|---|---|
| 1. | Students (Enrolled in schools) | 174 |
| 2. | Students (Completed school 2 years before) | 7 |
| 3. | Students (Did not complete higher secondary school) | 1 |
| 4. | Teachers | 38 |
| 5. | Parents | 32 |
| | Total of five group of respondents | 252 |

Source: Made by researcher

**TABLE 3.2**

**Schools Profile and Sample of Respondents School-Wise**

| Schools (S) | Type of School | Cate gory | Enrolled Students (Girls) | Total Students (Girls & Boys) | Students Completed Higher Secondary School | Students did not complete School | Teach-ers | Par-ents |
|---|---|---|---|---|---|---|---|---|
| S1 | Govern-ment | Co-ed | 28 | 56 | 2 | 1 | 11 | 8 |
| S2 | Govern-ment | Co-ed | 27 | 54 | 3 | - | 11 | 8 |
| S3 | Private | Co-ed | 11 | 22 | 1 | - | 8 | 8 |
| S4 | Private | Co-ed | 21 | 42 | 1 | - | 8 | 8 |
| | Total | | 87 | 174 | 7 | 1 | 38 | 32 |

Source: Made by researcher

## 3.4 TOOLS FOR DATA COLLECTION

Primary and secondary sources was used to collect data from the schools. The secondary sources provided data relating to enrolment, infrastructural facilities, availability of teachers, etc. These also included articles and reports related to women's education and empowerment. The tools used to collect data from the primary sources were the school information schedules, questionnaires for the students enrolled in secondary and higher secondary schools, observation schedules, in-depth interviews with parents and teachers, and case studies of students through in-depth interviews.

3.4.1 *In-depth Interviews:* In-depth interviews in a semi-structured form were conducted with various types of respondents. These interviews aimed to explain sensitive issues and unpack personal experiences, emotions and feelings that interviewees address in daily practices (Carvey, 2012). If so, much emphasis was laid on conducting interviews, it was because an interview offers access to one's ideas, thoughts and memories in their own words rather than in the researcher's words (Rainharz, 1992: 19). To explore the real-life stories of girls who are too naive and timid to disclose personal information and emotions, the interview method was found to be useful. An informal atmosphere is a prerequisite to obtain data from the perspective of rural girls. Semi-structured schedules allowed space for flexibility to accommodate new issues as addressed by the respondents. Semi-structured interviews can proceed with unstructured questions, depending upon the circumstances. In most of the qualitative interviews, "rambling" was encouraged to allow the interviewees to go "off on a tangent;" this helped to gain better insights into what the interviewees saw to be relevant and important (Carvey, 2012). In addition, this method supplements information about the respondents' personal characteristics, facial expressions and gestures, which is often of great value in interpreting results.

Semi-structured interviews were conducted as a major data gathering method. It was conducted with students, teachers and parents. in-depth interviews were conducted with the students who had completed or had not completed the senior secondary schooling to assess their views on the impact of education on empowerment of girls, schooling experience and social attitudes of women. The interview schedule for students consisted of 35 questions, out of which 11 questions were close-ended with multiple possible answers and 24 were open-ended questions. The teacher's interview schedule consisted of 22 questions, out of which 12 questions were close-ended with multiple possible answers and 10 were open-ended questions. In case of the interview schedule meant for parents, the number of such questions were 8 and 15 respectively. Interviews with teachers, principals, parents and SSA officials were conducted to find out the initiatives taken by the school for promoting girls' education. Multiple interviews were conducted with the respondents which helped them to open up. Interview questions were related to the social and economic backgrounds of the respondents, their perceptions on girls' education, schooling experiences, family backgrounds, work, decision, financial independence and empowerment.

3.4.2 *Interview Schedule:* The use of an interview schedule for the purpose in qualitative research work is not uncommon and it may be used with other social research methods such as focus groups (Cauvey, 2012). A interview schedule was used for girls of Class IX to XII to elicit their schooling experiences in schools, and for parents of the enrolled children. The interview schedule had both open-ended and close-ended questions. The interviews were conducted on students. There were multiple choice questions and a few of them had reasons for choosing the answers in brief. There were different sections in the interview schedule— to elicit information about the family, school and education; household activities, rights and awareness, mobility factors, family environment and financial matters.

3.4.3 *Focussed Group Discussion:* Another method of collecting data was the use of focussed group discussions among girls and boys in a school. They were separately asked questions on their schooling experience, social views and on the attitudes of teachers, general perceptions on schooling, social barriers and challenges in school. In a focus group discussion, the researcher was interested in how people respond to each other's views and build up a web of interactions within the group. This way we tried to learn about the participants' attitudes, values and behaviour patterns as the members of a group (Cauvey, 2012). In fact, groups can be interviewed about their experiences and attitudes which are suitable to unravel sensitive issues as people feel more comfortable while sharing in a group.

3.4.4 *Observation Schedule:* Observation technique is an important technique for collecting data on non-verbal behaviour. Observation is preferred when one wants to study in detail the behaviour that occurs in some particular setting or institution (Bailey, 1982). The researcher observed the day-to-day happenings in the sampled schools and recorded the meaningful comments, expressions, events and attitudes of students and teachers in relation to the present study. The analysis and interpretation of daily affairs off the school added to the findings. Observations of the schools in their natural settings and of the various components within the schools, such as relationship between students and teachers inside and outside classrooms, on the various facilities available in laboratories and libraries, and their functioning, were also noted down by the researcher in a separate diary. This method helped to yield data from natural settings and actions during the ordinary routine of life.

For this purpose, an unstructured observation schedule was prepared so as to observe and understand the behavioural patterns and interactions between students and teachers and between students and students within and outside the classrooms. At the school level, observations regarding infrastructure, staff and teaching learning materials were also made. The observation schedule was kept unstructured and the researcher added to the existing topics, depending on the situations in different schools.

3.4.5 *School Information Schedule:* The school information schedule was used as a check list to see the basic facilities available in a school. This schedule was administered on the selected sampled schools. The schedule was divided into sections. Section 1 consisted of basic information about the school such as village, block, etc. Section 2 dealt with the physical facilities such as the school building, teaching aids and physical aids, drinking water, toilet, mid-day meals and co-curricular activities available in school. It also included information related to schooling-related facilities like the classrooms, teaching learning materials, hostel facilities and medical facilities available in the school. Section 3 is about the teachers; Section 4 is about the non-teaching staff and Section 5 is about the school management committee.

3.4.6 *Village Information Schedule:* The village information schedule shows the basic services and facilities available in the village. The basic purpose was to get information about nearby areas around the school.

3.4.7 *Case Studies:* Case studies of the girls from rural areas, who had passed the senior secondary level of education and of those who were of the comparable age but had not passed this particular level, were made to find out what helps in in building the aspirations and self-esteem of girls for community development.

## 3.5 RELIABILITY AND VALIDITY

The reliability of the tools, particularly of the questionnaire and interview schedules, was checked through pilot survey. The first draft was reviewed by experts working in this field, including the academicians and peer group researchers. Each item in these tools was evaluated and the suggested changes were incorporated. Data was validated from secondary sources of information and crosschecked on the basis of tools used in the study through the process of triangulation.

## 3.6 PILOT STUDY AND ANALYSIS

A pilot survey is a mini survey where the researcher checks the tools and response pattern of the participants. It helps to overcome the challenges the main data collection process. The pilot survey undertaken was beneficial in improvising the tools of the study such as interview schedules of students and parents. The pilot survey enabled the interviewer to make suitable changes. The reliability and validity of the tools was checked.

The pilot study was conducted in the month of November and December 2015. An informal visit was made to the office of SSA (Sarva Shiksha Abhiyan) to discuss and get the list of schools in the Raiganj block of Uttar Dinajpur district. One government school was selected from the list of schools located in the rural areas. The sample collected from the government schools was based on 10 parents, 10 teachers and 20 students who were then interviewed (5 from each class) and 2 students who had completed the higher secondary schooling.

On the basis of the pilot study, certain changes were made in the questionnaires concerning students and parents. The students' questionnaire was lengthy and a few questions were repetitive. Those questions were changed. Students were not able to understand a few questions regarding health and hobbies. Hence necessary changes were made in the questionnaires. In the focus group discussions, students were not ready to share their views on any incidence of bullying and misbehaviour by certain boys. But once the questions were changed, they could easily share their views about such incidences.

The results of the pilot survey showed that many parents had no formal schooling or had studied till the primary level. Generally, mothers' education was lower than fathers' education. The schooling experience of students was found to be good as 62.5 per cent students responded. Teachers and parents were supportive. It was found that girls had to struggle and balance a lot between responsibilities at home and studies. Some 41.7

per cent of the girls stated that education has helped them in developing confidence and inculcating values and skills. Girls had to engage themselves in household activities after the school hours. In a patriarchal setup, decisions were taken mostly by male members of the family. Parents encouraged the boys more to study, compared to girls. The decisions about household savings and expenditures were taken by the male members of the family. Females are mostly involved in decisions regarding visiting their friends and relatives. Thus, primary decision-making in the family lies with the male members, and then a decision is followed by both male and female members.

There were considerable differences between the pilot and main survey. The main survey reflected that the parents encouraged both boys and girls to study. Parents with financial constrains encouraged the girls to pursue jobs, help them in household chores and farming activity. They preferred their sons to enter higher educational institutions over their daughters. It was found that time for study was limited for girls and boys in the government schools compared to private schools. Girls and boys got less time for extracurricular activities while private school children had no time due to excessive burden of studies. Decisions within family was taken by the male members but in consultation with the female members. Barring few family's girls had limited decision-making power. The major decisions were taken by the male member or the head of the family in consultation with females. Sometimes girls are given chances to make their choice and decisions. It depends on the social and economic background of the family. Thus, social and cultural norms determine the decision making with household in context of marriage and education.

## 3.7 PROCEDURE FOR DATA COLLECTION

The field study was carried out from February 2016 to April 2016 and August 2016 to December 2016 in different villages of Raiganj block of Uttar Dinajpur district which forms part of North Bengal. The field research was carried out in four villages in Raiganj block. These were Gouri VIII, Bahin IX, and Kalambari I-XIII. The researcher visited Vigayan Bhavan in West Bengal on October 2015 where she met the education officers in charge of the SSA and RMSA; earlier she had communications with them through various emails prior to the visit on the nature and purpose of the study. Before visiting the field, a letter was procured from the supervisor District Project Officers of SSA and RMSA in Uttar Dinajpur, about the purpose of the visit. The education officer gave us a list of schools. From this list, schools were selected on the basis of the following criteria: schools should be higher secondary, co-educational, having different kinds of management, and located in rural areas. The sampled schools were selected after a lot of discussions with the EMIS officer and his team who had visited those schools. They made the researcher aware of the unrest that was taking place in a few places around 50 kilometres from Raiganj and also about the areas where there were lacks of transport, communications and petrol pumps. A few schools were situated across the rivers. These were the anticipated barriers and challenges to be faced while selecting the schools. The researcher could have gone to the more interior rural villages by crossing the rivers in a boat, but she was advised not to take the risk of going alone.

The research method was primarily based on field work conducted in Uttar Dinajpur. Multiple methods were used to collect data from field sources. The primary collections were was done through questionnaires, interviews, focussed group discussions and by observation method. Questionnaires and interviews were personally administered on students, students who completed the higher secondary level, parents and teachers who agreed to be a part of the study. Apart from the questionnaires and semi-structured interview schedules, data were also collected through observations and focus group discussions. Focus group discussions were done in groups in the school premises --- with boys and girls separately.

Interviews with students who had completed the higher secondary school and parents were conducted at their homes and when they brought their children to the school. In some cases, multiple interviews were held with the respondents to fill certain important information gaps left after the earlier interviews. These conversations helped to develop a relationship with the respondents as they seemed to be giving personal information which they had not given during the previous meetings. Sometimes respondents also invited for tea at home. School principals were cooperative and shared the details of parents and students who had completed the senior secondary level of education. A few interviews took the form of telephonic conversations --- in the case of ones who were not staying in Raiganj. Interviews with teachers were conducted in the staff room during their free periods. The school principals arranged interviews with students during free periods, lunch breaks and after school timings so that classes were not disturbed. Secondary data on enrolment and achievement of the students were shared by the government schools while the private schools showed a degree of reluctance about disclosing these data.

## 3.8 ANALYSIS AND INTERPRETATION OF DATA

The collected data were then systematised so as to get answers to the research questions of the study. The data were analysed through certain relevant qualitative and quantitative data analysis processes. The data were organised through the analysis of transcription of interviews which were recorded, questionnaires, field notes and observational data. The data were categorised broadly through necessary scrutiny, and the repetitive and irrelevant data were dropped. The thus-edited data were classified according to the selected themes that were derived from the research questions. Transcripted data were then manually coded on the basis of the emerging themes. The categories were well defined in terms of indicators. Then a coding scheme was applied in order to tabulate the information.

To analyse and interpret the close ended questions, Statistical Packages for Social Sciences (SPSS), along with the MS excel sheets and manual methods, were used. The percentage of response for each question was thus found. Information obtained were tabulated separately to be analysed and interpreted. Open ended questions were analysed through the accumulation of similar points made during the interview and presented in a table form.

The broad theoretical guidelines followed while analysing qualitative data were obtained from Yin (2011) who arranged a qualitative analysis in a five-phase cycle, i.e., Compiling, Disassembling, Reassembling, Interpreting, and Concluding. During the phase of compiling, data gathered from different sources were sorted out and put in order. In the disassembling procedure, the compiled data were broken down into smaller fragments based on objectives of study and coding were done. Then was followed the process of reassembling by using the substantive themes. The rearrangements and recombination of the data were depicted graphically or in tabular forms. Both the disassembling and reassembling phases were used repeatedly. The fourth phase, that of interpretation work of the reassembled data and materials, was meant to create a new narrative text. In the last phase, conclusions were drawn from the entire study.

### 3.9 CONFIDENTIALITY

The participants of the study were assured in advance that their views, feelings and all the information provided by them during the interviews would not be disclosed anywhere. It was important for the researcher that the respondents speak up freely about their life at home or in school and about their personal affairs.

### 3.10 ETHICAL DILEMMA

Some ethical issues came up when the researcher visited the village for data collection. Most of the interviewees asked whether their interviews would bring about any positive gains for them. It was hard for the researcher to explain the reality that the study on the rural experiences and pain for was the purpose of our own study and not for any direct benefit for them. There are little chances of the research findings to be used in favour of the girls in that particular village where field study was conducted.

# CHAPTER 4

# THE STATE OF WEST BENGAL: UNDERSTANDING GIRLS' EDUCATION

## 4.1 INTRODUCTION

Literacy is a vital requirement for the educational development of women. Literacy is a tool to reduce poverty, control population and improve gender equality (Saha and Debnath, 2016). The literacy rate of West Bengal is close to the national literacy rate. According to the census 2011, however, the literacy rate was not even in the districts of West Bengal. The gender equality is highly skewed between the various districts. There was a significant change in the literacy pattern from Census 2001 to 2011 in the marginalised districts and female literacy was affected in these areas (Saha and Debnath, 2016). It has been an accepted fact that gender needs to be seen in a larger social context. It was found that Muslim or tribal girls from Kerala had better educational status than even the forward-caste the girls in Rajasthan and Uttar Pradesh. Thus, women's position varies from one social group to another, between different regions, and from urban to rural areas (Ramachandran, 2018). This context shows that urban and rural differences in literacy have much more to do with other factors than with gender differences.

## 4.2 THE PRESENT STATUS

In terms view of their educational status, some of the districts in West Bengal are backward. The centre and state government have to work towards their upliftment. The study of gross enrolment ratio (GER), net enrolment ratio (NER), gender parity index and educational infrastructure and other indicators do help to recognise the gaps in the secondary education.

The census of India 2011 states that West Bengal has the sex ratio[6] of 950 females per 1000 males. This sex ratio shows the numerical inequality of males and females in society, with various implication about preference for sons, differential child care within a family, skewed food distribution within family. The district of Uttar Dinajpur, including Raiganj block, shows that the sex ratio is lower here than the state average. See Table 4.1.

**TABLE 4.1**

**Sex Ratio in West Bengal, Uttar Dinajpur and Raiganj**

| State/District /Block | Sex Ratio |
|---|---|
| West Bengal | 950 |
| Uttar Dinajpur | 936 |
| Raiganj | 905 |

Source: Census 2011

**TABLE 4.2**

**Male and Female Literacy in West Bengal, Uttar Dinjpur and Raiganj**

| State/District/ Block | Total | Male | Female |
|---|---|---|---|
| West Bengal | 77.08 | 81.7 | 70.5 |
| Uttar Dinajpur | 59.07 | 65.52 | 52.17 |
| Raiganj | 63.52 | 60.19 | 48.32 |

Source: Census of West Bengal 2011 (Figures are in percentages.)

The state of West Bengal occupies the 20th rank on the literacy scale (census 2011). West Bengal has also ranked as 32nd position in Education Development Index constructed by NIEPA 2006-2007 (Basak &Mukherjee). Table 4.2 shows that female literacy in West Bengal is lower in comparison to male literacy. Uttar Dinajpur district has lower literacy level than the state. After the bifurcation of West Dinajpur in 1992, the more backward areas went to Uttar Dinajpur which further lowered its literacy level. This new district reflected a still lower female literacy rate. The rural areas reflected the lowest of them all. There is a high gender gap in literacy in Uttar Dinajpur and Raiganj block (the rural areas do not include Raiganj Municipality and Towns). According to the Census data of West Bengal (2011) the classification of towns is for urban areas and village for rural areas. A very low female literacy has been recorded in this district. It is a major concern in Raiganj block as well which also has lowest female literacy. According to the Census 2011, female literacy is the second lowest in the district, even after it has somewhat improved between 1991 and 2011. It has been observed that the low student teacher ratio, poverty and less educational institutions has pushed the literacy level down in comparison to the state average (District Census Handbook, 2011; Verma and Roy, 2019).

**TABLE 4.3**

**State, District and Block-Wise Rural and Urban Literacy Rates**

| State/District/ Block | Rural Literacy Rate | | | Urban Literacy Rate | | |
|---|---|---|---|---|---|---|
| | Total | Male | Female | Total | Male | Fe- male |
| West Bengal | 72.13 | 78.44 | 65.51 | 84.78 | 88.37 | 80.98 |
| Uttar Dinajpur | 55.99 | 68.82 | 48.72 | 80.28 | 83.91 | 76.32 |
| Raiganj | 62.78 | 69.59 | 55.54 | 81.69 | 84.42 | 78.65 |

Source: Census 2011, District Census Handbook 2011

(Figures are in percentages.)

Table 4.3 depicts that rural literacy is lower than the urban literacy at the all the three levels --- state, district and block. The female literacy declines when one moves from the state level to the block level. The fall in female literacy is higher in rural areas than in urban areas. As said, female literacy in Uttar Dinajpur is the lowest. It is mainly due to the fact that four blocks in Uttar Dinajpur --- Goalpokhar I, Goalpokhar II, Karandighi and Islampur blocks --- the literacy rates are below the district average (Verma and Roy, 2019). Female literacy continues to lag behind male literacy in the rural areas compared to the urban areas. The inter-block variations within the district make the rural and urban literacy rates better than the district average. There is a sharp difference in the overall male and female literacy in the rural and urban areas. The urban literacy is higher at the state level due to the availability of good infrastructure. However, literacy level varies from one district to another (Saha & Debnath, 2016). It has been found that the lowest literacy rate in Uttar Dinajpur is majorly due to the rural nature of the district where urban areas account fpr only 12 per cent of the population (Verma and Roy 2019). The rural literacy rate, especially the female literacy rate, in the block is not satisfactory. This makes the Uttar Dinajpur lag behind the other districts in West Bengal. There is a huge gender gap between male and female literacy in rural areas in all the blocks which then gets reflected at the district level. Islampur, Karandighi, Raiganj and Kaliagani blocks have low urban literacy is found. However, urban literacy in Raiganj is low compared to the other blocks (Verma and Roy, 2019).

## 4.3 ACCESS AND ENROLMENT PATTERNS

The government initiatives like the SSA, RMSA and DPEP have indeed improved the access to education and enrolment all over India. The Right to Education Act, 2009, made the provision of free and compulsory education for all. It focussed on the regular participation of children, qualified teachers and better infrastructure and academic facilities (Bandyopadhyay, 2018 *a* and *b*).

The attendance in schools is an important indicator according to the NFHS-4 for the age group 6-17 years in West Bengal. It has been observed that there is no gender disparity in the age group 6-14 years. However, gender disparity is found in the age group of 14-17 years. The number of girls attending school in the age group of 6-14 years is higher than the boys. But there is a drop in the number of girls attending school after 14 years. It is evident from the above table that there is a drop in the number of girls attending school in the age group of 16-17 years, as fewer girls have been attending school after

14 years. According to the NFHS data, the girls in their teen (44 per cent) with no education had to bear the child while only a small proportion of girls (6 per cent) of the ones who had completed 10 years of schooling were child-bearing. It was found that education was an important factor for population control and the burden of bearing child in the said age group (NFHS-4, 2015-16).

**TABLE 4.4**

**Percentage of Household Population by Age 6-17 Years, Attending Schools in West Bengal**

| Background Characteristics | Male | | | Female | | |
|---|---|---|---|---|---|---|
| Age | Urban | Rural | Total | Urban | Rural | Total |
| 6 - 10 (Primary) | 95.7 | 96.7 | 96.4 | 99.5 | 97.9 | 98.4 |
| 6 - 13 (Elementary) | 92.4 | 93.7 | 93.4 | 97.2 | 96.8 | 96.9 |
| 11 - 13 (Upper Primary) | 88.2 | 88.9 | 88.7 | 93.5 | 95 | 94.6 |
| 14 - 15 (Secondary) | 77.7 | 69.6 | 72 | 83.2 | 78.7 | 80 |
| 16 - 17 (Higher Secondary) | 57 | 54.7 | 55.4 | 63.5 | 49.4 | 53 |

Source: NFHS-4 2015-16 (Figures are in percentages.)

**TABLE 4.5**

**GER and NER (2016-17) in Uttar Dinajpur and West Bengal**

| District/ State | GER | NER |
|---|---|---|
| Uttar Dinajpur | 64.14 | 32.72 |
| West Bengal | 80.21 | 48.55 |

Source: UDISE 2016-17 (Figures are in percentages.)

**TABLE 4.6**

**GER and NER (2019-20) in West Bengal**

| School Level | GER | NER |
|---|---|---|
| Secondary | 77.9 | 50.2 |
| Higher Secondary | 51.4 | 32.3 |

Source: Udise+2019-20 (Figures are in percentages.)

According to the data (Table 4.5 & 4.6), Gross Enrolment Ratio and Net Enrolment Ratio (2016-17) in the district were lower than the state averages. The Net Enrolment Ratio was less than 50 per cent at both state and district levels. There was a sharp decline in the Gross Enrolment Ratio and Net Enrolment Ratio from the secondary to the higher secondary level in West Bengal during 2019-20. The overall picture shows that gross enrolment and net enrolment has improved in the subsequent years.

**TABLE 4.7**

**Proportion of Girls in School at State, District and Block Levels (2016-17)**

| State/District/ Block | Total Enrolment | Girls (%) |
|---|---|---|
| West Bengal | 16144562 | 50.7 |
| Uttar Dinajpur | 669357 | 52.6 |
| Raiganj | 99560 | 50.3 |

Source: UDISE 2016-17 (Figures are in percentages.)

**TABLE 4.8**

**Enrolment of Girls and Boys at the State and District Levels (2019-20)**

| State/District | Girls (%) | Boys (%) | Total Enrolment |
|---|---|---|---|
| West Bengal | 52.9 | 47.1 | 6551538 |
| Uttar Dinajpur | 58.3 | 41.7 | 253945 |

Source: Udise+2019-20 (Figures are in percentages.)

Table 4.7 shows that the proportion of girls in schools is almost equal to the proportion of the boys. The proportion of girls in schools is a little more than 50 per cent at district level. The highest proportion of girls' enrolment was found at the district level. Reports show that girls of rural areas could not attend school due to the distance between the school and home, lack of safety, absence of female teachers and lower preference for girls' education (NFHS Report, 2015-16, Bandyopadhyay, 2019). If we look upon the data (Table 4.8) the enrolment of girls has increased from 2016-17 to 2019-20 at the state level and at the district level. Table 4.8 shows that enrolment of girls are more than boys at the district level, followed by the state level.

**TABLE 4.9**

**Age Specific Enrolment of Girls and Boys at the State Levels (2019-20)**

| Age wise Enrolment | Girls | Boys | Total |
|---|---|---|---|
| 11-13 | 91.1 | 86 | 88.5 |
| 14-15 | 92.4 | 76.7 | 84.4 |
| 16-17 | 60.2 | 48.2 | 54.1 |

Source: Udise+2019-20 (Figures are in percentages.)

The table 4.9 shows age specific enrolment at the state level. There is not much variation in the enrolment of girls from 11-15 years of age. A decline in the enrolment 16-17 years age group can be observed.

**TABLE 4.10**

**Gender Parity Index at Secondary and Higher Secondary Level**

| State/District/ Block | Year | Secondary | Higher Secondary |
|---|---|---|---|
| West Bengal | 2016-17 | 1.2 | 1 |
| Uttar Dinajpur | 2016-17 | 1.4 | 1.3 |
| Raiganj | 2016-17 | 1.2 | 1.1 |
| West Bengal | 2019-20 | 1.2 | 1.2 |

Source: UDISE 2016-17, Udise+2019-20

Table 4.10 indicates that girls' enrolment was higher than the boys in the state level in 2016-17. Gender parity index at the higher secondary level improved at the state level in 2019-20. The gender parity index was calculated here to know the number of girls in school. Uttar Dinajpur has a higher gender parity index among all the districts of West Bengal. Raiganj block displays a lower gender disparity as compared to the district average.

**TABLE 4.11**

**Percentage of Schools in West Bengal, Uttar Dinajpur and Raiganj**

| State/District/ Block | Urban | Rural | Total (n = 100) |
|---|---|---|---|
| West Bengal | 13.6 | 86.4 | 97828 |
| Uttar Dinajpur | 5.5 | 94.5 | 3246 |
| Raiganj | 0.4 | 99.6 | 521 |

Source: Udise+2019-20 (Figures are in percentages.)

It is evident from Table 4.11 that the percentage of rural schools is higher than the urban schools. The percentage of rural schools in Raiganj block exceeds the corresponding figures at the district and state levels. All this shows that there is a greater urbanization at the district level. Other probable factors are the greater number of primary schools at the district and block level. However, the 64 round of NSSO (GOI, 2010) revealed that a few habitations of disadvantaged groups were still not covered.

It is a significant factor that the percentage of state government schools in Uttar Dinajpur exceeds the state average. At the state level the percentage is more than 80 per cent. However, the per centage of private schools is more at the state level than at the district and block level. It is a noteworthy factor that the percentage of government schools is more than other schools with a different kind of management. The presence of government primary schools within one kilometre radius from a habitation exceeds the number of government schools at the district and block levels. The proportions of aided and other management schools are lesser.

**TABLE 4.12**

**Schools by Management Categories in West Bengal, Uttar Dinajpur and Raiganj**

| State/District/ Block | Government | Private | Aided | Others |
|---|---|---|---|---|
| West Bengal | 84.7 | 12.04 | 0.13 | 3.12 |
| Uttar Dinajpur | 90.3 | 8.5 | 0.2 | 0.8 |
| Raiganj | 89.6 | 9.2 | 0.3 | 0.7 |

Source: UDISE 2018-19 (Figures are in Percentages.)

**TABLE 4.13**

**Schools with Various Basic Facilities**

| State/ District/ Block | Drinking Water | Boys' Toilet | Girls' Toilet | Boundary Wall | Play Ground | Ramp | Kitchen Shed | Electricity Connection |
|---|---|---|---|---|---|---|---|---|
| West Bengal | 98.4 | 97.7 | 99.7 | 44.5 | 40.8 | 35.4 | 71.8 | 81.6 |
| Uttar Dinajpur | 99.9 | 99.7 | 100 | 29.7 | 42.9 | 19.3 | 64.1 | 92.6 |
| Raiganj | 99.8 | 100 | 100 | 42.6 | 39.3 | 28.3 | 64.2 | 100 |

*Source: Flash Statistics, 2016-17, NIEPA* (Figures are in Percentages.)

**TABLE 4.14**

**Schools with Other Basic Facilities**

| State/ District/ Block | Computers | Building | Library | Hand wash Facility | Midday Meals | Approachable by Road |
|---|---|---|---|---|---|---|
| West Bengal | 13.1 | 99.8 | 77 | 62.1 | 86.5 | 86.5 |
| Uttar Dinajpur | 8.4 | 100 | 65.5 | 35 | 88.7 | 80.6 |
| Raiganj | 8.1 | 100 | 54.1 | 40.3 | 88.8 | 79.8 |

*Source: Flash Statistics, 2016-17, NIEPA* (Figures are in Percentages.)

These data (Table 4.13 and 4.14) show that 90 per cent of the schools in the district are state board schools which lack the basic physical facilities. It has been noted that 36 per cent schools do not have a kitchen shed. A majority of the schools do not have boundary walls. It has been noticed a few schools do not have electricity at the district and state level. A huge proportion of schools lack computer facilities due to power shortage. A significant proportion of the schools does not have roads and does not receive midday meals. More than half of the schools do not have the handwash facility. Lacking the basic facilities, these schools do not provide a conducive environment for the students. The lack of library and computer facilities affects their classroom environment. A considerable proportion of schools are not approachable by road at the block and district level. Parents do not send their girls to school where the environment is not safe. There are considerable variations in the infrastructure facilities available at the state district and block level.

**TABLE 4.15**

**Pupil Teacher Ratio (PTR) and Student Classroom Ratio (SCR)**

| State/District/Block | SCR | PTR |
|---|---|---|
| West Bengal | 30 | 29 |
| Uttar Dinajpur | 37 | 36 |
| Raiganj | 34 | 31 |

*Source: Flash Statistics, 2016-17, NIEPA* (Figures are in Percentages.)

It has been observed that the pupil teacher ratio is higher at the district level than the state level. The student classroom ratio is higher at the district level. The U Dise + 2019-20 reflects the pupil teacher ratio at different levels. It shows that the pupil teacher ratio at the secondary level is 1:29 and at the higher secondary level it is 1:30 in the district. However, the ratio seems to be higher at the primary and upper primary level.

Similarly, at the block level the pupil teacher ratio is higher at the primary level than at the higher secondary level.

**TABLE 4.16**

**Pupil Teacher Ratio at Different Levels (2019-20)**

| State/District/ Block | Primary | Upper Primary | Secondary | Higher Secondary |
|---|---|---|---|---|
| West Bengal | 30 | 28 | 19 | 28 |
| Uttar Dinajpur | 35 | 44 | 29 | 30 |
| Raiganj | 37 | 31 | 20 | 23 |

*Source: U Dise+2019-20*

The proportion of female teachers (table 4.17) is less than male teachers at the secondary and higher secondary levels. There exists a huge variation between district and block levels. The number of teachers varies at the state level and the district level.

**TABLE 4.17**

**Percentage of Female Teachers at Secondary and Higher Secondary Level**

| State/ District | Secondary | | | Higher Secondary | | |
|---|---|---|---|---|---|---|
| | Female | Male | Total (n = 100) | Female | Male | Total (n = 100) |
| West Bengal | 36.9 | 63.1 | 152851 | 37.8 | 62.2 | 68678 |
| Uttar Dinajpur | 26.8 | 73.2 | 3631 | 27.6 | 72.4 | 1758 |

*Source: U Dise+2019-20* (Figures are in Percentages)

## 4.4 REPETITION, TRANSITION AND DROPOUT

The major indicators to assess the gender inequality are dropout, repetition and transition rates. It has been found that the dropout rates are higher for girls at the secondary and higher secondary levels in India. The transition rate helps to know whether the same proportion of girls are able to transit to the next level as the boys. The transition rate declines at the secondary and higher secondary level (Bandyopadhyay, 2018 *a* and *b*).

The repetition rate of students is higher among girls at the secondary and higher secondary level in the state. At the district and block levels, the repetition rate is low. However, it is evident from the data that there are fewer repetitions among girls at the higher secondary level.

**TABLE 4.18**

**Repetition Rates of Students at Secondary and Higher Secondary Levels**

| State/District/ Block | Secondary | | Higher Secondary | |
|---|---|---|---|---|
| | Boys | Girls | Boys | Girls |
| West Bengal | 0.92 | 1 | 1.4 | 1.24 |
| Uttar Dinajpur | 0.31 | 0.15 | 0 | 0.06 |
| Raiganj | 0.06 | 0.06 | 0 | 0.04 |

Source: Flash Statistics, 2016-17, NIEPA

**TABLE 4.19**

**Dropout Rates, Repetition Rates and Transition Rate for Girls and Boys**

| Gender | Dropout Rate | | Repetition Rate | | Transition Rate | |
|---|---|---|---|---|---|---|
| | West Bengal | Uttar Dinajpur | West Bengal | Uttar Dinajpur | West Bengal | Uttar Dinajpur |
| Girls | 13.6 | 24 | 7.3 | 3.3 | 79 | 72.6 |
| Boys | 14.1 | 22.4 | 6.8 | 3.2 | 79 | 74.3 |
| Total | 13.8 | 23.4 | 7 | 3.2 | 79 | 73.3 |

*Source: U Dise+2019-20* (Figures are in Percentages)

The data from Table 4.19 show that the dropout rate of girls is lower at the state level than the district level. Similarly, repetition rate is higher among the girls at the state level. The transition rate of girls is lower at the district level.

**TABLE 4.20**

**Transition Rates from Upper Primary to Higher Secondary Levels**

| State/ District/ Block | Upper Primary to Secondary | | | Secondary to Higher Secondary | | |
|---|---|---|---|---|---|---|
| | Boys | Girls | Total | Boys | Girls | Total |
| West Bengal | 87.5 | 94 | 90.9 | 74.9 | 68.4 | 71.4 |
| Uttar Dinajpur | 67.9 | 77.7 | 73.5 | 59 | 56.8 | 57.8 |
| Raiganj | 74.6 | 77.9 | 76.4 | 71.8 | 67.2 | 69.3 |

*Source: Flash Statistics, 2016-17, NIEPA* (Figures are in Percentages)

The transition rate of girls is higher in the secondary level in the state, followed by the district and block levels. However, the transition rate of girls is lower than the boys at higher secondary level. The transition rate of girls is considerably lower in the district, compared to state and block level. The overall transition rate is lower for girls at the higher secondary level.

## 4.5 CONCLUSION

In West Bengal, Uttar Dinajpur is the only district which has a huge gap between urban and rural literacy. Most of the secondary and higher secondary schools, the institutions of higher education, are located in the urban areas. There are primary schools in the rural areas. However, the secondary and higher secondary schools woefully lack adequate educational facilities in rural areas compared to the urban areas. Due to the high inter-district and inter-block variation, Uttar Dinajpur has been divided into four zones of gender disparity --- high, moderate, low and very low. The highest disparity was found in Goalpokhar I and the lowest in Hemtabad block. It was revealed the Raiganj had only moderate male-female disparity (District Census Handbook, Uttar Dinajpur, 2011, Hira & Das,

2018). A significant conclusion from the above findings is that male-female disparity needs to be treated as a major concern in this district and the block. It has been found from records that highest girls' enrolment has been found in Uttar Dinajpur, followed by other districts. The proportion of girls' enrolment is, in fact, higher than the boys' enrolment which reflects that the Kanyashree scheme has been effective among parents and community members (Mollah, 2018). The average repetition rate has increased from the secondary to the higher secondary level. Logically, the transition level has decreased from the primary to the higher secondary level. The dropout of girls is higher more at the district level. Though there are improvements in the infrastructure facilities, still the government schools need to go a long way.

This chapter shows the prevailing situation at the state and district level. The empirical data will be presented in the following chapter.

CHAPTER 5

# FACTORS DETERMINING GIRLS' EDUCATION AND EMPOWERMENT

## 5.1 INTRODUCTION

*Women in much of the world lose out by being women.*
*Their human powers of choice and sociability*
*are frequently thwarted by societies in which they must*
*live as the adjuncts and servants of the ends of others,*
*in which their sociability is deformed by fear and hierarchy*

**– Martha C. Nussbaum.**

The author claims that women should claim their power of choice and the opportunities should be realised and augmented. If women fail to attain a higher level of capability, it has been cited as a "problem of justice." The capability approach measures the quality of life when different nations are compared.

The present chapter focusses on various factors that lead to girls' education and empowerment. It is divided into three sections. The first section deals with the profile of teachers, parents and students. It includes the social and economic background of the girls. The second section deals with the various factors leading to girls' education and empowerment. It includes the decision-making process in family about educational matters and other social factors that determine the possibility of education for girls. The social factors which affect the girl's education are related to household chores, patriarchal norms such as early marriage, dowry system. The third section discusses the educational factors that leads to girls' education at the secondary level of schooling. The study explores the factors behind the education and empowerment of girls. There are a few factors that prove to be impediments in the course of acquisition of education by girls and force them to leave school midway.

## SECTION I

## 5.2 PROFILE OF PARENTS, STUDENTS AND TEACHERS

The profile of teachers includes the social category, educational and professional background, and the experience of teaching in schools. The students' profile includes the social category-wise distribution of the students in schools under different managements, age groups of the students, their educational qualification and the economic condition in which they are living.

### 5.2.1 TEACHERS PROFILE

**TABLE 5.1**

**Total Number of Teachers**

| School Type | School Code | Male | Female | Total |
|---|---|---|---|---|
| Government | School 1 | 9 | 2 | 11 |
| | School 2 | 8 | 3 | 11 |
| | Total (%) | 17 (77.2) | 5 (22.7) | 22 |
| Private | School 3 | 7 | 1 | 8 |
| | School 4 | 4 | 4 | 8 |
| | Total (%) | 11 (68.7) | 5 (31.3) | 16 |
| | Total | 28 (73.7) | 10 (26.3) | 38 |

*Source: Field Data*

Interviews were conducted with 38 teachers in all. From the government schools, 22 teachers and 16 teachers from private schools were selected purposively on the basis of their availability and their willingness to participate. Out of the total number teachers, 28 were males and 10 females. In the government schools 17 male and 5 female teachers were interviewed. In private schools, 11 male and 5 female teachers were selected for interview. It was found that the number of female teachers was low here.

**TABLE 5.2**

**Educational Qualification of Teachers**

| School Type | School Code | Graduate | | Post Graduate & Above | | Total |
|---|---|---|---|---|---|---|
| | | Male | Female | Male | Female | |
| Government | School 1 | 1 | 0 | 8 | 2 | 11 |
| | School 2 | 3 | 1 | 5 | 2 | 11 |
| | Total | 4 | 1 | 13 | 4 | 22 |
| Private | School 3 | 3 | 0 | 4 | 1 | 8 |
| | School 4 | 0 | 2 | 4 | 2 | 8 |
| | Total | 3 | 2 | 8 | 3 | 16 |
| | Total | 7 | 3 | 21 | 7 | 38 |

*Source: Field Data*

It was found that the teachers needed a master's degree as the educational qualification in private schools. A majority of male teachers in government schools and a few female teachers held this degree. There were two teachers with the Doctor of Philosophy (PhD) degrees --- one from a government school and another from a private school. The number of teachers with graduate degree is more in private schools.

The table below shows that a majority of government school teachers had a B. Ed. (Bachelor of Education) or equivalent degree, followed by the private school teachers. The proportion of teachers with no professional qualification or B. Ed. degree was higher among the male teachers than female teachers in private schools. A few teachers in government schools had degrees equivalent to B. Ed.; it was seen in case of the computer science teachers. According to the data from DISE (District Information System for Education), the school profile of the sampled schools revealed that government school teachers were more professionally qualified (had a B. Ed. degree). In private schools, a majority of teachers did not have a B. Ed. degree or any equivalent degree.

**TABLE 5.3**

**Professional Qualification of Teachers**

| School Type | School Code | No Professional Qualification | | B. Ed. or Equivalent Professional Qualification | | Total |
|---|---|---|---|---|---|---|
| | | Male | Female | Male | Female | |
| Government | School 1 | 1 | 0 | 8 | 2 | 11 |
| | School 2 | 3 | 1 | 5 | 2 | 11 |
| | Total | 4 | 1 | 13 | 4 | 22 |
| Private | School 3 | 1 | 0 | 6 | 1 | 8 |
| | School 4 | 0 | 2 | 4 | 2 | 8 |
| | Total | 1 | 2 | 10 | 3 | 16 |
| | Total | 5 | 3 | 23 | 7 | |

Source: Field Data

It was observed that a majority of male teachers in government schools had accumulated more experience than female teachers. In private schools, a majority of teachers fell under the 0-5 years and 6-10 years categories of experience. The number of teachers with more than 10 years of experience was less in private schools. The average experience of female teachers remained low in government and private schools. Among the teachers of government and private schools, four principals had more than 10 years of teaching experience --- two from government schools and two from private schools. Chart 5.1 presents the overall work experience of these teachers, including principals. It is clear from data that government school teachers are more educationally qualified and experienced than private school teachers.

**TABLE 5.4**

**Teaching Experience of Teachers**

| School Type | School Code | 0-5 years | | 6-10 years | | 11-15 years & Above | | Total |
|---|---|---|---|---|---|---|---|---|
| | | Male | Female | Male | Female | Male | Female | |
| Government | School 1 | 2 | 1 | 2 | 1 | 5 | 0 | 11 |
| | School 2 | 4 | 2 | 1 | 0 | 3 | 1 | 11 |
| | Total | 6 | 3 | 3 | 1 | 8 | 1 | 22 |
| Private | School 3 | 2 | 1 | 3 | 0 | 2 | 0 | 8 |
| | School 4 | 0 | 2 | 0 | 2 | 3 | 1 | 8 |
| | Total | 2 | 3 | 3 | 2 | 5 | 1 | 16 |
| | Total | 8 | 6 | 6 | 3 | 13 | 2 | 38 |

*Source: Field Data*

**CHART 5.1**

**Teaching Experience-Wise Distribution of Teachers**

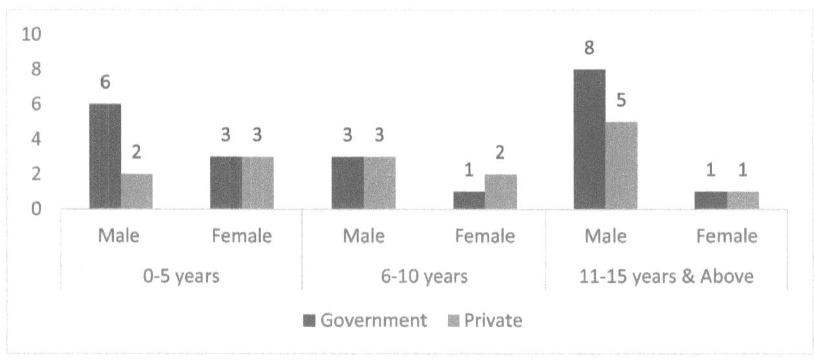


Source: Field Data

### *5.2.2 Parents Profile*

**TABLE 5.5**

**Total Number of Parents**

| School | Number of Parents |
|---|---|
| Government schools | 16 |
| Private schools | 16 |
| **TOTAL** | **32** |

*Source: Field Data*

Thus, 32 parents were selected for the study, out of which 16 parents had their children studying in government schools and 16 in private schools. There were 8 mothers and 8 fathers selected from the government and private schools.

### *5.2.3 Students Profile*

The students selected for the study included both girls and boys. It covered the background information about the students which included age, grade and social milieu to which they belonged, the economic background of their parents that further determines their selection of schools and regulates their aspirations and employment status. It was found that in the rural areas the economic conditions of a family largely determine to what extent its girls are able to access schools.

**TABLE 5.6**

**Total Number of Students**

| School | Boys | Girls | Total |
|---|---|---|---|
| Government | 55 | 55 | 110 |
| Private | 32 | 32 | 64 |
| Total | 87 | 87 | 174 |

*Source: Field Data*

As said earlier, the total number of students considered for the study was 174 --- 110 students were selected from government schools and 64 from private schools. An equal number of girls and boys were interviewed in the case of both, i.e., the government and private schools. The girls were selected purposively and an equal number of boys was taken to compare their responses.

### CHART 5.2

### Age-Wise Distribution of Students in Government Schools

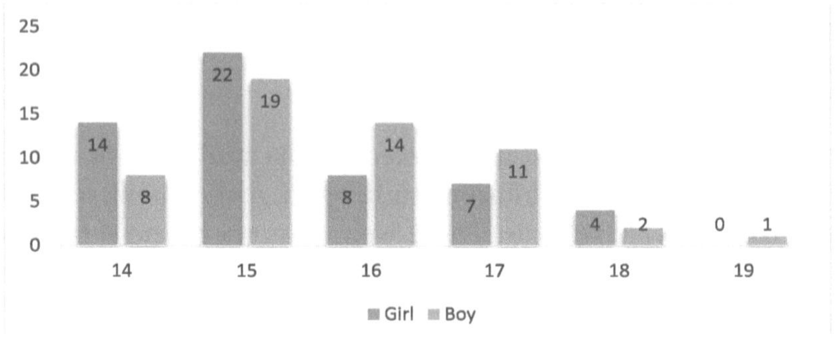


Source: Field Data

It was observed that a majority of the selected students from the government schools were 15 years of age; out of them, 22 were girls and 19 boys. Then, there were 22 students who were 14 and 16 years of age. A few of them were 17 years of age. Six students were 18 years of age and one was 19 years of age. On the whole, a majority of girls were aged 14 to 17 years.

### CHART 5.3

### Age-Wise Distribution of Students in Private Schools

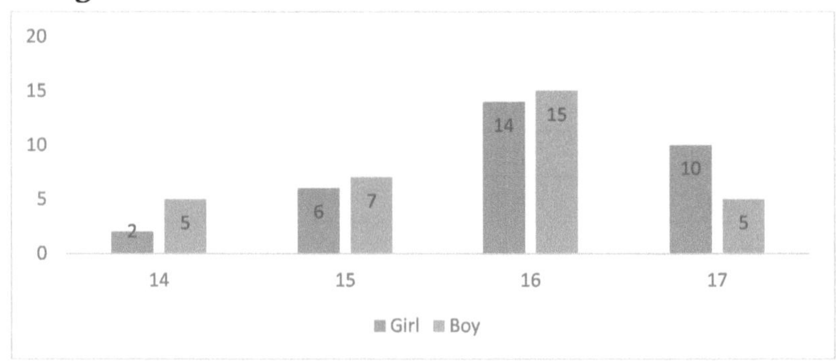


Source: Field Data

A high proportion of students in private schools were 16 years of age, followed by those of 17 years of age. A small proportion of students were 15 years and 14 years of age.

**CHART 5.4**

**Grade-Wise (Secondary and Higher Secondary) Distribution of Students in Schools with Different Managements**

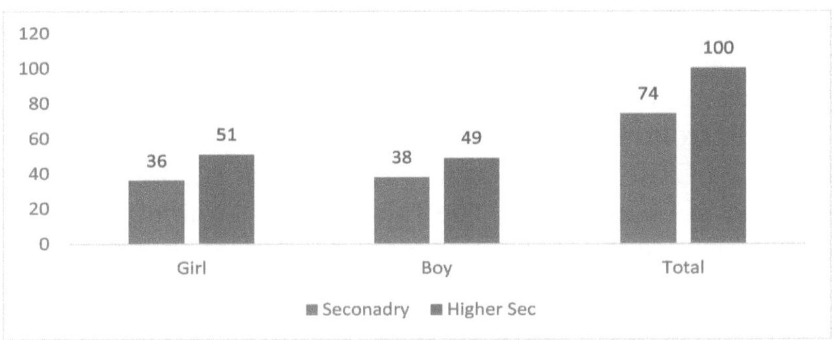


*Source: Field Data*

A high proportion of the students were selected from the higher secondary level. In all, 36 girls and 38 boys were selected from the secondary level, and 51 girls and 49 boys from the higher secondary level from schools under different managements. As is the usual practice, the secondary level included both Classes IX and X while the higher secondary level meant Classes XI and XII taken together.

**TABLE 5.7**

**Social Category-Wise and Gender-Wise Distribution of Students**

| Caste | Girl | Boy | Total |
|---|---|---|---|
| ST | 3.4 | 1.1 | 2.3 |
| SC | 35.6 | 34.5 | 35.1 |
| OBC | 8.0 | 6.9 | 7.5 |
| Muslim | 13.8 | 17.2 | 15.5 |
| General | 39.1 | 40.2 | 39.7 |
| Total (N = 100) | 87 | 87 | 174 |

*Source: Field Data* (Figures in Percentages)

An effort was made to find out the socioeconomic backgrounds of the children belonging to various social groups during the interview conducted by the present investigator. The profile of the students showed that a large proportion of students belonged to the Scheduled Castes, Muslims, Other Backward castes and Scheduled Tribes categories. The proportion of girls belonging to the general category and of those from the Scheduled Castes were higher than those from other social categories. The concentration of the Scheduled Caste communities was heavier in fact due to the migrated Scheduled Caste workers into Uttar Dinajpur from Bangladesh after the Partition. However, the Scheduled Caste population in Raiganj block is comparatively less than in other blocks. The rural literacy attainment is low here because of the concentration of deprived Scheduled Caste and Muslim communities in this region. The females from the Scheduled Castes, Scheduled Tribes and Muslim communities were in fact worse affected than other communities in this region (District Human Development Report, Uttar Dinajpur, 2010). In the rural areas of Raiganj, uneven concentration of diverse social communities was observed. A sizeable proportion of the Scheduled Caste and Muslim communities constitutes the agricultural workforce in these blocks. These social communities are mostly landless agricultural labourers who are engaged in various activities, apart from farming, during the off seasons.

The table 5.8 depicts the social category-wise distribution of students in government and private schools. It was found that the percentage of Scheduled Tribe students was low in all the schools. The percentage of Scheduled Caste girls was higher in the government schools (43.6 per cent) compared to the private schools (21.9 per cent). The proportion of Schedule Caste and Muslim girls attending government schools was higher than those in the private schools. In the private schools, the percentage of Scheduled Caste girls was higher as compared to Scheduled Caste boys. The proportion of students hailing from the general category was higher in private schools compared to the government schools. A majority of general category girls attends private schools.

**TABLE 5.8**

**Social Category-Wise Distribution of Students in Schools under Different Managements**

| Social Category | Government | | Total | Private | | Total |
|---|---|---|---|---|---|---|
| | Girls | Boys | | Girls | Boys | |
| ST | 0.0 | 1.8 | 0.9 | 9.4 | 0.0 | 4.7 |
| SC | 43.6 | 45.5 | 44.5 | 21.9 | 15.6 | 18.8 |
| OBC | 10.9 | 3.6 | 7.3 | 3.1 | 12.5 | 7.8 |
| Muslims | 20.0 | 21.8 | 20.9 | 3.1 | 9.4 | 6.3 |
| General | 25.5 | 27.3 | 26.4 | 62.5 | 62.5 | 62.5 |
| Total (N = 100) | 55 | 55 | 110 | 32 | 32 | 64 |

*Source: Field Data* (Figures in Percentages except in the Last Row)

A smaller proportion of girls in the general category attends the government schools. This table clearly indicates that girls belonging to the Scheduled Caste, Other Backward Caste and Muslim categories goes to attend the government schools. It has also been observed that there is a wide gap in the proportion of girls attending government schools and those attending private schools from the Scheduled Caste, Other Backward Caste and Muslim categories. Studies have shown that in the north eastern states where Scheduled Caste and Scheduled Tribe populations are in a majority, children belonging to these social groups have low years of schooling (Thangjam and Ladusingh, 2018). In some case, it has been noted that the proportion of boys belonging to the deprived social categories (Other Backward Castes and Muslims) are higher than girls in private schools while the proportion of Other Backward Caste boys attending private schools is also higher than the boys attending government schools. Thus, the choice of school depends largely on the parents' economic status in various social categories. The data reflect inequality in the parents' choice of schools for the girls and boys. In literature, we find several similar references on the rising inequalities in school education and the disparities; moreover, these have not yet come down to any acceptable levels (see, for instance, Govinda & Bandyopadhyay, 2019). The concentration of Schedule Tribe girls and boys is low in Raiganj block and the same is being reflected in schools.

The choice of school has been discussed in details in the later pages.

### *Parents' Educational Qualifications*

According to the District Human Development Report for Uttar Dinajpur (2010), the district happens to be one of the least literate districts in West Bengal. The male literacy is lowest in Uttar Dinajpur while it is ahead of only one district in female literacy. Education backwardness is a major problem in this district, with a large proportion of illiterates being rural women. Urban population constitutes only around 12 per cent. Thus, a huge part of the district is rural without the satisfactory availability of many of the amenities.

The students background can be better understood with the help of parents' educational qualification and occupation. The proportion of fathers with no formal education schooling is higher among the socially disadvantaged categories. The Scheduled Castes have the highest proportion of fathers with no formal schooling. In the socially disadvantaged categories (ST, SC and Muslims), a majority of the fathers, if at all educated, have only primary and secondary level of education. Only a small proportion of the Scheduled Caste and Muslim parents were graduates and postgraduates. It is worth noting that Other Backward Castes have been ahead of the other socially disadvantaged categories in the matter of higher education --- postgraduation and above. The bulk of the population who are graduates and postgraduates are from the urban parts of Raiganj.

The educational qualifications of fathers in the Scheduled Tribe category lag far behind not only those of the general category but even of the other social disadvantaged categories. Several fathers belonging to this category had no higher education. The reason behind this could well have been their poverty. They did not get financial support from the government either. Families' demand for physical work in the fields or any other occupations could have been the other reasons. The data revealed that several OBC and Muslims fathers (of boys) did have higher education --- graduation and postgraduation. Some of the girls' fathers from the socially disadvantaged categories are graduates. The maximum educational qualification of fathers was postgraduation, followed by other educational qualifications. Those who fall in this category of other educational qualifications are generally doctors, engineers and PhDs. A majority of them are from the general category; few of them are from the Scheduled Castes. Thus, the social category does have an impact on educational qualifications and occupations of individuals which, in turn, regulates their school selection for children. If we look at the data, educational backwardness is higher among the girls' fathers than the boys' fathers.

The table 5.10 below shows that an overwhelming proportion of the mothers had had no formal schooling. But a majority of these mothers are from the socially and economically disadvantaged categories. It was also seen that most of the first-generation learners were girls' mothers. Education backwardness is also higher among the Scheduled Castes, Scheduled Tribes and Muslims. It is a striking feature that boys from Other Backward Castes have mothers with higher education followed by the girls whose mothers mostly have senior secondary education. It was found that a few girls' mothers from the in socially disadvantaged categories were graduates and above. Girls' mothers belonging to the general category were mostly graduates and postgraduates or had other higher educational qualifications. The data represent that mothers belonging to the general, Other Backward Caste and Muslim categories have, overall, higher education. Researches show that in a few states of India educational attainment among Muslim females is high (Z. Hasan & R Menon, 2005). It has been observed that a few graduates and postgraduates were from the Muslim community, which shows that educational backwardness is related to the deficiency of education system rather than the community affiliations (DHDR 2010).

**TABLE 5.9**

**Social Category-Wise Distribution of Fathers' Educational Qualification of Girls and Boys**

| Gender | Social Category | No formal Schooling | Primary | Secon dary | Senior secon dary | Graduate & above | Total (N = 100) |
|---|---|---|---|---|---|---|---|
| Girls | ST | 0.0 | 33.3 | 33.3 | 33.3 | 0.0 | 3 |
| | SC | 9.7 | 22.6 | 16.1 | 25.8 | 25.8 | 31 |
| | OBC | 14.3 | 28.6 | 0.0 | 14.3 | 42.8 | 7 |
| | Muslims | 16.7 | 25.0 | 41.7 | 8.3 | 8.3 | 12 |
| | General | 2.9 | 20.6 | 8.8 | 20.6 | 47 | 34 |
| | Total | 8.0 | 23.0 | 16.1 | 20.7 | 32.2 | 87 |
| Boys | ST | 0.0 | 0.0 | 100.0 | 0.0 | 0 | 1 |
| | SC | 20.0 | 33.3 | 20.0 | 13.3 | 13.3 | 30 |
| | OBC | 16.7 | 16.7 | 0.0 | 0.0 | 66.7 | 6 |
| | Muslims | 0.0 | 40.0 | 20.0 | 0.0 | 40 | 15 |
| | General | 0.0 | 17.1 | 17.1 | 5.7 | 60 | 35 |
| | Total | 8.0 | 26.4 | 18.4 | 6.9 | 40.0 | 87 |

*Source: Field Data* (Figures in Percentages except in Last Row and Column)

## TABLE 5.10

## Social Category-Wise Distribution of Mothers' Educational Qualification of Girls and Boys

| Gender | Social Category | No Formal Schooling | Primary | Sec-ondary | Senior Second-ary | Graduate & above | Total (N = 100) |
|---|---|---|---|---|---|---|---|
| Girls | ST | 0.0 | 0.0 | 33.3 | 66.7 | 0.0 | 3 |
| | SC | 19.4 | 19.4 | 29.0 | 16.1 | 16.1 | 31 |
| | OBC | 28.6 | 28.6 | 28.6 | 14.3 | 0.0 | 7 |
| | Muslims | 33.3 | 25.0 | 33.3 | 0.0 | 8.3 | 12 |
| | General | 2.9 | 23.5 | 11.8 | 29.4 | 32.4 | 34 |
| | Total | 14.9 | 21.8 | 23.0 | 20.7 | 19.5 | 87 |
| Boys | ST | 0.0 | 100.0 | 0.0 | 0.0 | 0.0 | 1 |
| | SC | 26.7 | 36.7 | 23.3 | 6.7 | 6.7 | 30 |
| | OBC | 0.0 | 33.3 | 0.0 | 0.0 | 66.7 | 6 |
| | Muslims | 6.7 | 53.3 | 6.7 | 13.3 | 20.0 | 15 |
| | General | 8.6 | 11.4 | 22.9 | 5.7 | 51.4 | 35 |
| | Total | 13.8 | 29.9 | 18.4 | 6.9 | 31.0 | 87 |

*Source: Field Data* (Figures in Percentages except in Last Row and Column)

## TABLE 5.11

## Fathers' Educational Qualifications and School-Wise Distribution of Students

| School Type | Gender | No Formal Schooling | Primary | Secondary | Senior Second-ary | Graduate & above | Total (N = 100) |
|---|---|---|---|---|---|---|---|
| Government | Girls | 12.7 | 34.6 | 18.2 | 21.8 | 12.7 | 55.0 |
| | Boys | 12.7 | 38.2 | 27.3 | 5.5 | 16.3 | 55.0 |
| | Total | 12.7 | 36.4 | 22.7 | 13.6 | 14.5 | 110.0 |
| Private | Girls | | 3.1 | 12.5 | 18.8 | 65.6 | 32.0 |
| | Boys | | 6.3 | 3.1 | 9.4 | 81.2 | 32.0 |
| | Total | | 4.7 | 7.8 | 14.1 | 73.4 | 64.0 |

*Source: Field Data* (Figures in Percentages)

It is disheartening to see that a high proportion government school students are the first-generation learners. A substantial proportion of fathers in government schools has primary, secondary and senior secondary education. Moreover, a small proportion of the fathers are graduates and postgraduates in government schools. At the same time, a majority of children in the private schools has qualified fathers who were graduates and postgraduates. Overall, private schools have more educationally qualified fathers than government schools.

In Raiganj, the general population send their children to private schools. It was found that private schools are situated near the Raiganj Municipality building. According to Thangjam and Ladusingh, 2018), more children from the economically sound households are enrolled at the secondary and higher secondary level than children from economically weaker households. Their study also highlighted that although three fourths of the children were enrolled in public schools in rural areas, their patronisation for private schools is increasing. Some secondary sources[7] show that there is a dearth of secondary and higher secondary schools in rural areas while overwhelming facilities for secondary and higher secondary schooling are available in the urban areas of Raiganj, especially at the municipal headquarters. There is a huge gap in the number of schools and literate population in the rural and urban areas of Raiganj.

**TABLE 5.12**

**Distribution of Mothers' Educational Qualification of Boys and Girls in Schools under Different Managements**

| School Type | Gender | No Formal Schooling | Primary | Secondary | Senior Secondary | Graduate & above | Total (N = 100) |
|---|---|---|---|---|---|---|---|
| Government | Girl | 23.60 | 34.50 | 25.50 | 9.10 | 7.30 | 55 |
| | Boy | 21.80 | 43.60 | 29.10 | 3.60 | 1.80 | 55 |
| | Total | 22.70 | 39.10 | 27.30 | 6.40 | 4.50 | 110 |
| Private | Girl | | 0.00 | 18.80 | 40.60 | 40.60 | 32 |
| | Boy | | 6.30 | 0.00 | 12.50 | 81.20 | 32 |
| | Total | | 3.10 | 9.40 | 26.60 | 60.90 | 64 |

*Source: Field Data* (Figures in Percentages except in Last Column)

The education of the mothers is equally important for sending their girls and boys to school. But a significant proportion of mothers with no formal education or with a minimum level of education were sending their girls to government schools. Be they educated or non-educated, mothers always want their girls to be educated. Similarly, a significant proportion of mothers had primary and secondary education in government schools. It is worth noting that only a small proportion of the girls enrolled in the government schools had mothers with higher educational qualifications --- senior secondary and graduates. There was a high proportion of educationally qualified mothers (senior secondary, graduates, and postgraduates with other professional degrees) in private schools. It is noteworthy that 28 per cent of the girls' mothers were postgraduates and professional degrees holders.

This clearly indicates a positive impact of a mother's educational qualification on her daughter's education on the one hand, and selection of choice of school irrespective of gender on the other hand. A majority of qualified mothers with graduate and postgraduate degrees send their children to private schools. However, the enrolment of such girls in private schools is low. The data indicate that parents of 15 per cent children enrolled in secondary and senior secondary classes had no formal education and the parents of more than 60 per cent children had higher education (secondary, senior secondary, graduate and above). Recent research on the parental gradients and educational attainment by Thangjam and Laduisingh (2018), conducted in the north eastern states of India, revealed that parental education, particularly mothers' education, enhances the years of schooling of their children. Their finding is that the economic wellbeing of a household is an insignificant factor of educational outcome in the regions where mothers' literacy is restricted.

### *Occupational Patterns of Parents*

Like everywhere else, the occupational pattern in Uttar Dinajpur district consists of three categories --- the primary sector, secondary sector and tertiary sector. According to the Human Development Report 2010, the main source of rural livelihood is agriculture in Uttar Dinajpur and a majority of the rural workforce primarily depends on it. According to the DHRD report (2010), a large chunk of the main workforce has been forced to move from farm-based activities to non-farm-based activities, leading to impoverished effects on the people of the district. The Census 2001 had a fourfold classification of occupations --- cultivators, agricultural labours, household industry workers and other workers. Among them, cultivators and agricultural labours fall under the primary sector, household industry workers come under the secondary sector and those in services come under the tertiary sector.

**TABLE 5.13**

**Fathers' Occupations and School-Wise distribution of Girls and Boys**

| School Type | Gender | La-bourer | Agricul-ture | Self- Em-ployed | Private job | Govern-ment Job | Total (N = 100) |
|---|---|---|---|---|---|---|---|
| Govern-ment | Girl | 1.8 | 38.2 | 40.0 | 5.5 | 14.5 | 55 |
| | Boy | 14.5 | 29.1 | 38.2 | 7.3 | 10.9 | 55 |
| | Total | 7.3 | 33.6 | 40.0 | 6.4 | 12.7 | 110 |
| Private | Girl | | 6.3 | 34.4 | 18.7 | 40.6 | 32 |
| | Boy | | 12.5 | 6.3 | 18.8 | 62.5 | 32 |
| | Total | | 9.4 | 20.3 | 18.7 | 51.6 | 64 |

*Source: Field Data* (Figures in Percentages)

If we look at the data on the occupational pattern, a majority of fathers are involved in agricultural activities since it is predominantly an agricultural region. There was a small proportion of fathers who were daily wage labourers. Some of the them were involved in agricultural activities and self-employed. The fathers who are self-employed run their own small-scale businesses. These may be categorised as large- and small-scale businesses, like grocery shops, bicycle repair business, etc. Some of them own huge tracts of land from which they sell vegetables in the market. It was found from the data that the proportion of fathers engaged in services such as government and private jobs was higher in private schools than in government schools. A few of the fathers whose children were enrolled in government schools were engaged in clerical jobs and peon jobs. However, the fathers' occupational pattern also showed that some of the children in government schools were from well to do families. In case of the private school children, their fathers were engaged in services, like police officers, doctors, bankers and state civil servants.

**TABLE 5.14**

**Mothers' Occupations and School-Wise Distribution of Girls and Boys**

| School Type | Gender | Unemployed | Daily Wage Labour | Agriculture | Self-employed | Private job | Government job | Total (N = 100) |
|---|---|---|---|---|---|---|---|---|
| Government | Girl | 60 | 18.20 | 7.3 | 3.60 | 1.8 | 9.1 | 55 |
| | Boy | 78.1 | 5.50 | 5.5 | 1.80 | 3.6 | 5.5 | 55 |
| | Total | 69.1 | 11.80 | 6.4 | 2.70 | 2.7 | 7.3 | 110 |
| Private | Girl | 71.8 | | 0.0 | | 9.4 | 18.8 | 32 |
| | Boy | 59.4 | | 3.1 | | 25.0 | 12.5 | 32 |
| | Total | 65.6 | | 1.6 | | 17.2 | 15.6 | 64 |

*Source: Field Data* (Figures in Percentages)

The data (Table 5.14) indicate that mostly mothers were homemakers in both types of schools. These mothers, irrespective of their educational qualifications, preferred to manage the household chores. It was found that a majority of mothers of the government school children are daily wage labours, agriculturists or self-employed. In government schools most of the mothers was working as daily wage labourers. A considerable proportion of mothers from private schools was engaged in services (government and private jobs) in comparison to the government schools. The proportion of working mothers of girl children are more in government schools than in private schools.

## SECTION II

## 5.3 DECISION-MAKING PROCESS IN EDUCATION AND FAMILY

The process of decision-making within the family depends not only upon the agreement of the family members but also on the head's ability to convince the members of the family. The study explores the impact of education on the decision-making ability of the girls and how far it is different from the boys. It tries to understand the difference in the decision-making ability of girls and boys, and also the role of parents in the guidance and support of their children. The decisions concerned the choice of school and the choice of subject which differed in the government and private schools.

### *5.3.1 Decision on School Choice*

The choice of school and of subject is an important factor that impacts the decisions regarding further educational possibility. The choice of school depends largely on who has access to what kind of school.

The study tries to understand the girls' and boys' access to different kinds of schools. Girls from diverse backgrounds have different preferences about schools. Similarly, parents from diverse social classes and categories have differential preferences about the choice of school. There were two categories of respondent.

Category I included ones who were convinced about the parents' choice of school. In this category girls and boys from private schools were convinced about their parents' choice of school. A chunk of students belonging to the government schools came under this category. There was not much difference between the responses of girls and boys in private schools, as they felt their parents had made the most preferable educational choices for them. It was found from the enrolment that a small proportion of girls belonging to elite background could reach the private schools. Hence the proportion of girls' enrolment was found to be less in the private schools than in government schools.

In case of the government schools, girls were aware of the difficulties which their parents face while sending them to school. Hence the choice of school remained limited to them. Government school girls felt that the facilities provided by their schools were suitable to their needs. The girls and boys from government schools explained that the schools are good in terms of studies and excels in sports.

Category II consisted of ones who were not convinced with their parents' choice of school. Girls from government school fell in this category. To understand why the girls of government schools were not satisfied with the choice of school, they were further questioned by the researcher to understand the type of schools which they preferred and the reasons behind it. The data revealed a high proportion of girls who preferred private schools. The preference on choice of school can be better understood by looking through their lens.

A girl studying in a government school desired to study in a private school. She belongs to the Muslim minority and was studying in a secondary class in a government school. Her father buys and sells grains from the field. The father had only primary education while the mother was secondary educated. The mother were home makers. They lived in a semi-*pucca* house which has gas and electricity connections. She stated: "*The government school remains closed most of the time. Sometimes there are no classes. We miss our classes and cannot complain about it. Private schools are better. In our school, teachers are less and in rainy season classes are waterlogged. Hence the school remains closed during the rainy season.*"

The school is in a low lying and gets water logged in the rainy season. This government school is not able to follow the minimum number 220 instruction days as a mandatory RTE mandate in an academic year.

There was a 16 years old girl from a low middle class family. Her father runs a small grocery shop and mother is a housewife. She lives in a *kutcha* house which has electricity but no gas connection. She explains her dependence on the facilities and incentives provided in the government schools to complete her education: "*I prefer government schools where poor intelligent students, who desire to study, can study without spending money and get facilities for completion of schooling such as books, mid-day meals, etc.*"

There was a girl, 15 years old, who belongs to a socially and economically disadvantaged category. Her father works in the fields. She is from a low-income group, belongs to the SC category and studies at the senior secondary level. Both here parents are senior secondary educated. The father owns some land and lives in a semi-*pucca* houses in which the roof is made of tin or asbestos. She has electricity and gas connections in her house. She prefers a private school over a government school. The family's financial condition and location of the school are the two main factors for the choice of a school but she is aware of the facilities available in private schools. She said: "*All government schools are nearby and private schools are far away. I desire to study in a private school but could not do so because of their location.*"

A 16 years boy belongs to a socially and economically disadvantaged category. His father is primary educated and works in the fields, while his mother has no formal education and works in fields. They have their own land, live in a *kutcha* mud-thatched houses which has electricity but no gas connection. He explained the reason for his choice of school. He said: "*I had to choose a government school due to poor living conditions and low family income.*"

A 17 years old boy is a first-generation learner belongs to a socially disadvantaged group. His parents have no formal schooling; father is a cultivator and mother is a daily wage labourer who works in the fields of others. He lives in a *kutcha* house which has electricity but no gas connection He intends to study in a private school but cannot study because of the financial constraints. He is a first-generation learner and helps father in the fields after school in all the seasons. He stated: "*In government schools children gets different types of benefits. They give importance to education over money. Though I desire to study in a private school because of good educational facilities there, the government school provides us with the basic standard education.*"

Other girls from government schools expressed that teachers were good and teach patiently. They are highly experienced and cooperative. Teachers solve our problems and provides a healthy environment for studies.The responses given by students on the choice of schools has been thematically categorised under certain broad themes. These are (a) school location, (b) educational facilities and incentives, and (c) quality of education.

***Category 1: School Location***

The proportion of private schools is quite small. The girls have to walk down to some far-flung, deserted areas. Government schools are located within one kilometre radius from the habitation. It was found that a majority of girls and a few boys of the government schools favoured a school in a nearby locality. One of the girls in a government school said that all government schools were located nearby while the private schools were far away.

***Category 2: Availability of Facilities and Incentives***

Data from the field revealed that a majority of girls belonging to the low-income groups were aware that their financial conditions and the availability of incentives in government schools played an important role in their schooling. The fees in government school quite low and there are a lot of facilities available. The government provides stipends for girls in these schools. During the interviews, the girls stated that in private schools a lot of money was required. It was difficult for their parents to bear such expenditures.

One of the girls responded: "*My parents are not very affluent, so I have to study in a government school. The financial condition of the family does not permit me to study in a private school where the fees and expenditure are high.*"

Another girl stated: "*My parents will not be able to send me to a private school because of our financial condition and they are more worried about my future and try to provide me the best option they can afford.*"

In government schools, we find more availability of the educational facilities and incentives, and a majority of girls and boys enrol in these schools even if they wish to study in a private school. One of the girls stated that she preferred a government school where poor children who are intelligent and desire to study can study without spending much money and also get facilities like textbooks and mid-day meals for completion of schooling.

Another girl responded: "*......in government schools children get different types of benefits and facilities. They give importance to education over money and other things. Government schools provides us with standard education.*"

A majority of the students said a government school offers a lot of educational facilities --- stipends, books and clothes. It has been observed that since the girls are poor and belong to the weaker sections of society, they depend on government schools for their education. The incentive schemes provide a lot of support to these schools. As a result, girls are interested and have aspirations of continuing their education if they get support from the government. Some other views which they shared were that teachers are cooperative and there is a healthy and helpful environment for study.

Another government school student made a different remark. He said: "*Most students think that in government schools' studies and teaching are good but they are unaware of the facilities in private schools. Being children of poor parents, they cannot afford to go to private schools.*"

*Category 3: Quality of Education Provided in Schools*

A small proportion of girls from government schools responded that private schools were better than the government schools. All the children enrolled in private schools favoured their schools.

The girls opined that *"a majority of students think that studies and teaching are good in government schools but they are unaware of the facilities in private schools. Being children of poor parents, they cannot afford to go to private schools."*

These girls admire the school culture and discipline. There was one girl who had studied in a government school and had then shifted to a private school. She thus shared her views and experiences: *"I have been studying in a government school earlier from class one to five and then in a private school and, according to my experience, private schools have better educational facilities. Teachers, rules and everything is very strict and students are brought up in a proper and disciplined and organised manner."* Another girl stated: *"I have been attending government schools since childhood and cannot think of any other alternatives."*

**CHART 5.5**

**Reasons for School Preference of Boys in Government Schools**

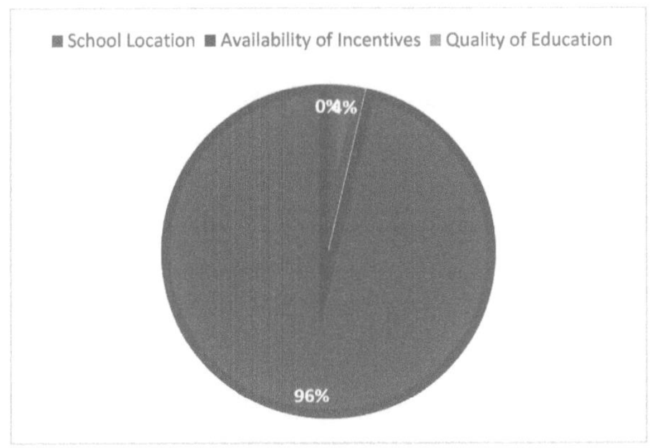


*Source: Field Data*

A majority of girls in private schools mentioned that the education system in a private school is more helpful for a student to grow. Private schools offer proper systematic study. Students have good experiences and learn new things in these schools.

**CHART 5.6**

**Reasons for School Preference of Girls in Government Schools**

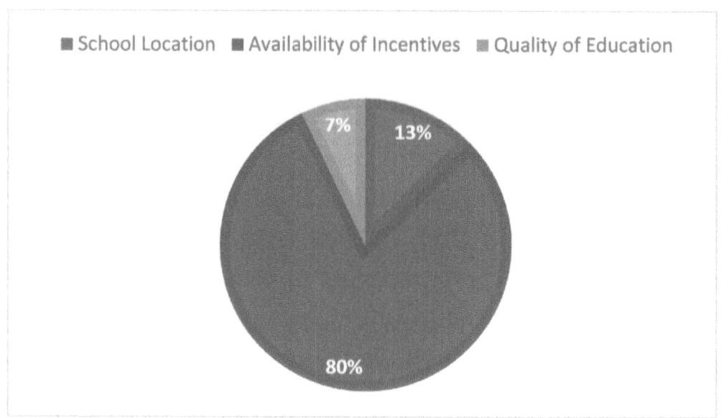


*Source: Field Data*

### *5.3.2 Parents Perception on Choice of School*

It was observed that parents' perception varied in government schools. The parents of government school girls proclaimed that the school was the best school in the locality. One of the girls' parents stated: "*It is a good school; I have studied in this school and I want my daughters to study here.*" A father, who runs a small bicycle business and is from a socially deprived group, has two children --- a boy and a girl. He said: "*It is a good school, I have studied in this school and both my children are studying here.*" Parents of a few girls said the school was near their home. Other parents felt that the school provided cheapest education and was nearer home.

In private schools, a majority of the parents felt that the school was the best school in the locality. The parents of one of the girls stated that "*the school is near our home and good in all respects.*" The parent of a girl studying in a private school said: *"The school is good; I come all the way in an auto to drop her."* It was observed that a school in the proximity, within a radius of one kilometre or so, or nearer home, remains a preference of all the girls' parents, irrespective of the type of school they are sending their girls to.

### *5.3.3 Decision on Choice of Subject at Secondary Level*

The choice of a subject is based on one's ability to take decisions for their career and aspirations. The researcher tried to probe the respondent girls and boys on the choice of a subject which they had either made or will be making in the near future.

If we look at the data, a majority of girls (56.4 per cent) in government schools chose humanities as a subject than science subjects. The proportion of girls choosing science as a subject was less. There was a higher proportion of boys choosing science and commerce as a subject. In private schools, a high proportion of girls and boys selected science as a subject. A few girls selected humanities, followed by commerce, at the senior secondary level. Studies have shown that girls and boys make subject preferences depending upon the gender, career and higher education preferences (Vleuten & Jaspers, 2015). It was found that boys made subject choices based on their preferences for occupation and higher education. Girls are household makers and their choice of subjects are more feminine. It was found by these researches that boys and girls make different choices of subjects depending on their social environment, peers, parents, teachers and schools. Adolescents internalises the gender role expectations in their ideology, and it plays an important role in choice of subject. However, even though girls selected subjects that are considered masculine, such as science, for boys it was difficult to enter the feminine domain. Traditional discourses show that a majority of secondary school students select gender-stereotypical subjects. It was claimed that both the sexes were good at both the types subjects. Our study seeks to discover the subject preferences for different genders and whether the reasons for the selection of subjects are based on ability or anything else (Francis, 2000).

## CHART 5.7

## Choice of Subjects at Senior Secondary level in Government Schools

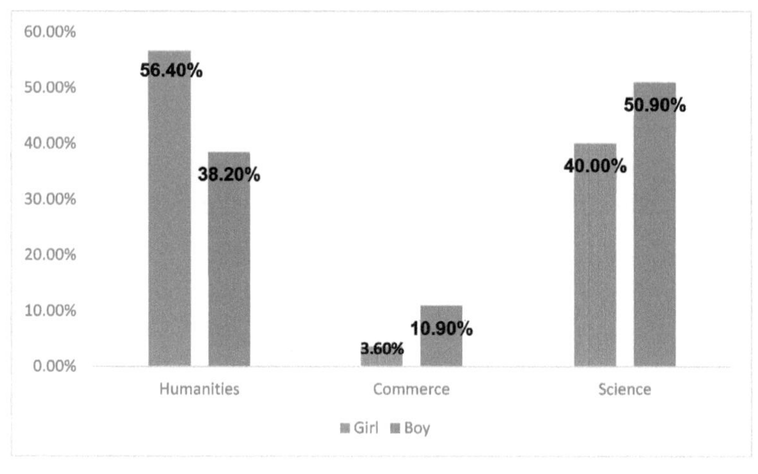


*Source: Field Data*

## CHART 5.8

## Choice of Subjects at Senior Secondary level in Private Schools

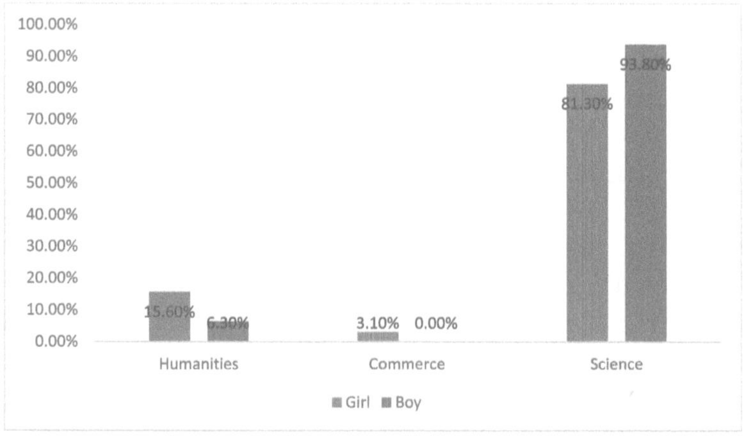


*Source: Field Data*

Discussions with the respondents show that the decisions regarding subject choices made by the girls had the following reasons

First, the choice of a subject was based on the peer pressure. Girls who were unable to make their own choices mostly depend on their friends or peer groups to seek guidance about it. These children choose subjects which a majority of the children select in the class. They are unclear about their own choice, have low aspirational levels and are indecisive about career choices. It is seen that girls opt for subjects like humanities and boys opt for science under the peer pressure. Generally, it is found that peer pressure works more among boys than girls. A smaller proportion of girls selected a subject because of peer pressure.

Second, the choice of a subject is made by parents. It was found that parents selected humanities for girls. But the proportion of parents selecting science for girls is significant in government schools. Similarly, the proportion of boys' parents who selected science as a subject was higher than girls. A small proportion of parents selected science for the boys of private schools. Parents whose girls are in private schools selected science for the senior secondary level. In West Bengal, parents choose subject on behalf of their children on the basis of their own aspiration levels rather than the girls' aspiration levels. In most parts of West Bengal, science as a subject is given more preference over commerce and humanities. Parents who belong to the working class prefer their girls to become school teachers and doctors, and boys to be doctors and engineers. Overall, the proportion of parents who prefer their girls to study science is less than that in the case of boys. The guidance given by their parents shows that decisions regarding the choice of subject and career are mostly taken by the parents. This is more evident in case of the parents who are working and affluent.

One of the respondents stated that "*at home parents give us the feedback and guidance in selection of the subject and I agree with them and like their decisions. I believe they are more experienced than us and are our well-wishers.*"

Another respondent from a government school said that she liked studying science but was forced to take humanities because her sisters had studied the same subject. They thought she would not be able to cope up with the science subject. Most of the parents visualise that they would get their daughters married after graduation. Hence, they persuade their daughters to select humanities as they would not be able to bear the expenses of science education after the school level. In rural areas. girls and boys believe that their parents' decisions regarding schooling and choice of subject was ultimate and that they made correct choices of career for them. One girl mentioned that she had chosen this subject because of her parents and that her teachers believed that she could make a better career and be motivated.

Thirdly, a choice based on interest. In this regard, choices are made by girls based on their interest and understanding of the subject. It was seen that a majority of the girls decided about their subject choice on the basis of their own understanding of the subject. A respondent explained that she desired to study a subject of her own choice and score well and get selected in a good college of her choice and make her parents proud. Another girl stated that "*the subject I have chosen for study is one in which I am interested. I will give my heart and soul to learn the subject because of my inquisitiveness and passion for it.*" A girl studying in a government school said that "*education is not for employment; to be knowledgeable and to know about a subject one needs to select the subject on the basis of own choice and not anyone else choice.*"

A significant factor is that the proportion of girls who had made their own choices of the subjects is more than that of the boys in private schools. In government schools, a high proportion of girls and boys had their choice of subjects based on interest. In government schools, girls selected humanities followed by science while boys selected science followed by humanities. Similarly, in private schools, girls selected science followed by humanities.

Fourthly, the choice was decided by the prospect of entering higher education. There is a small proportion of girls who select a subject on the basis of their ideas about higher education. Mostly, girls selecting science as a subject fall under this category. A girl who had selected science as a subject said that "*I like studying this subjects and desire to be a doctor. I seek to clear the Joint Entrance Exam and get selected in a medical college.*"

Fifth, the choice was based on the career aspirations. It was evident from the data that the girls studying in private schools selected science as a subject on the basis of career aspirations. Similarly, boys studying in private schools selected a science subject on the basis of career aspirations. A small proportion of girls in government schools selected subject such as humanities on this very basis. One of the respondents stated that she had selected humanities as this subject selection would enable her to excel at the next level. She said this subject would help her to grow in career in future. A girl studying in a government school said: "*I will become an engineer and will make my parents proud. I like this subject and will work in this area after completing my studies.*" Another girl opined that "*I want to pass my graduation and take admission in the B. Ed. programme to become a teacher.*"

Sixth the choice based on availability of subjects in schools. In this context an important factor is non availability of different subjects like science, mathematics, history and vocational subjects. The girls and boys in private schools preferred subjects like fashion technology, fashion designing, forensic science, film making/ dramatics, photography and international languages. There is a growing demand of these subjects in schools. The girls and boys demand for these subjects at higher secondary level and continue them in higher institutions.

A boy from a private school said that the choice of subject he desired to study was not available in the school and locality where he was studying. He preferred to study film making which is commonly not available in schools.

In the sample school's science, commerce and humanities are available in the sample schools. However, some specific subject may not be available. For instance, a 17 years old boy, is studying in a government school at senior secondary level. He belongs to the Scheduled Caste category. His father has primary education, and works on his own agricultural land and mother has no formal schooling, she looks after the household work and helps her husband in the fields. They live in a *kutcha* house with electricity but no gas connection. His choice has been limited due to non-availability of subject in the school. He said: "*I desired to become a historian in future. But in this school humanities department does not have History subject and I cannot change the school because of my family's financial condition.*"

Hence some students are not able to select a particular subject which is not available in the department.

In government schools, a smaller proportion of girls made the choice of subject for the sake of a career as compared to boys. On the contrary, a large proportion of girls in private school made the choice of subject based on career. But their proportion was smaller than the boys.

### *5.3.4 Personal Preferences and Decision-Making Ability*

The choice of subject is, on the one hand, based on the ability to take decisions for their future career aspirations and on personal preferences, on the other hand. Science is the most preferred subject choice among boys and girls in private schools, but it is less so in the government schools. In fact, a high proportion of girls selected humanities compared to boys in government schools. The preference for selecting a subject at the senior secondary schools is based on interest, career choices and higher education. The data revealed that a significant proportion of girls do not prefer to study humanities at the secondary level in private schools. Similarly, a proportion of girls do not prefer to select science as a subject. But a majority of students in private schools have their own preferences in selection of the subjects. The proportion of students who do not have personal preferences in subject selection, is lower in case of the private schools. The researcher tried to understand the perceptions of girls and boys for preferring or not preferring a particular subject in schools under different managements.

**TABLE 5.15**

**Gender-Wise Distribution of Subject Choices and Personal Preferences of Students Enrolled in Government Schools**

| Gender | Subject Choice | Personal Preferences of Students Enrolled in Government Schools | | Total (N = 100) |
|---|---|---|---|---|
| | | No | Yes | |
| Girl | Humanities | 5 | 26 | 31 |
| | | 16.1 | 83.9 | 100.0 |
| | Commerce | 0 | 2 | 2 |
| | | 0.0 | 100.0 | 100.0 |
| | Science | 8 | 14 | 22 |
| | | 36.4 | 63.6 | 100.0 |
| | Total | 13 | 42 | 55 |
| | | 23.6 | 76.4 | 100.0 |
| Boy | Humanities | 4 | 17 | 21 |
| | | 19.0 | 81.0 | 100.0 |
| | Commerce | 0 | 6 | 6 |
| | | 0.0 | 100.0 | 100.0 |
| | Science | 5 | 23 | 28 |
| | | 17.9 | 82.1 | 100.0 |
| | Total | 9 | 46 | 55 |
| | | 16.4 | 83.6 | 100.0 |

*Source: Field Data* (Figures in Percentages)

However, in government schools, a considerable proportion of students do not have personal preferences while selecting the subject. But the academic achievement tends to be higher for the students who have personal preferences for a subject. Studies show that academic achievement has a direct link with the personal preference for the subjects. As 76.4 per cent girls and 83.6 per cent boys in government schools and 93.8 per cent girls and 78.1 per cent boys in private schools have personal preferences in subject selection, and this impacts their achievement level.

### TABLE 5.16

### Gender-Wise Distribution of Subject Choices and Personal Preferences of Students Enrolled in Private Schools

| Gender | Subject Choices | Personal Preferences of Students Enrolled in Private Schools | | Total (N = 100) |
|---|---|---|---|---|
| | | No | Yes | |
| Girl | Humanities | 1 | 4 | 5 |
| | | 20.0 | 80.0 | 100.0 |
| | Commerce | 0 | 1 | 1 |
| | | 0.0 | 100.0 | 100.0 |
| | Science | 1 | 25 | 26 |
| | | 3.8 | 96.2 | 100.0 |
| | Total | 2 | 30 | 32 |
| | | 6.3 | 93.8 | 100.0 |
| Boy | Humanities | 2 | 0 | 2 |
| | | 100.0 | 0.0 | 100.0 |
| | Science | 5 | 25 | 30 |
| | | 16.7 | 83.3 | 100.0 |
| | Total | 7 | 25 | 32 |
| | | 21.9 | 78.1 | 100.0 |

*Source: Field Data* (Figures in Percentages)

The researcher tried to probe the views held by respondent girls and boys on the choice of subject. It was critical to understand whether the choices of subject made by the girls and boys were under the guidance of their parents, purely on their own or their parent's choice. From the qualitative interviews conducted with the girls and boys, the responses were further categorised.

**Table 5.17**

**Gender-Wise Distribution of Students on Decision-Making on Subject Choices**

| School Type | Gender | Decision taken by parents | | | Decision taken by students | |
|---|---|---|---|---|---|---|
| | | Parents selected but students were not convinced | Parents selected the subject students were convinced | Parents selected the subject and students were partially convinced | Students' choice; Parents support | Students' own choice without any support |
| Government | Girl | 4 | 13 | 19 | 7 | 12 |
| | Boy | 6 | 9 | 26 | 3 | 11 |
| | Total | 10 | 22 | 45 | 10 | 23 |
| Private | Girl | 0 | 2 | 14 | 9 | 7 |
| | Boy | 1 | 7 | 1 | 18 | 5 |
| | Total | 1 | 9 | 15 | 27 | 12 |
| Total | Girl | 4 | 15 | 33 | 16 | 19 |
| | Boy | 7 | 16 | 27 | 21 | 16 |
| | Total | 11 | 31 | 60 | 37 | 35 |

*Source: Field Data*

***Category I: Decision Taken by Parents, Students were Convinced***

The proportion of students belonging to this category was higher in government schools than in private schools. These students did not have their own personal preferences and followed the decisions taken by their parents. A majority of them opted for the subjects preferred by their parents. One of the girls from a government school stated: "*My parents' choice is my choice.*" A similar statement given from a private school girl was: "*I am convinced about my parents' choice of subject and school as they have taken correct decisions for me.*" A boy from a government school said: "*I have chosen this subject because my parents and teachers motivated me to do so.*"

***Category II: Decision Taken by Parents and Students were Partially Convinced***

A majority of students belong to this category. But the proportion of such students was higher in government schools than in private schools. Though these students had their personal choices, they went by their parents' choice of subjects. The factors behind this kind of choice are the profession of parents and the prospects for their children regarding the same profession, the possibility of entrance to higher education, interest in the subject and better learning environment in schools. There were a few students in private schools who opined that these schools had facilities and laboratories for learning science. One student from a government school said that teachers were knowledgeable and school provided facilities for studying science which were not available in other government schools. A girl from a government school said: "*At home I have to listen to my parents and hence they have taken their choice of subjects.*" Another girl from a government school was of the opinion: "*I am convinced with my parents' choice because the school is well equipped and provides facilities for studying science. Teachers of these government schools are qualified. They help us to understand the topic and resolve our problem.*" A boy from a private school stated that "*I prefer to become a doctor like my parents and my parents supported me.*"

### *Category III: Decision Taken by Parents but Students were not Convinced*

There were a few students who had their personal preference in selection of subjects but their parents forced them to select a different subject which was of their choice. The students' own preference was based on interest and the prospects for higher education. The proportion of these students was higher in government schools. A girl from a government school, belonging to a socially disadvantaged category, desired to study science but selected humanities under her parents' pressure. "*No one in my family will agree to my subject choice. Everyone has a different choice,*" said a government school girl.

Similarly, a boy who belonged to a socially disadvantaged category, one whose father had no formal education and was a daily wage labourer while his mother was a housewife, stated that "*I do not have a personal preference while choosing the subject. My parents forced me to take science and I do not understand the subject. It has many difficult terms which I am unable to interpret.*"

However, it has been noticed that choice of subjects is sometimes not available with the schools and locality or block. Hence students are not convinced with the subjects available in schools. They have to agree with the parent's choice as they are unable to switch to another school.

### *Category IV: Decision Taken by Students with Parents Supporting Their Choice.*

The proportion of such students was high in private schools as compared to government schools. Another striking feature is that the more private school boys belong to this category. There is a high proportion of girls who selected science, as compared to humanities, in private schools. Similarly, the proportion of girls selecting humanities was higher in government schools. It was evident that all such students had their own personal preferences. One of the girls from a private school stated that "*I had preference in choosing the stream in consultation with my parents, I have chosen science as I like the subject.*" Another boy from a private school stated: "*I have my personal preference while choosing the stream. I aspire to become a lawyer so I took political science and law.*"

A private school boy explained: "*I am not only convinced but also extremely happy and thankful to the decisions made by our parents regarding the choice of school. This school in Raiganj is the best of its kind in the town and being affiliated to the ISC and ICSE it allows a wider scope of knowledge. I had been supported by my parents to take up humanities after the 10th standard and therefore I have nothing to complain.*" He then added: "*The choice of subject completely depended upon me and my parents supported it.*"

***Category V: Decision Taken by Students without the Guidance and Support of Parents***

In this category, a high proportion of girls and boys opined that they had taken their own decisions in the selection of a subject. There was no involvement of parents. The proportion of students who had chosen their subjects was higher was in government school than in private schools. A majority of girls had chosen humanities in government schools and science in private schools. These students had their own personal preference in the selection of subject. In government schools there are two girls who belonged to socially disadvantaged groups, were the first-generation learners and has selected subjects of their own choice. They opined that they have selected subjects of their choice because their parents could not guide them at all. The parents were informed of their choice of the subject.

"*My parents did not study in school, hence I decided to choose a subject on my own,*" told a government school girl. One of the students opined: "*I have selected my own subject for the purpose of my study.*"

The girl from a private school said: "*Humanities is my choice of subject and with these I want to excel to the next level. I will study this subject in future and grow in my career.*"

*Category VI: Decision Taken by Students in consultation with Teachers and Peers*

Few girls and boys from government school took the guidance of teachers and even consulted their peers.

It is evident from the data that a majority of the students who selected subjects on their own did so on the basis of career prospects, interest, higher education prospects, or peer pressure. On the contrary, some did not have any personal preference while selecting the subjects.

### *5.3.5 Parental Guidance in Subject Selection*

Parental guidance in the selection of subjects at the senior secondary level was higher in case of girls in private schools. Parents sending their children to government schools agreed that they provided personal guidance to the girls in selection of subjects after the secondary level. The proportion of girls who did not receive any kind of guidance in the choice of subject remained low in government schools. The boys received parental guidance in selecting the subjects, irrespective of the kind of their schools, at the higher secondary level. However, the type of guidance provided by government school parents was different from those of the parents of private school students. Private schools had specialized counselling department to help the students after secondary level. Some of the parents from government schools did not provide any guidance to their children in the selection of their subjects. These parents supported the girls in order that they become emotionally strong and independent. Many of such parents were uneducated and daily wage earners. One of them said "*We do not know anything about education and the subjects, and we left it to their children as to what they wanted to study.*" Parents sending their children to government schools stated that children had made their own choice of stream with the help and guidance from teachers in school.

One of the government school parents who had studied till the eighth standard and runs a small bicycle business, said: "*Yes,*

*I have supported my children about the choice of stream, but it was just for guidance. My own educational background is not strong enough to provide any type of academic guidance.*"

### *5.3.6 Decision on Choice of Profession*

The decisions on choice of profession are related to the subjects selected at the senior secondary level. It was observed that respondents gave opinion on subject choices on the basis of their future choice of profession. It may be observed from Table 5.18 below that a majority of girls in government schools selected the teaching profession. This is because it is considered to be the most respectable and safe profession for girls. A small proportion of the girls also selected the doctor's profession. Only a small proportion of girls selected business, engineering and other professions. Similarly, a high proportion of the boys in government school selected teaching as a profession, followed by engineering, medicine and others. There are a large proportion of girls who, having selected humanities and a few girls who selected science subjects at the senior secondary level, chose the teaching profession. A few boys from government schools studying humanities chose the teaching profession. A majority of boys studying science at the senior secondary level chose the profession of doctors and school teachers. However, a majority of the girls who had selected science as a subject in private schools chose the profession of doctors, followed by engineers. Similarly, boys in private schools studying science subjects at the senior secondary level preferred to become engineers and doctors. Some of the girls from government schools chose other professions such as Service Selection Board Officer, police, writer in a popular magazine, etc. Similarly, some of the boys desired to become painters, writers, camping professionals and filmmakers. A considerable proportion of girls in private schools had had other professional choices. If some of them aspired to become a writer pr army officer, others desired to become a journalist or a professor. One of the girls stated: "*I would like to join the administrative sector; something like intelligence bureau would be highly satisfying.*" Another girl said: "*I would like to start an NGO.*" Some of the boys studying in private schools had other choices and desired to become IAS officers; one of the boys studying science at the senior secondary level desired to work in the area of forensic sciences.

Thus, government school girls generally have aspirations to become school teachers, irrespective of the subjects they are studying. A majority of the girls desired to become a school teacher and only a small proportion of them aim to become doctors, engineers and other professionals. On the contrary, in private schools, a large proportion of girls aspired to become doctors, engineers, lawyers, and forensic experts, journalists and police officers.

**TABLE 5.18**

**Gender-Wise Distribution and Choice of Profession in Government Schools**

| Gender | Any Other | Business | Engineer | Doctor | School Teacher | Total (N = 100) |
|---|---|---|---|---|---|---|
| Girl | 5.5 | 5.5 | 3.6 | 12.7 | 72.7 | 55 |
| Boy | 12.7 | 5.5 | 23.6 | 14.5 | 43.6 | 55 |
| Total | 9.1 | 5.5 | 13.6 | 13.6 | 58.2 | 110 |

*Source: Field Data* (Figures in Percentages)

**TABLE 5.19**

**Gender-Wise Distribution and Choice of Profession in Private Schools**

| Gender | Any other | Engineer | Doctor | School teacher | Total (N = 100) |
|---|---|---|---|---|---|
| Girl | 31.3 | 18.8 | 46.9 | 3.1 | 32 |
| Boy | 15.6 | 53.1 | 25.0 | 6.3 | 32 |
| Total | 23.4 | 35.9 | 35.9 | 4.7 | 64 |

*Source: Field Data* (Figures in Percentages)

### *5.3.7 Parents' Perception on Choice of Profession*

It is clear from the data that parents preferred the girls to be school teachers in government schools. One or two of them preferred other jobs such as doctors. Similarly, in the case of private schools, parents opted for a school teacher job for their girls. Only a few of the parents chose the profession of doctors or engineers for their girls. The parents favoured government jobs for their boys which were permanent jobs. Some of the parents preferred their boys to be engineers and school teachers in government schools. In private schools, parents preferred that their boys enter the teaching, doctor and engineer jobs.

**TABLE 5.20**

**School-Wise Distribution of Parents' Choice of Profession for Girls and Boys**

| School Type | Gender | School Teacher | Doctor | Engineer | Any Other | Total |
|---|---|---|---|---|---|---|
| Government | Girls | 6 | 1 | 0 | 1 | 8 |
| | Boys | 3 | 0 | 1 | 4 | 8 |
| | Total | 9 | 1 | 1 | 5 | 16 |
| Private | Girls | 3 | 1 | 2 | 2 | 8 |
| | Boys | 5 | 1 | 1 | 1 | 8 |
| | Total | 8 | 2 | 3 | 3 | 16 |

*Source: Field Data*

Some of the parents were liberal-minded and said that they had not yet decided about it; that their children would themselves decide their profession. The father of one of the girls stated: "*None of the options I would like the child to work according to their own choice and his or her intelligence.*" Another girl's parent stated: "*Teaching which she also likes.*" A boy's parent stated: "*Whatever job the child likes to do.*"

### ***5.3.8 Aspirations for Entering Higher Education***

It is evident from the data that in government schools a higher proportion of girls had the aspiration to continue their education after the senior secondary level and pursue higher education. Yet it was observed that the proportion of girls who opted for higher education remained low compared to the boys. It was heartening to know that a considerable proportion of girls had aspirations to work after completing school education. The proportion of these girls was higher than the boys. A small proportion of girls for socially and economically disadvantaged category chose the household chore after completing the school. It was observed that several students (girls) did not feel they would be able to convince their parents about higher education and therefore were content with the household chore or some minor job after passing the school. It was found that these respondents, who hailed from the socially backward and economically weaker sections, did not opt for higher education due to the family pressure and chose to look after the household chores or do some outside work and support them financially.

One of the girl respondents from a socially disadvantaged group, whose parents had no formal education (father worked in the fields and mother was a daily wage earner), chose to stay at home to help mother with the household chores. They live in a *kutcha* house which has electricity but no gas connection and they use firewood to cook food.

Another girl respondent belongs to a socially deprived group. Her father is primary educated and mother is illiterate, both work in fields and live in a *kutcha* house agreed to do household work and help parents in the fields after schooling.

A boy, whose parents work on an agricultural land, lives in thatched house which has no electricity and gas connection. This boy had his own choice of subject at the senior secondary level and was not sure whether he would be able to convince his parents for higher education. He desires to take up a job after the senior secondary level to support his family financially. He said: "*After passing from school, I will work and try to overcome the financial crisis of my family.*

## CHART 5.9

## Aspiration of Girls and Boys after Senior Secondary Education in Government Schools

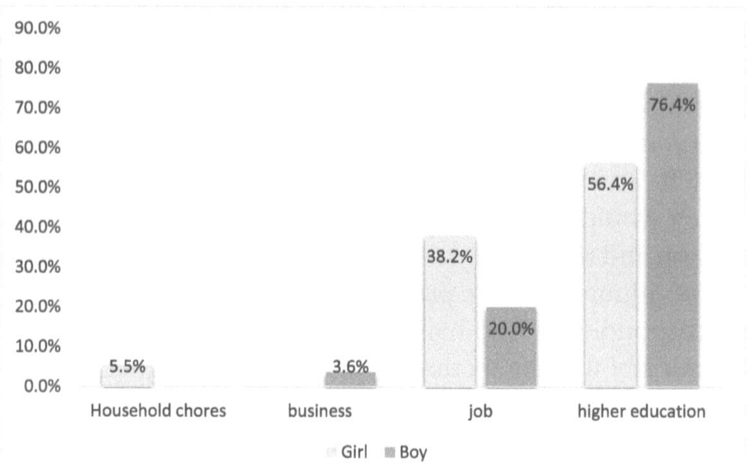


*Source: Field Data*

## CHART 5.10

## Aspirations of Girls and Boys after Senior Secondary Education in Private Schools

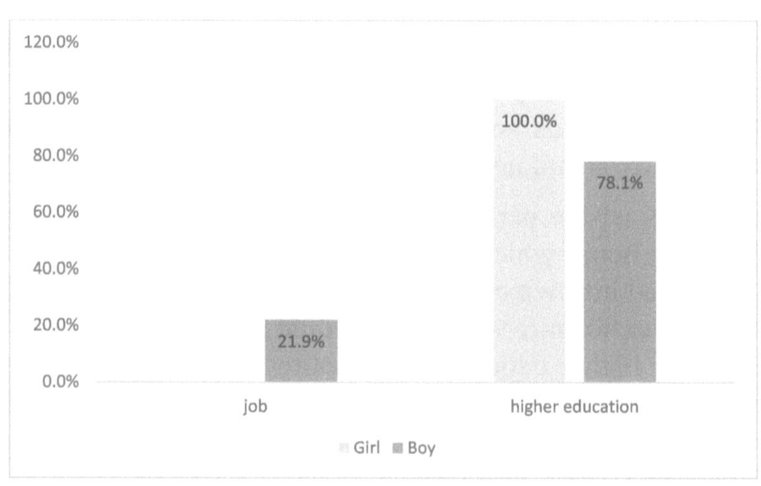


*Source: Field Data*

It is clear from the data gathered from private schools that a majority of the girls wanted to pursue higher education. Though most of the boys preferred to go in for higher education, a considerable proportion of the boys preferred to work after completing their senior secondary education. All the private school students felt that that they would be able to convince their parents about pursuing higher education. A majority (98.2 per cent) of the government school students also opined they would be able to convince their parents for higher education. But a few students felt that they would not be able to convince their parents for higher education due to their poor economic background.

### *5.3.9 Parent's Aspiration on Higher Education and Economic Factors behind Girls' Education*

A majority of the parents proclaimed that they would send their children for higher education. They stated that it was for their children to decide whether they would continue their education further. Some of them said they will help their daughters to study up to the school level. Another parent opined that he would try to give his wards higher education after Class XII if they get some financial support. Other parents believed that their children should get education according to their will and aspiration. They said they would help and promote the girls to get higher education. A parent said that "*girls can become independent and fearless by getting education. They should be educated so that they can live a better life and shape a better society.*" Parents also felt that girls would get special recognition in their future families after completing higher education. Some believed that higher education is not the only factor; special recognition comes once the girl starts earning money. One of the parents sighed deep and said that "*after higher education they have to earn money and manage household work, so special recognition is just a term used for respect.*"

The parents were further questioned whether they would let their daughters have higher education in case they were offered a job or a marriage proposal. They believed that studies were essential for girls. A majority of the parents proclaimed that they would let their girls pursue higher education. It was disheartening to know that a few parents of government school girls felt that marriage was a better option. They thought that girls could study even after marriage. However, in case of the boys, all the parents believed that they should pursue higher education; as an exception one of the parents who that his son had stopped studying of his own will and had no interest in studies. They were insisting upon him to complete the senior secondary level at least.

**CHART 5.11**

**Parents' Willingness to Let Girls Continue Education after Senior Secondary Level**

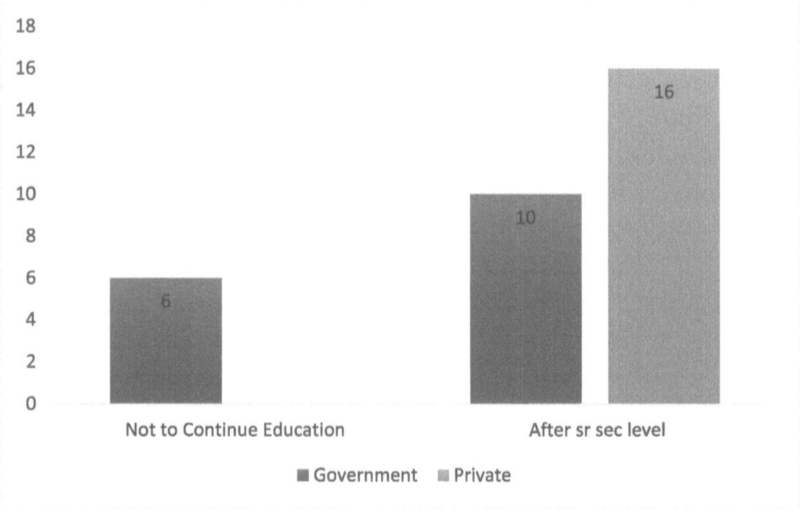


*Source: Field Data*

It is evident from the chart 5.12 that a majority of the parents did not face any hardship while sending their girls to school. It was disheartening to know that a small proportion of government school parents said they were facing financial loss and labour loss while sending their girls to school. One of them stated: "*We are suffering both financial and labour losses. If only she were with us, she could help us in farming activity.*" Another parent (mother) felt that there was labour loss; she said: "*I have to do a lot of physical labour. Since there is no male member in the family, so I think there is labour loss.*" One of the mothers stated that "*the father feels there is loss of labour in the fields but I feel there is no loss in educating her.*"

**CHART 5.12**

**Gender Wise Distribution on Hardship Suffered by Parents**

*Source: Field Data*

It was found that a majority of the parents were of the opinion that girls should work after completing school education or higher education. One of the parents said that girls have to work after completing their studies and it is one of the reasons for sending them to school. A small group of parents do not want their girls to work. A couple, who have two children, a girl and a boy, expressed their opinion on the girl's choice of work. They specifically believed that the boys should work and girls not. They thought that the boys should become doctors or engineers or hold high positions in government jobs but girls should not work; rather they should manage the household chores after studies. One of the parents, who had a girl and a boy, desired his son to become a doctor but did not want his daughter to do any job.

**CHART 5.13**

**Parents' Opinions on Letting Girls Work after Completing Education**

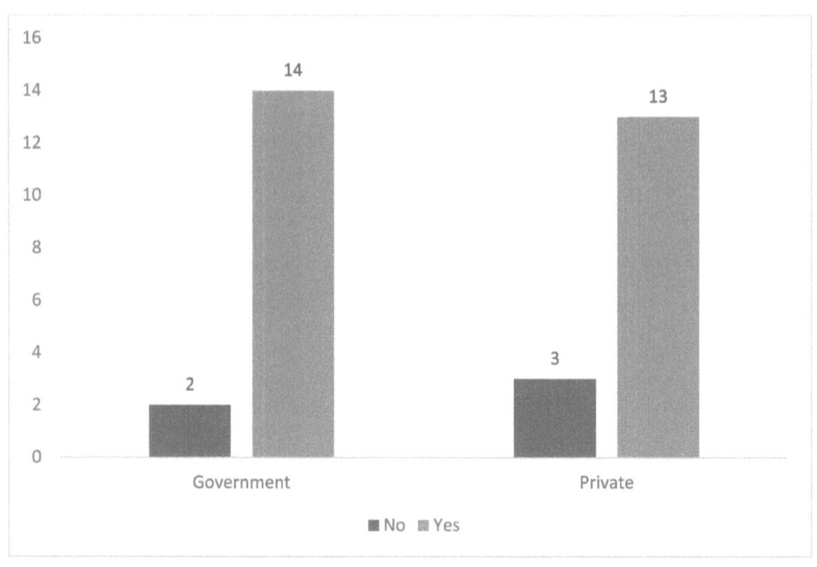


*Source: Field Data*

Some of the parents belonged to the socially deprived categories and the children of some were first generation learners. They work in farms or owns small businesses such as selling vegetables in the market to sustain themselves. They felt girls should work after completing their senior secondary education so that they could sustain their families. Some of the poor parents were found suffering a lot of hardships while sending their daughters to school.

## 5.4 HOUSEHOLD FACTORS AND OTHER FACTORS INFLUENCING EDUCATION

The household factors and other factors influencing decision-making includes the girls' involvement in household chores, patriarchal family environment, decisions on marriage and choice of partners, studying time, voicing opinion, mobility factors and financial independence.

***5.4.1 Household Chores:*** It is evident from the data that a majority of the children of government schools are engaged in household chores such as sweeping the floor. It was found that a significant proportion of girls were doing all the household chores. Similarly, a significant proportion of the boys were involved in all the household chores. The common household activities which the girls are performing are looking after siblings, sweeping the floor, helping in kitchen, fetching water and helping parents in the fields. The boys were involved in activities such as sweeping the floor, fetching water, feeding animals and washing clothes. It was found that a majority of boys were involved in activities outside home such as helping parents in the fields and small-scale family businesses (grocery shops, cycle business) after the school. These boys assist their father in the shops, and study, and play games in free time. One of the boys said: *"I do not work at home; my parents do all the work by themselves."* Another boy stated after school he helped his parents in the paddy fields.

It was clear that both boys and girls studying in government schools were involved in the household chores. But a small proportion of girls who were not involved in any household chores and they said they play and study after school time.

In private schools, a significant proportion of girls helped their parents in kitchen. A small proportion of the girls are involved in household chores such as fetching water, washing plates and all household activities. A high proportion of boys are involved in activities apart from household chores these included purchasing household items such as vegetables and medicines from the market. A small proportion of girls are involved in activities such as watering the plants and arranging the clothes in the cupboard.

### TABLE 5.21

### Household Activities of Girls and Boys from Government Schools (Figures in Percentages)

| Gender | Nothing | Looking after Small Children | Sweeping in the House | Helping in Kitchen | Fetching Water | Feeding Animals | Tailoring | Washing | Any Other | All the Above | Total (N= 100) |
|---|---|---|---|---|---|---|---|---|---|---|---|
| Girl | 3.6 | 7.3 | 38.2 | 10.9 | 7.3 | 1.8 | 1.8 | 0.0 | 7.3 | 21.8 | 55 |
| Boy | 3.6 | 5.5 | 20.0 | 3.6 | 5.5 | 10.9 | 0.0 | 9.1 | 25.5 | 16.4 | 55 |
| Total | 3.6 | 6.4 | 29.1 | 7.3 | 6.4 | 6.4 | 0.9 | 4.5 | 16.4 | 19.1 | 110 |

*Source: Field Data*

### TABLE 5.22

### Household Activities Performed by the Students of Private Schools (Figures in Percentages)

| Gender | Sweeping in the House | Helping in Kitch-en | Fetching Water | Washing Plates | Feeding Animals | Washing Clothes | Any Other | All the Above | Total (N = 100) |
|---|---|---|---|---|---|---|---|---|---|
| Girl | 0.0 | 40.6 | 18.8 | 6.3 | 3.1 | 6.3 | 18.8 | 6.3 | 32 |
| Boy | 6.3 | 0.0 | 12.5 | 0.0 | 0.0 | 12.5 | 65.6 | 3.1 | 32 |
| Total | 3.1 | 20.3 | 15.6 | 3.1 | 1.6 | 9.4 | 42.2 | 4.7 | 64 |

*Source: Field Data*

## CHART 5.14

### Household Chores of Girls and Boys from Government Schools

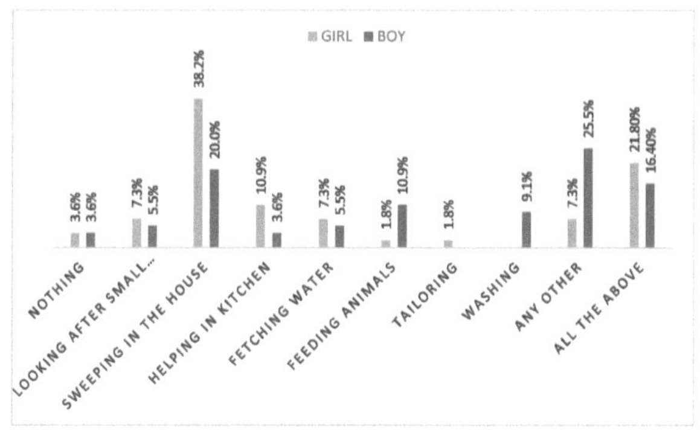


## CHART 5.15

### Household Chores of Girls and Boys from Private Schools

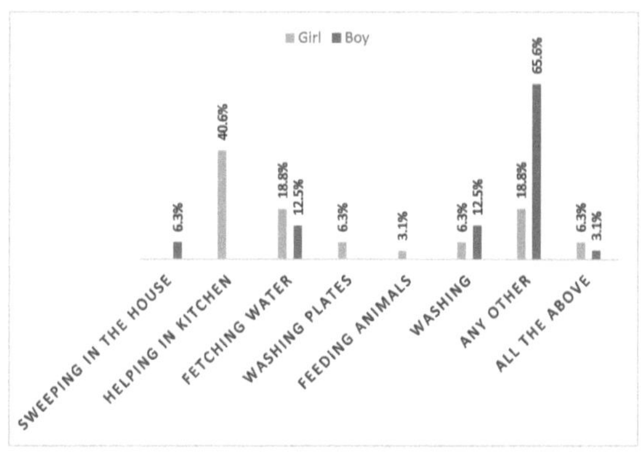


***5.4.2 Time to Study:*** After having enquired about the involvement of girls and boys in household chores, the researcher tried to find out whether the girls had enough time to study at home. It was learnt that the proportion of boys spending time on studies was higher than the girls in government schools. In private schools a significant proportion of girls had time to study, but it was lower in comparison to boys. It was disheartening to know that a considerable proportion of girls in government schools and a good many in the private schools, did not have time to study. In case of the government schools, data revealed that girls who were involved in more than one activity at home did not have sufficient time for studies. Conversely, it was also found that girls who were involved in lesser activities at home had comparatively more time for studies. Similarly, in private schools, a small proportion of girls who were involved in more household activities did not have sufficient time for studies. The boys involved in all the household activities had lesser time to study in both kinds of schools.

**TABLE 5.23**

**School-Wise Distribution of Students' Studying Time**

| School Type | Gender | Studying Time | | Total (N = 100) |
|---|---|---|---|---|
| | | No | Yes | |
| Government | Girl | 29.1 | 70.9 | 55 |
| | Boy | 20.0 | 80.0 | 55 |
| | Total | 24.5 | 75.5 | 110 |
| Private | Girl | 21.9 | 78.1 | 32 |
| | Boy | 12.5 | 87.5 | 32 |
| | Total | 17.2 | 82.8 | 64 |

*Source: Field Data* (Figures in Percentages)

In government schools a substantial number of girls had had no time to study. Another category of girls had less than one hour to study, but their proportion was low. It was found that a good chunk of the girls had less than two hours to study at home. A majority of the girls in government schools had two to three hours to study. However, a small proportion of boys too had no time, or less than one hour time, to study. A high proportion of the boys had two hours or more time to study. In private schools a higher proportion of the girls had two hours or more than two hours studying time. A small number of girls had less than one hour to study and a few girls had no time to study. A majority of boys in private schools had two hours and more than two hours studying time. But the proportion of boys who had less than one hour to study was low compared to the girls. In a private school, we found only one boy who had no time to study at home.

**TABLE 5.24**

**Gender-Wise Distribution on Time Devoted to Studies in Government Schools**

| Gender | No Time | Less than 1 Hour | 1-2 Hours | 2-3 Hours | Total |
|---|---|---|---|---|---|
| Girls | 12 | 2 | 13 | 28 | 55 |
| Boys | 9 | 6 | 25 | 15 | 55 |
| Total | 21 | 8 | 38 | 43 | 110 |

*Source: Field Data* (Figures in Percentages)

**TABLE 5.25**

**Gender-Wise Distribution on Time Devoted to Studies in Private Schools**

| Gender | No Time | Less than 1 Hour | 1-2 Hours | 2-3 Hours | Total |
|---|---|---|---|---|---|
| Girls | 2 | 6 | 10 | 14 | 32 |
| Boys | 1 | 5 | 14 | 12 | 32 |
| Total | 3 | 11 | 24 | 26 | 64 |

*Source: Field Data* (Figures in Percentages)

***5.4.3 Time Spent on Extra-Curricular Activities:*** A majority of girls chose painting and dance as their extra-curricular activities while some of the girls chose sports and games or other activities similar to those of a majority of boys. A few boys preferred extra-curricular activities like painting, dance and music. A significant proportion of girls in government schools mentioned that they liked other activities such as listening to poems, writing about experiences, gardening, etc. Some of them mentioned that they were fond of studying. Similarly, some of the boys preferred studying and while a portion of these did

**TABLE 5.26**

**School-Wise and Gender-Wise Distribution of Students and Their Choice of Extra-Curricular Activities**

| School Type | Gender | Any Other | Painting | Dance | Music | Sports | Total (N = 100) |
|---|---|---|---|---|---|---|---|
| Govern-ment | Girl | 19 | 12 | 5 | 13 | 6 | 55 |
| | | 34.5 | 21.8 | 9.1 | 23.6 | 10.9 | 100.0 |
| | Boy | 6 | 12 | 2 | 3 | 32 | 55 |
| | | 10.9 | 21.8 | 3.6 | 5.5 | 58.2 | 100.0 |
| | Total | 25 | 24 | 7 | 16 | 38 | 110 |
| | | 22.7 | 21.8 | 6.4 | 14.5 | 34.5 | 100.0 |
| Private | Girl | 3 | 3 | 7 | 15 | 4 | 32 |
| | | 9.4 | 9.4 | 21.9 | 46.9 | 12.5 | 100.0 |
| | Boy | 1 | 1 | 0 | 8 | 22 | 32 |
| | | 3.1 | 3.1 | 0.0 | 25.0 | 68.8 | 100.0 |
| | Total | 4 | 4 | 7 | 23 | 26 | 64 |
| | | 6.3 | 6.3 | 10.9 | 35.9 | 40.6 | 100.0 |

*Source: Field Data* (Figures in Percentages)

*NOTE*: The second row in each case above shows the percentage distribution.

not have free time as they thought they did not have enough time for studies. The private school girls preferred cooking and reading books while the boys liked watching plays.

In the government schools, a majority of girls stated that they had sufficient time for extra-curricular activities. But A considerable proportion of students claimed they did not have sufficient time for extra-curricular activities. A majority of girls from private schools stated they did not have time for extra-curricular activities. This could be due to the pressure of studies in private schools.

**TABLE 5.27**

**School-Wise and Gender-Wise Distribution of Students and Time Spent on Extra- Curricular Activities**

| School Type | Gender | Hardly Any | Not Sufficient | Suffi-cient | Total (N = 100) |
|---|---|---|---|---|---|
| Govern-ment | Girl | 3.6 | 36.4 | 60.0 | 55 |
| | Boy | 12.7 | 47.3 | 40.0 | 55 |
| | Total | 8.2 | 41.8 | 50.0 | 110 |
| Private | Girl | 18.8 | 43.8 | 37.5 | 32 |
| | Boy | 15.6 | 50.0 | 34.4 | 32 |
| | Total | 17.2 | 46.9 | 35.9 | 64 |

*Source: Field Data* (Figures in Percentages)

***5.4.4 Experience in School:*** It was observed that a significant proportion of government school girls had to struggle with responsibilities at home and studies. The proportion of such boys was low compared to girls in government schools. The proportion of girls struggling between responsibilities at home and at school was quiet low as compared to boys in private schools. However, the overall proportion of girls who had to struggle between responsibilities at home and at school was much higher. A considerable proportion of girls viewed their schooling experience as very good because of helpful teacher and supportive parents. The proportion of girls in this category was higher in private schools. A small proportion of girls in government and private schools agreed that their teachers were kind and helpful. Some of government school girls even explained that teachers taught them well and were kind and supportive enough to help them with doubts. A few girls of government schools stated that the teachers and their teachings were good. Since they were highly qualified teachers, they were recruited in government schools. They also said that the attitude of the teachers was good and they help in solving their problems in their concerned subjects. A few private school girls and boys viewed their schooling experience as wandering with friends and a memorable stage of their life.

A majority of girls and boys in government schools felt that education enabled them to inculcate positive values. The proportion of such girls was higher in private schools. An equal proportion of girls and boys in private schools thought that positive values were inculcated through education. A high proportion of girls in government schools opined that they gained confidence through education and could now speak to people confidently. A few boys of government schools felt that education developed confidence. A small proportion of girls in private schools said that they developed confidence because of education. Some of the girls in both government and private schools thought that education would help them in seeking a good job. Such responses from boys were higher compared to girls in both government and private schools. One of the girls in a private school said: "*Education introduced me to a better life and imaging myself; to be uneducated produces anxiety.*"

**TABLE 5.28**

**School-Wise and Gender-Wise Distribution of Students' Experiences in Schools**

| School Type | Gender | Struggled to Balance with Home Responsibilities & Studies | Helpful Friends | Supportive Teacher | Supportive Parents & Teachers | Total (N = 100) |
|---|---|---|---|---|---|---|
| Government | Girl | 32.7 | 1.8 | 18.2 | 47.3 | 55 |
| | Boy | 14.5 | 0.0 | 30.9 | 54.5 | 55 |
| | Total | 23.6 | 0.9 | 24.5 | 50.9 | 110 |
| Private | Girl | 9.4 | 18.8 | 9.4 | 62.5 | 32 |
| | Boy | 12.5 | 18.8 | 6.3 | 62.5 | 32 |
| | Total | 10.9 | 18.8 | 7.8 | 62.5 | 64 |

*Source: Field Data* (Figures in Percentages)

TABLE 5.29

**School-Wise and Gender-Wise Distribution of Students on Benefits of Education**

| School Type | Gender | Help in Seeking Job | Develops Confidence | Incul-cates Values | Total (N = 100) |
|---|---|---|---|---|---|
| Govern-ment | Girl | 9.1 | 40.0 | 50.9 | 55 |
| | Boy | 14.5 | 25.5 | 60.0 | 55 |
| | Total | 11.8 | 32.7 | 55.4 | 110 |
| Private | Girl | 6.3 | 6.3 | 87.5 | 32 |
| | Boy | 12.5 | 0.0 | 87.5 | 32 |
| | Total | 9.4 | 3.1 | 87.5 | 64 |

*Source: Field Data* (Figures in Percentages)

***5.4.5 Patriarchal Family Environment:*** The data show that the family culture and environment is male dominated. A majority of household works, such as distribution of food, is the mother's responsibility as compared to anyone else in the house. A small proportion of girls and boys choose to distribute food themselves. Though there is not much difference in the eating patterns of girls and boys, it was found that a majority of girls and boys prefer to have food together. The responses of girls showed that a majority of them have food together and not before and after the family. This showed that even if a girl were hungry, she would have to wait and have food with everyone.

TABLE 5.30

**Gender-Wise Opinion of Students on Food Distribution at Home**

| Gender | You | Mother | Father/ brother | Anyone of u | Total (N = 100) |
|---|---|---|---|---|---|
| Girls | 2.3 | 89.7 | 0.0 | 8.0 | 87 |
| Boys | 3.4 | 87.4 | 2.3 | 6.9 | 87 |
| Total | 2.9 | 88.5 | 1.1 | 7.5 | 174 |

*Source: Field Data* (Figures in Percentages)

**TABLE 5.31**

**Gender-Wise Opinion of Students on Eating Pattern in Family**

| Gender | Members have Food Together | | Total (N = 100) |
|---|---|---|---|
| | No | Yes | |
| Girls | 12.6 | 87.4 | 87 |
| Boys | 11.5 | 88.5 | 87 |
| Total | 12.1 | 87.9 | 174 |

*Source: Field Data* (Figures in Percentages)

**TABLE 5.32**

**Gender-Wise Opinion of Students on Females Eating Pattern**

| Gender | After Male Members | Everyone Together | Before Male Members | Total (N = 100) |
|---|---|---|---|---|
| Girl | 16.1 | 80.5 | 3.4 | 87 |
| Boy | 23.0 | 73.6 | 3.4 | 87 |
| Total | 19.5 | 77.0 | 3.4 | 174 |

*Source: Field Data* (Figures in Percentages)

The data reveal that a majority of females in the family have food with everyone. The responses of girls in this category were higher than the boys. Some of the girls and boys responded that females in the family had food after the male members. The percentage of boys' responses in this category was higher than the girls. The percentage of females having food before male members was quite low. It shows that females had to wait for the other members of the family before having food, and it is they who distribute the food among the family members. Thus, a majority of the families are patriarchal in nature.

***5.4.6 Voicing Opinion:*** It was disheartening to see that a considerable proportion of girls were not able to express their opinion at home or at school. The percentage of girls who were not able to voice their opinion was higher in private schools as compared to government schools. Similarly, a significant proportion of boys could not voice their opinion at home and in school. It is worth mentioning that the percentage of girls and boys who were able to voice their opinion was higher in government schools than the private ones.

**TABLE 5.33**

**Ability to Express Opinion of Girls and Boys**

| School Type | Gender | Cannot Express Opinion | Express Opinion | Total (N = 100) |
|---|---|---|---|---|
| Government | Girls | 16.4 | 83.6 | 55 |
| | Boys | 21.8 | 78.2 | 55 |
| | Total | 19.1 | 80.9 | 110 |
| Private | Girls | 21.9 | 78.1 | 32 |
| | Boys | 34.4 | 65.6 | 32 |
| | Total | 28.1 | 71.9 | 64 |

*Source: Field Data* (Figures in Percentages)

During the focus group discussions, students responded that they engaged freely in a mixed company. But it was only limited to friends, especially to the girls. The girls responded that they did not discuss any problems with their parents as they were strict and had, in some cases, even stopped sending their daughters to school. Some of the boys responded that they used to discuss problems with the teachers. But only a few girls discussed their problems with the teachers; their number was much less compared to the boys. The government school girls were reluctant to share their problem with their parents. They said they only discussed problems with their friends. These girls explained that at home no one listened to them and so they did not share their opinions with parents. Girls from the private schools were of the opinion they could express their opinion before their parents and friends. Also, they could easily share their ideas in a mixed company but they were not able to share their ideas with teachers. They said: "*We discuss the problems with teacher, if needed.*" And they did discuss their problems with the teachers but not always.

In the other government school, girls proclaimed that they could not speak freely in school. At home the girls were generally scared of their fathers and hardly spoke to them. A few girls opined they were close to their mothers and could share their problems whenever needed. But in most of the cases they could not share their problems and opinion with their parents. They shared their views with friends. In a mixed company, girls were hesitant to speak with boys and share their opinions. Moreover, a conversation between boys and girls are not taken a positive light by all the teachers, friends and parents.

***5.4.7 Decision on Marriage and Choice of Partners:*** It was clear from the data that decisions about marriage depended on the parents. A huge proportion of girls in private schools responded that they would take a decision on marriage in consultation with their parents. A significant proportion of the students in government schools depended solely on their parents and grandparents. Government school girls felt that the decisions made by other family members was significant. However, a majority of the girls hoped that they would be allowed to take a decision in consultation with their parents. Though the proportion of boys are higher that decisions of marriage will be taken in consultation with the parents.

**TABLE 5.34**

**Gender-Wise Distribution on Decision on Marriage**

| Gender | Yourself | Consultation with Parents | Parents | Grand Parents | Other Family Members | Total (N = 100) |
|---|---|---|---|---|---|---|
| Girls | | 59.8 | 21.8 | 3.4 | 14.9 | 87 |
| Boys | 1.1 | 65.5 | 25.3 | 2.3 | 5.7 | 87 |
| Total | 0.6 | 62.6 | 23.6 | 2.9 | 10.3 | 174 |

*Source: Field Data* (Figures in Percentages)

**TABLE 5.35**

**Gender-Wise Distribution on Choice of Marriage outside Community**

| Gender | No Choice of Marriage Outside Community | Choice of Marriage Outside Community | Total (N = 100) |
|---|---|---|---|
| Girls | 78.2 | 21.8 | 87 |
| Boys | 58.6 | 41.4 | 87 |
| Total | 68.4 | 31.6 | 174 |

*Source: Field Data* (Figures in Percentages)

**TABLE 5.36**

**Gender-Wise Distribution on Choice of Partner**

| Gen-der | Educated till Higher Secondary Level | Graduate with a Job | Educated with a Good Job | Total (N = 100) |
|---|---|---|---|---|
| Girls | 3.40 | 9.20 | 87.30 | 87 |
| Boys | 34.40 | 23.00 | 42.50 | 87 |
| Total | 19.00 | 16.10 | 64.90 | 174 |

*Source: Field Data* (Figures in Percentages)

It is evident from that data that decisions on marriage outside community remained restricted for the girls as well as the boys. When they were further questioned about the decision of marriage outside community, a big percentage of girls said they would not be allowed to marry outside their community. The case was similar for the boys. However, a considerable proportion of boys believed that they could marry outside the community. Though a few girls agreed they could marry outside the community, their percentage remained low.

The data revealed that a majority of the girls preferred a partner with a good job. Some of the government school girls preferred a partner who are graduate with a good job. Only a few of the girls desired grooms educated till higher secondary. On the contrary, preferences of boys were different. A considerable proportion of the boys preferred brides educated up to the higher secondary level. Some of the boys preferred graduate brides with a job. In fact, there was a significant proportion of boys who preferred educated brides with a good job.

***5.4.8 Custom of Early Marriage:*** It is evident from the data that many of the girls lacked awareness about the legal age of marriage. Boys were found to be more aware of the legal age of marriage. There were girls with awareness on marriageable age but their percentage remained half of the sample size. It was found from the responses of boys and girls that the correct age of marriage was not being followed in Raiganj in Uttar Dinajpur district. The girls were married at an early age. A disheartening feature was that a majority (65 per cent) of girls and boys informed about the practice of early marriage in the villages. The girls were married before attaining the age of 18 years. The responses showed that only a few girls were married at the right age. This shows signs of the prevalent norm of early marriage in West Bengal. Such early marriages were practised mostly among the poor villagers, the Scheduled Castes and the Scheduled Tribes. Studies show that poor people force their girls to marry early in order to reduce the pressure of their economic responsibilities. There exists a strong relationship between child marriage and community affiliation. The tradition of early marriage continues to be a crucial factor for the poverty stricken, unemployed, landless, and illiterate people, and a lack of awareness leads to the continuation of this social practice. The kinship ties, social and religious obligations do not let individuals to rise above this tradition (Ghosh, 2010).

**TABLE 5.37**

**Gender-Wise Distribution on Awareness of Marriageable Age**

| Gender | Wrong Age | Right Age | Total (N = 100) |
|---|---|---|---|
| Girl | 40.2 | 59.8 | 87 |
| Boy | 47.1 | 52.9 | 87 |
| Total | 43.7 | 56.3 | 174 |

*Source: Field Data* (Figures in Percentages)

**TABLE 5.38**

**Gender-Wise Distribution on Early Marriage (Figures in Percentages)**

| Gender | Correct Age of Marriage | | Total (N = 100) |
|---|---|---|---|
| | Not Followed | Followed | |
| Girl | 65.5 | 34.5 | 87 |
| Boy | 44.8 | 55.2 | 87 |
| Total | 55.2 | 44.8 | 174 |

*Source: Field Data*

**Picture 5.1: At an inter-district sports meet, the researcher observed that a few girls performing cultural functions were wearing the traditional bangles (shakha and palla) worn by married Bengali women. These girls were studying at the higher secondary level and were married. This picture is clear evidence of the custom of early marriage.**

These data can be further substantiated with a poem on early marriage of girls, received while interviewing a male English teacher in a government school during a field visit.

**Bornomala**

*(A poem based on the practice of early marriage)*

*Mathay Kalshi niye je meyeti mile peroy*
*Ektu joler jonno protidin lomba pay hete*
*Banglar teacher hobe ekdin, boro ichhe chilo*
*Class fiver beshi bornomala egote pareni*

*Jekhane kochuripana bedonay gobhir beguni*
*Shei niribili theke bohu dure chilo high school*
*Pother bipod chilo shalbon, bolgachara truck*
*Majhe majhe tup kore gile nito school balikake.*

*Tader bhoy baba biye chan, porate chan na*
*Kintu shei jedi me go dhoreche korbena biye*
*Barir lokera take dhore bendhe pirite boshale*
*Shey chute paliye jay tepantorer rupkothar deshe*
*Shey chute asroy ney gramer local thanai*
*Aamke bachao kakoo, aami chai iskule jete*
*Aamar maa er moton borkhar jibon chaina*
*Meye tar chokhe jole bornomalar hajar watt.*

**– Syllabary (Version in English)**

The girl with a pitcher on her head walked on long legs every day, for miles for water. She wished to become a Bengali teacher someday but could not advance the alphabets beyond fifth standard. High school was far from the solitude where the water hyacinth was deep purple in pain. The danger of the path was dense forest and unrestrained trucks or vehicles that often gulped down (kidnapped) the school going girls. Fearing this the father wants to get his daughter married, the girl with strong will power would not let go her education. Relatives grabbed her, tied her up and tried to force her for marriage. Soon the girl ran away to the land of fairy tales. She ran away to the local police station of the village. "Uncle, I want to go to school. I don't want a burkha (traditional dress of Muslims) like my mother. "The girl's tears had a shine of thousand watts of alphabets that ran down her cheeks.

This poem depicts that girls from rural India are still facing challenges of an early marriage. The societal norms prevent them from continuing their education and force them to marry at an early age. Some of them are determined to have higher education and rebel against the societal obstacles in order to move ahead and fulfil their dreams. The dreams of these girls are shattered when they are married away at an early age.

***5.4.9 The Practice and Problems of Dowry System:*** The practice of dowry makes the position of women vulnerable in society. Undoubtedly, it is a crucial factor in women's disempowerment and adversely impacts the status of women in society. In the capitalist economy and amid the growing unemployment in society, men tend to exploit women and seek for themselves a comfortable position in society. The custom of dowry manifests the power of men over women in society. The Dowry Prohibition Act 1980 makes the practice illegal in society, though the law has been grossly violated an umpteen number of times, especially in the rural areas, due to the social customs and ignorance of the law (Bilkis, 2005). Dowry is supposed to be a collection of gifts given by the bride's family, and it includes jewellery, luxury items, furniture and other consumer goods. But, in practice, it involves an element of force. The practice of dowry is prevalent among all sections of society, whether rich or poor, upper caste and lower caste, educated or illiterate (Ghosh, 2010). The prevalence of the dowry system is a serious concern in many states of India including West Bengal.

An attempt has been made here to understand the respondents' views on the issue of dowry. The girls and boys were aware of the problems of dowry. The practice of dowry confirms the tradition of patriarchy in rural Bengal. As the parents are under tremendous pressure to fix the marriage of their girls, such practices are only strengthened. This practice of dowry brings pressure on the parents, including the poorest of parents, to give cash, jewellery and goods to the groom. Some of the girls believe that such a practice is immoral as their parents have already invested money on their studies. One of the girls said: "I do not believe in dowry as our parents are raising us with a lot of difficulties."

According to some of the girls, everyone is not affluent enough to pay dowry. Many of the girls claimed that they did not believe in dowry. One said her parents had spent and invested money on her upbringing and hence she would not like them to pay money at the time of her marriage. Girls mentioned that all parents are not rich, that some of them sell their valuables for marriage, and spend their hard-earned money. Parents have to go through a tough time. Dowry should not be given at the time of marriage. A proportion of students was aware that dowry is against the law. They revealed that parents quiet often discussed about the practice of dowry; they were afraid of this custom of giving away a part of their wealth at the time of a daughter's marriage and the humiliation which daughters of the poor parents' face by her husband and in-laws if they fail to keep the custom. Parents prefer boys over girls for fear of this very custom. Some parents are uneducated and unaware of the government laws. Many girls and boys referred to dowry as a crime. Girls felt that men and women hold an equal position in society and that dowry is a punishable offence. The boys' family demands dowry for their own purposes, e.g., to start a business. But girls as well as boys were aware that this practice often leads to domestic violence. They believed such practices should be forbidden in society. A girl from a private school said: "There are many deaths occurring in our society for such obsolete customs, killing women physically and emotionally. Women are valued only for the amount of money paid at the time of marriage, which is a deliberate insult to them."

Many girls from private schools viewed dowry as an obsolete system though followed by the people even today. The boys from private schools were sensitive about it. One of them emphasised: "*Girls are treated as a commodity for getting money in marriage. They should be independent enough to settle down themselves.*"

It is a known practice that a marriage cannot be settled without settling the dowry issue first. There are many instances in which a boy's family sent a query about dowry to a girl's family even before coming to her house. The respondents told us that there are times when girls' parents are unable to settle the dowry claim. It leads to a divorce or a broken marriages where girls are not accepted in the wider society. A majority of the respondents told us that dowry should be altogether forbidden. But several of the girls whose parents were involved in cultivation supported dowry as a social norm. One of the girls claimed that dowry meant a girl's future assets. Studies have shown that parents do not give girls equal property rights after marriage and make a one-time marriage settlement with the groom's family. The settlement is termed as dowry and justified as a social norm. Some girls stated that boys did not marry without dowry and it was made a compulsion. There were a few girls studying in government schools believed that girls and boys hold an equal position in society. Similarly, the boys felt that girls can even be independent and earn their living after marriage. Some of the boys and girls expressed that dowry suppresses the women in a patriarchal society. It values business over love. Girls mentioned that dowry overpowers women and kills their self-respect in society, which should not be acceptable.

It was observed that girls and boys from private schools generally belonged to the middle and higher class, and they keenly discussed about the inequality and power structure of society. A girl from a private school proclaimed: "*I am totally against dowry system. It is a form of perpetrating female's suppression and dominance of men over women. It shows we are living in a patriarchal society. It shows how women are still deprived of all facilities which are available to men. It undermines the dignity of women in society.*"

Another girl said: "*Although I do not want to marry, I do want to comment on it. I am against the dowry system. This custom is against the self-respect of my individuality and my family. I honour my gender. I am a burden to no one. A relationship on the basis of money is fake and unacceptable."*

The girls of this part of Uttar Dinajpur asserted that educated and modernised people should not follow the dowry system. They believed it is a system prevalent among the uneducated and the poor, and some cruel members of society perpetuate this tradition.

***5.4.10 Mobility:*** It is evident from the data that girls' physical mobility is restricted in Uttar Dinajpur district of West Bengal. A high proportion of girls rarely go out of their limited area. The proportion of girls who go out only occasionally is higher compared to those who go out frequently. The proportion of girls who frequently go for outing, is small. However, the proportion of boys who go out frequently is higher than that of the girls. There are a few boys who go out rarely but their proportion is small.

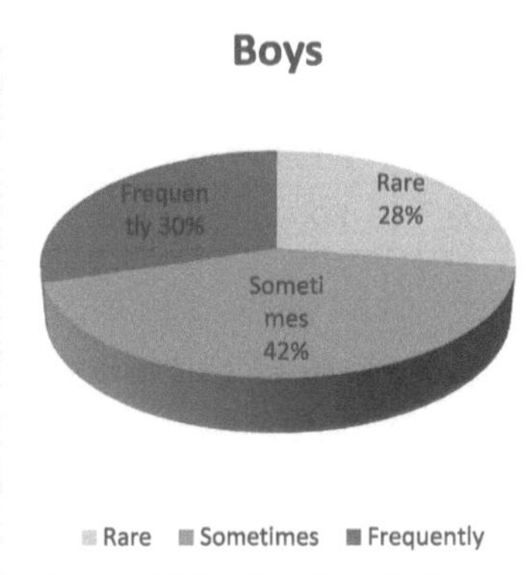


**CHART 5.16**

Boys' Mobility

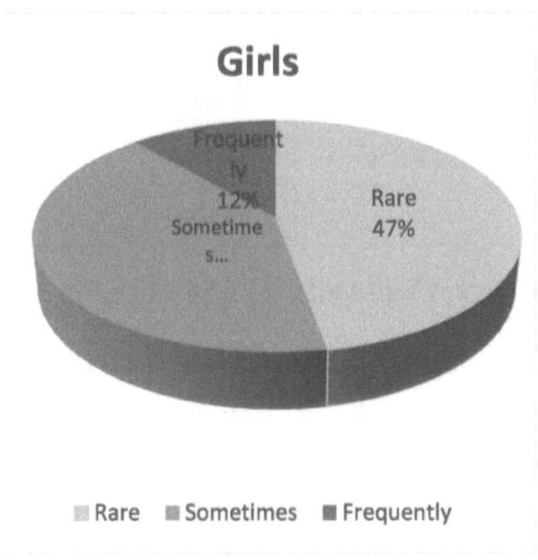


**CHART 5.17**

Girls' Mobility

Source: Field Data

It is clear from the data given below that a majority of girls go out only with their family members. The proportion is higher in case of the government school girls than the private school girls. It was found that a girl going out alone is very rare in case of the government schools. However, the proportion of boys going out with family members is low. A striking feature is that the proportion of girls going out with friends is higher than the boys in case of the private schools. It was found that very few girls from government schools go out alone. The proportion of boys going out alone with friends is higher. Thus, it was found that girls in rural areas go out with friends and family members while the boys often move alone. The common reason behind it the concern for safety of the girls moving alone.

**TABLE 5.39**

**School-Wise Girls and Boys Accompanied for Outing**

| School Type | Gender | Family | Friends | Alone | Total (N = 100) |
|---|---|---|---|---|---|
| Government | Girls | 87.3 | 9.1 | 3.6 | 55 |
| | Boys | 49.1 | 30.9 | 20.0 | 55 |
| | Total | 68.2 | 20.0 | 11.8 | 110 |
| Private | Girl | 71.9 | 28.1 | 0.0 | 32 |
| | Boys | 62.5 | 15.6 | 21.9 | 32 |
| | Total | 67.2 | 21.9 | 10.9 | 64 |

*Source: Field Data* (Figures in Percentages)

***5.4.11 Mode of Transportation from School to Home:*** In government schools, it was seen that a higher proportion of girls travel alone from home to school though their proportion is lower than that of the boys. It was found that a considerable proportion of girls travelled with their siblings from home to school. A small proportion of girls were accompanied by their parents and friends. The data reveal that a majority of boys travel alone from home to school. Some of the boys are accompanied by siblings and friends. However, in private schools, a majority of girls travel with their siblings or their parents. Few girls move out of home alone. There are a large proportion of boys in private schools who travel alone. A few boys travel with their siblings and some of them travel with parents.

## CHART 5.18

## Students Accompanied from Government Schools to Home

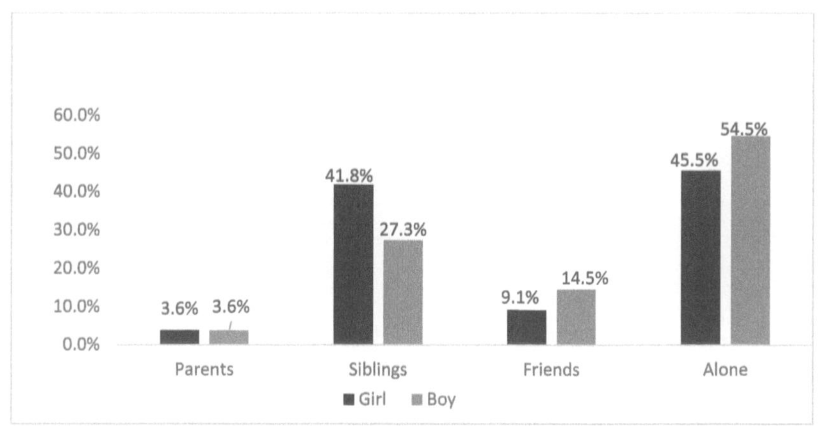


Source: Field Data

## CHART 5.19

## Students Accompanied from Private Schools to Home

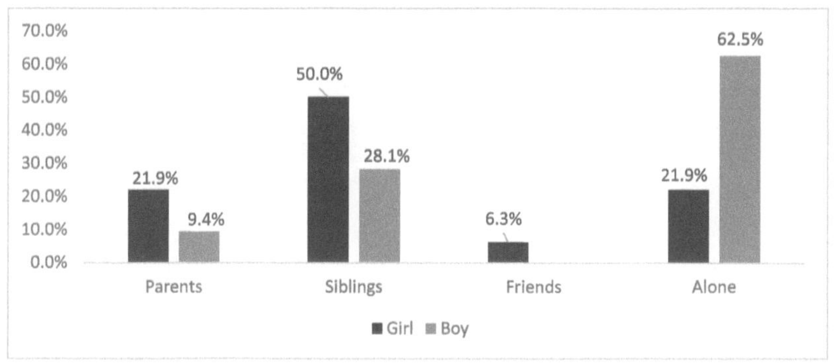


Source: Field Data

It was found from data (see Chart 5.20 below) that a majority of government school girls walk down to school. A small proportion of the girls go to school by a bicycle provided by the state government. These bicycles were provided by the government of West Bengal. While they were distributed in some schools, other schools had withheld them waiting for the distribution ceremony.

**Picture 5.2 : Bicycle of the Students**

**Picture 5.3 : Government school waiting for the distribution ceremony of the bicycles**

## CHART 5.20

## Gender-Wise Mode of Transportation from a Government School to Home

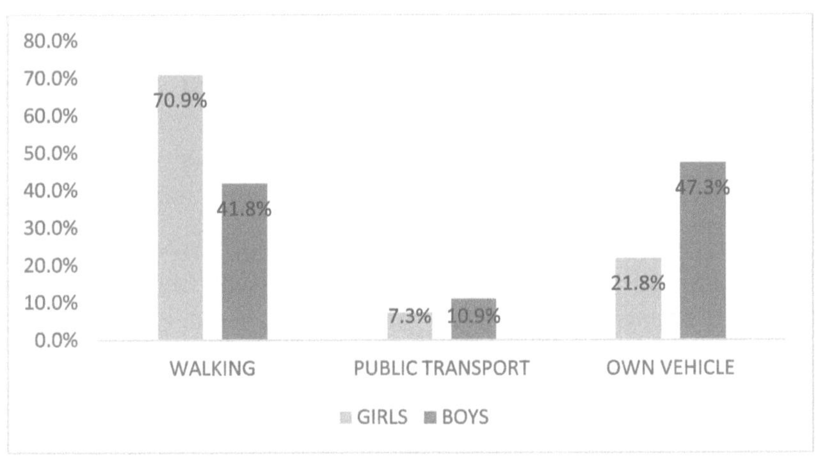


Source: Field Data

## CHART 5.21

## Gender-Wise Mode of Transportation from a Private School to Home

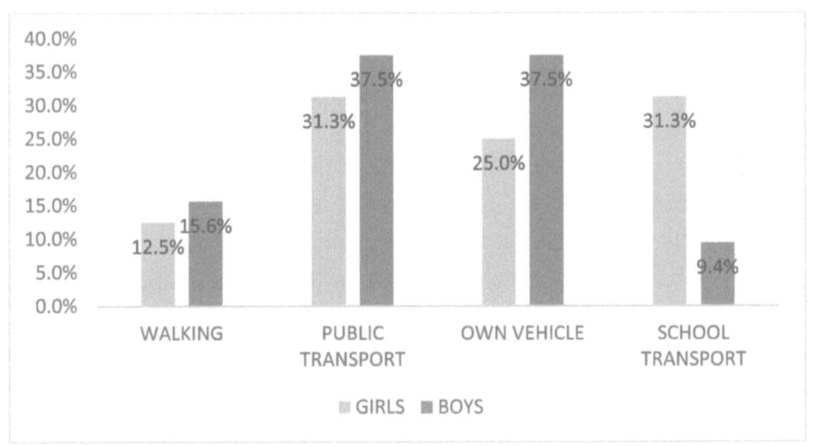


Source: Field Data

It was also found that in government schools, girls who walk down from home to school are mostly accompanied by siblings and a few of them are accompanied by friends or alone. Many of the boys walking down from home to school, using the public transport and own vehicles are accompanied by friends or siblings; only some of them travel alone.

In private schools, a considerable proportion of the girls go to school-by-school transport or public transport. Some of the girls travel by their own vehicles. Few of them go home walking. A high proportion of the boys in private schools' travels from home to school either by their own vehicles or public transport.

In case of the private schools, girls and boys are accompanied by friends and siblings while walking down from home to schools. Only a few of them walk back alone. The girls are accompanied by parents, siblings and friends in public transport. A large proportion of the girls are travelling by school transportation with their siblings. Private school buses were engaged by the girls' parents in consultation with the school principals for safe pick-and-drop service. A few boys of private schools also availed this service. But the choice was restricted to the affluent parents who pay for this service.

The location of a school is another important factor. Private schools are located in the urban areas of Raiganj. The distance from a village to a school is large and cannot be covered without transport. Girls staying in remote areas have to walk down to get the local transport in order to go to school. Transportation facilities in remote villages are not good. Hence children belonging to government schools were provided with bicycles from the state government. Parents from private schools arrange their own means of transportation for their children, but it is not possible for poor parents. On the contrary, most of the government schools are located in rural areas and parents prefer to send their children to a nearby school. The private schools are located in far off areas and they are very few in number. Moreover, the safety concerns for girls are another factor. These areas are not only unsafe but prone to inter-community conflicts and conflicts over land holdings. Hence both boys and girls find it unsafe to travel through such areas.

***5.4.12 Scholarships and Part-Time Jobs:*** It was clear from data that a large proportion of government school girls received scholarships from the government. The girls belonging to the socially and economically disadvantaged fell under this category. Some of the boys received scholarships, but their proportion was low. These scholarships are a part of the schemes which the state government has launched for the girls' education.

**TABLE 5.40**

**Scholarships Received by Boys and Girls of Government Schools**

| Gender | Do not Receive Scholarship | Receive Scholarship | Total (N = 100) |
|---|---|---|---|
| Girls | 29.1 | 70.9 | 55 |
| Boys | 50.9 | 49.1 | 55 |
| Total | 40.0 | 60.0 | 110 |

*Source: Field Data* (Figures in Percentages)

But a noteworthy feature is that among the girls the awareness about the school fees was found to be low. A majority of the boys were aware about their school fees in the government schools. Some of the girls stated that the school fee was Rs 250 a month in a government school; it was Rs 1500 a month in private schools. Our data showed that girls in private schools were more aware of the school fees than the boys. It was found that a majority of government school girls and boys had had bank accounts as their scholarship amounts are transferred directly to their bank accounts. A small proportion of girls and boys in private schools hold bank accounts which were opened by their parents and not by the government.

**TABLE 5.41**

**School-Wise Distribution of Students Aware of Their School Fees**

| School Type | Gender | Do not Know School Fees | Know School Fees | Total (N = 100) |
|---|---|---|---|---|
| Gov-ern-ment | Girls | 56.4 | 43.6 | 55 |
| | Boys | 27.3 | 72.7 | 55 |
| | Total | 41.8 | 58.2 | 110 |
| Private | Girls | 12.5 | 87.5 | 32 |
| | Boys | 18.8 | 81.3 | 32 |
| | Total | 15.6 | 84.4 | 64 |

*Source: Field Data* (Figures in Percentages)

**TABLE 5.42**

**School-Wise Proportion of Girls and Boys Having Bank Accounts**

| School Type | Gender | No Bank Account | Bank Account | Total (N = 100) |
|---|---|---|---|---|
| Government | Girls | 18.9 | 78.1 | 55 |
| | Boys | 30.9 | 69.1 | 55 |
| | Total | 25.0 | 75.0 | 110 |
| Private | Girls | 62.5 | 37.5 | 32 |
| | Boys | 65.6 | 34.4 | 32 |
| | Total | 64.1 | 35.9 | 64 |

*Source: Field Data* (Figures in Percentages)

It was evident from another set of data that a small proportion of girls as well as boys work on a part time basis. But a teacher from a government school explained that only a small proportion of students work while and studying. Nowadays, till the eighth standard, students get a fixed amount of money. Still there are some girls who were found working part time.

These girls and boys belong to the socially and economically disadvantaged categories and are poverty stricken. It was found that the money earned by the girls is spent either by their parents or, sometimes, in consultation with their parents. Parents working in fields force their children to work part time in order to get some support for their living. The daughters of many of them were found working part time.

## CHART 5.22

### Girls and Boys Working Part Time

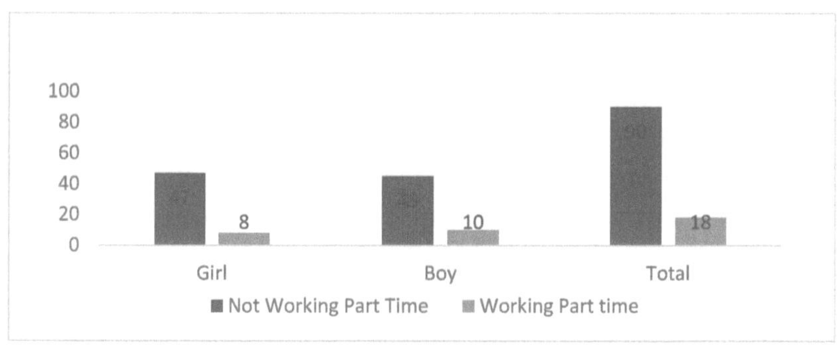


Source: Field Data

## CHART 5.23

### Decision on Spending and Savings of Girls and Boys Working Part Time

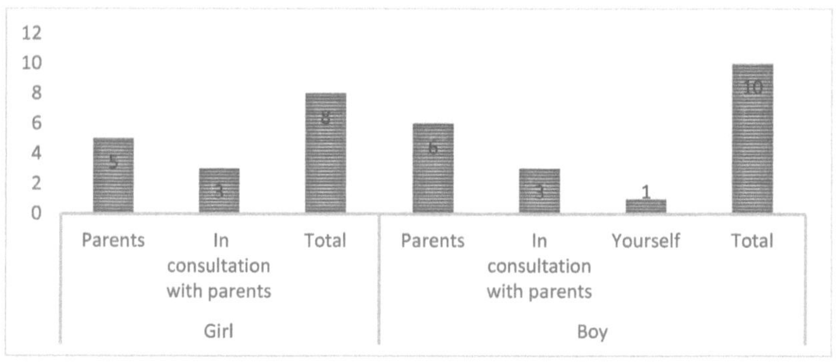


Source: Field Data

## SECTION III

### 5.5 EDUCATIONAL FACTORS: ARE SCHOOLS GENDER FRIENDLY?

Several educational factors throw light on the profile of the schools selected for the study. Here we have focussed on the location and background of these schools and the availability of physical infrastructure and academic facilities there. We have also tried to find out whether these schools were gender friendly. There is a close association between a school's location and quality of education on the one hand and the children's access to and participation in the school on the other hand. Parents find it difficult to send their girls to a school which lack the basic facilities such as drinking water, toilets and female teachers. The presence of female teachers in a school provides a sense of security to parents and the girls. Female teachers also act as the role models for girls (Bandyopadhyay, 2012). For this aspect of the study, four schools were selected from the Raiganj block. Two schools of them were government schools and two were private schools. These schools are coded as School 1, School 2 (government schools), and School 3, School 4 (private schools).

#### *5.5.1 Location, Background, Physical and Academic Facilities of Government Schools*

*Government School 1:* The District Project Officer of the Sarva Siksha Abhiyan granted us permission for the school visit. It had been raining heavily since the early morning when the researcher visited the school. It was located in Gauri village, Raiganj block, in Uttar Dinajpur. The educational block of the school is known as Raiganj South.

The school was established in the year 1960 and is run by a state board. It is one of the oldest rural schools of Raiganj. This school is located in Gauri VIII. The panchayat of the village is based in Gauri. The village is located 15 kilometres away from Raiganj which houses both the district and subdistrict headquarters above Gauri village. It belongs to the Jalpaiguri division. There were *kutcha* roads and mud houses with thatched roofs in the school's vicinity. The road which led to the school was very narrow, with paddy fields on both sides. Bicycles and battery driven rickshaws were plying there. The village is located three kilometres to the north from the district headquarters.

Gauri is a large village in Raiganj block. The geographical area of the village is 409.3 hectares. There was then a total of 980 households in Gauri village. The total population is 4,588 --- 2,282 males and 2,306 females --- as per the Census of 2011.

Literacy rate of Gauri village is lower compared to the average rate for West Bengal. The literacy of Gauri village was 63.51 per cent --- male literacy was 71.32 per cent and female literacy was 55.68 per cent. As per the Constitution of India and the Panchayati Raj Act, the village is administered by a Sarpanch (the head of the village). The languages spoken are Bengali and Maithili.

A majority of the parents were paddy cultivators. Apart from paddy cultivation, they were involved in part time jobs. They farmers sell their crops in the evening markets held in the locality or to small grocery shops in the village.

*Availability of Physical and Academic Facilities:* This is a co-educational school, while there is another higher secondary school within one kilometre distance for boys. The school provides education from class VI to XII. The student teacher ratio is 44:1. The medium of instruction in the school is Bengali. The school building was spacious and spread over a large area in a circular shape. The school had boundary walls. There was a small ground but it remained waterlogged. The school had had an electricity connection but power cuts were normal during heavy rains.

There was no room for the Head Teacher who had to share the staff room with other teachers. The staff room was dark and not well ventilated. Teachers were sitting outside the staff room.

When the researcher visited the school, the Head Teacher was not present in the school. He was out for some official work and the school was being supervised by the Deputy Head Teacher. Some classes were ongoing while students from other classes were roaming in the veranda as there was a power cut. Some of the teachers were not taking their classes.

There were separate toilets for girls and two for boys, and both of them were functional. But these toilets did not have water facility. Sanitation was poor and it was difficult for girls to maintain cleanliness and hygiene. Tap water was provided for drinking. A medical chest was maintained by a teacher and it had common medicines for cold and fever, bandage, cotton and Dettol.

The place where mid-day meals was served was unhygienic. The kitchen shed was used to distribute the food. There was no room for the students to sit and have their meals. The kitchen shed where the meal was served had no link with the main building. Students had to cross the pool of water accumulated in the playground to take their meals.

The school had 16 classrooms and each classroom was big and well ventilated. But many of the windows were broken. Three classrooms were under construction. The classroom walls were painted in black, so as to be used as black boards. There were benches for the children but they were not in a good condition. There was no display of teaching learning materials. Some of the classrooms had paintings on the wall. The school had an integrated physics, chemistry and biology and geography laboratory but it was not properly equipped. The dusty condition of the materials showed poor usage of the teaching learning materials. A beehive was found outside the laboratory; classroom corridors showed the poor maintenance of the school. It was dangerous for the students. The school had a small library with books and magazines. But there was no ventilation in the library. Students crowded over the tables to read books in the dark. One candle was kept on each table.

*Location and Background of School 2:* The school is a government higher secondary school located in Bahin-IX village. It was established in 1952. The village is located 12.1 km from the district headquarters. The total geographical area is 233.12 hectares.

According to the Census 2011, the village had 547 households. The total population of the village was 2,793, of which 1,367 (48.9 per cent) was the female population. The girl child population of the village (0-6 years) was 47.5 per cent. The Census 2011 showed that the village literacy level was 44.7 per cent, and female literacy rate was only 19.5 per cent. The schools are under the state's Department of Education (West Bengal Board), had upper primary to higher secondary classes. The medium of instruction is Bengali.

*Availability of Physical and Academic Facilities:* The school building has adequate space for its proper functioning. The school was situated near the highway. At the entrance, there is a huge statue of Subhash Chandra Bose, situated in an open area. Behind this statue is the school building.

The school do not have a boundary wall. There is no playground in the school. There is some space in front of the school to play. During the rainy season water gets accumulated in the front area and in the classrooms. The school is in a low-lying area and water from the highway comes into the school ground and classrooms. There are two hand pumps; one hand pump is in front of the entrance gate. There are two toilets for boys and one for girls. In the toilets, however, cleanliness is not maintained. There is no water in the toilets.

There are 18 classrooms in the school. Some of them need to be repaired. The benches were broken and in some classrooms the researcher saw broken fans. There were four classrooms which required new furniture. The walls of the classroom were without any teaching aid or chart. The rooms were dark and did not have adequate lighting.

Separate rooms were available for teachers, Head Teacher and office staff. Teaching learning material was available in the science laboratory and geography laboratory for social science. Library and computer lab were maintained in good condition. There was a room for the mid-day meals which were cooked and served in the school, and the food was cooked by some volunteering mothers. The principal told us that some of the parents were poor and had joined the school as *Asha Karmis* on the daily wage basis. They prepared food for the children in the school kitchen. There was a separate room where the food was served to the students. It had tables where the students stood in groups and had food.

The school do not have any security or medical attendants. Medical aids are provided by the teachers. Medical chests were maintained with medicines and sanitary napkins. The school organises health check-up camps every five months.

On the day we visited the school, a strikingly good feature was noticed --- the principal was conducting a meeting with the parents where the examination papers of Classes IX and XI were shown and discussed with the aim of improving the performance of the students. After this meeting, the researcher met a few parents who were School Management Committee members and who participated equally with the principal in the development of the school. They, along with the principal, meet the village panchayat members for bringing more children to school, to stop early marriages, and collect funds for school improvement. The village panchayat helps the school by raising funds and enrolling the children from the nearby villages. Hostel facilities are available for boys as girl's parents do not let them stay in the hostel at night.

Picture 5.4 : Government School 1

Picture 5.5 : Government School 2

**Picture 5.6 : Infrastructure of Government Schools**

**Picture 5.7 : Head Teacher room combined with staff room**

**Picture 5.8 : Geography Laboratory in Government School**

**Picture 5.9: Biology Laboratory in Government School**

**Picture 5.10 : Water logged Government School campus during Rain**

**Picture 5.11 : Computer Laboratory in Government School**

**Picture 5.12 : Art Gallery in Government School**

**Picture 5.13 : Library in Government School**

**Picture 5.14 : Mid Day Meal in Government School**

**Picture 5.15 : Students having Mid Day Meal in Government School**

**Picture 5.16 : Drinking water facility in Government School**

### *5.5.2 Location, Background, Physical and Academic Facilities of Private Schools*

#### *Location and Background of School 3 and School 4*

Kamalabari is a large sized village divided into Phases I to XIII. School 3 and School 4 are located in Kamalabari village. The district headquarters, Raiganj, is located 7.5 km away from Kalambari village. The total geographical area is 282.58 hectares. The total number of households is 456 in the village. As per the Census 2011, the male population was 1,064 and the female population was 919. The literacy rate of the village was 71.69 per cent, which is lower than the West Bengal average of 76.26 per cent. In this village 839, 287 are cultivators and 359 are agricultural labourers. Kamalabari village has 3 schools, out of which one is a government school and two are private schools. School 3 is located in Sudarshanpur, Raiganj. It is a co-educational school affiliated to the CBSE since 1999. The school operates under the Sarda Seva Trust of Raiganj. The school says it underlines the principles of spirituality and morality.

*Availability of Physical and Academic Facilities in School 3:* This school was established in 1995. The medium of instruction is English. The school building is well planned, with a garden in front of the building. The school has a *pucca* boundary wall. The school maintained a good security service. It was found that a record register was maintained at the gate for the visitors. No playground was found in the school. Drinking water was provided in the school through the filters. Aqua guards were installed for drinking water. There were eight separate toilets for girls and boys. But it was found that these toilets did not have water and were stinking. Foul smell even reached the classrooms located near the toilets. The classrooms and the corridors were cleaned at regular intervals. It was found that students and teachers entered the classes by removing their shoes outside. On the day of our school visit, the principal did not agree that researcher should meet the teachers and students. But the teachers, students and parents were cooperative.

The pupil teacher ratio was 24:1. The classrooms were well ventilated and in a good condition. A few classrooms had a time table in the form of charts put on the walls. Mid-day meals were not provided in this school. There were separate rooms for the principal, teachers and administrative employees.

The school had a medical room for the students to rest and the medical box was maintained by a teacher. Health check-ups were conducted twice a year. The library and computer lab were well maintained. The computer lab was used for learning purposes. The laboratories were integrated. But the dust in laboratories showed there was no proper usage. The school provided transport facilities and buses were available for the students.

*Availability of Physical and Academic Facilities School 4:* School 4 was founded and run by "The Jesuits of Santal Society," a minority Christian Society registered under the Society's Registration Act 1860. Its headquarters were at Dumka. The **Society of Jesus** has since long been active in the field of education. At present, it is running as many as 878 high schools and 88 university colleges all around the world.

This school was established in the year 1999. It has classes from primary to higher secondary. The distance of the school from main habitation, Hemtabad, is 3 kilometres. It is a private Christian Minority School, affiliated to the Council for Indian School Certificate Examinations, New Delhi. The medium of instruction is English.

The school building is spacious and well maintained. The school has boundary walls. There were 36 classrooms and all were in a good condition. Separate rooms for the principal, teachers and administrative staff were available. The school had four coolers with aqua guard services and separate toilets for girls, boys and teachers. This school did not have any mid-day meals facility. The school notice boards displayed the notices and children's work. The school had a well-organised library, an integrated science laboratory and a computer lab for computer aided learning. The school maintained the record of visitors.

On the day of our visit the school was closed as it was a holiday though a few teachers were holding extra classes for Class XI and XII. Also, Classes IX and X were being shown *The Merchant of Venice*, a movie related to the English syllabus. The school is proactive in co-curricular activities. Special karate classes were organised for girls aged 8 years and above to learn self-defence. The school had a proper mode of transportation for students, arranged by the parents through mutual cooperation.

There is one medical room in the school with a trained nurse, and the medical kit is kept with her. Health awareness camps are organised in the school and in the villages with the help of parents who are doctors. These are the school-organised campaigns on prevention of dengue and malaria.

**Picture 5.17 : Private School 3**

**Picture 5.18 : Private School 4**

**Picture 5.19 :Outside view of Principal room in Private School**

**Picture 5.20 : Classroom in Private School**

**Picture 5.21 : Corridor in Private School**

Picture 5.22 : Computer Laboratory in Private School

Picture 5.23 : Library in Private School

Picture 5.24 : Chemistry Laboratory in Private School

### *5.5.3 Participation of Girls in Schools*

The NFHS report throws light on various national level data on girls in rural areas. The table below shows the proportion of girl's enrolment in School 1, School 2 (government schools) and School 3, School 4 (private schools). It was observed from the table that the enrolment of girls was high in the government schools, compared to the other schools. A change in the literacy rate were seen from 2001 to 2011, in the traditionally backward districts like Purulia, Malda and Uttar Dinajpur which had a higher rate of literacy growth than the state average. To develop the literacy rate in these districts, special emphasis was laid on the different government programmes (Saha & Debnath, 2016).

School 1 is located in Gauri VIII which is a large village in Raiganj block. It caters to the village and surrounding areas such as Hemtabad, as it is the only senior secondary school in that area. Studies have shown that there is a high degree of inter-block variation in Uttar Dinajpur district. The most literate block in the district is Hemtabad, followed by Raiganj. In the blocks in rural areas, with the exception of Hemtabad, the gender literacy gap widens as the literacy rate increases and males have better educational opportunities than females. In rural areas with a lower gender disparity, female literacy is pushed up by male literacy. This shows that school located near Hemtabad, which has a higher male literacy, supports female literacy as well. There is a positive relationship between male literacy and female literacy, the female workforce participation and female literacy. As education reduces inequalities within families (Hira and Das, 2018). This may be one of the reasons for higher enrolment of girls. Another reason could be that there was only one senior secondary school in the catchment area.

#### *Girls Enrolment*

The following tables, 5.43 and 5.44 represent the grade wise enrolment of girls, show that an increase in the grade is accompanied by a decline in the enrolment of girls. A majority of schools show more gender disparity in higher grades.

**TABLE 5.43**

**Proportion of Girls Enrolment in Sample Schools**

| Schools | Boys Enrolment | Girls Enrolment | Total Enrolment |
|---|---|---|---|
| School 1 | 812 | 897 | 1709 |
| School 2 | 1446 | 648 | 2094 |
| School 3 | 657 | 459 | 1116 |
| School 4 | 1079 | 508 | 1587 |

Source: Field Data

One of the government schools showed (Table 5.44) a drastic decline in the enrolment of girls. The enrolment of girls in Grade XII was found to be nil. The school almost remained closed in the rainy season. As there is a senior secondary school for girls in the village, parents prefer to enrol their daughters in that school. The location of the school near the highway could be another factor.

The table 5.45 indicates that grade-wise the proportion of girl's enrolment is lower than boys' enrolment in government as well as private schools with the exception of a government school. The schools showed high gender disparity between girls and boys. The data also show a higher gender disparity in the higher grades. The most probable reason is that the social and economic backwardness do not allow girls to continue their schooling.

**TABLE 5.44**

**Grade-Wise Percentage of Girls Enrolment in Sample Schools**

| Schools | IX | | X | | XI | | XII | |
|---|---|---|---|---|---|---|---|---|
| | Girls | Total (N = 100) | Girls | Total (N = 100) | Girls | Total (N = 100) | Girls | Total (N = 100) |
| School 1 | 55.5 | 364 | 50 | 164 | 62.9 | 186 | 61.2 | 147 |
| School 2 | 26 | 311 | 21.7 | 217 | 28.8 | 229 | 0 | 115 |
| School 3 | 38 | 63 | 40 | 72 | 43.3 | 60 | 29 | 31 |
| School 4 | 29.7 | 121 | 31 | 152 | 37 | 186 | 34.4 | 157 |

*Source: Field Data* (Figures in Percentages)

**TABLE 5.45**

**Percentage of Girls Enrolment in Sample Schools**

| Schools | I -VIII | | | IX-XII | | |
|---|---|---|---|---|---|---|
| | Girls | Boys | Total (N = 100) | Girls | Boys | Total (N = 100) |
| School 1 | 47.8 | 52.2 | 848 | 57 | 43 | 861 |
| School 2 | 37.2 | 62.8 | 1222 | 22.2 | 77.8 | 872 |
| School 3 | 41.8 | 58.2 | 890 | 38.5 | 61.5 | 226 |
| School 4 | 31 | 69 | 971 | 33.4 | 66.6 | 616 |

*Source: Field Data* (Figures in Percentages)

**TABLE 5.46**
**Year-Wise Girls Enrolment in Schools**

| Schools | 2014-15 | | 2015-16 | | 2016-17 | |
|---|---|---|---|---|---|---|
| | Total Enrolment | Girls Per centage | Total Enrolment | Girls Per centage | Total Enrolment | Girls Per centage |
| School 1 | 1722 | 49.2 | 1680 | 51.7 | 1709 | 52.5 |
| School 2 | 2152 | 34.8 | 2175 | 33.9 | 2094 | 30.9 |
| School 3 | 1008 | 39.2 | 1008 | 39.2 | 1116 | 41 |
| School 4 | 1005 | 51.7 | 1079 | 52.9 | 1587 | 32 |

*Source: Field Data*

(Figures in Percentages)

**TABLE 5.47**
**Age-Wise and Gender-Wise Distribution of the Students in Government Schools**

| Grade-Wise | Gender | Age of Students | | | | | | Total |
|---|---|---|---|---|---|---|---|---|
| | | 14 | 15 | 16 | 17 | 18 | 19 | |
| Secondary Level | Girls | 14 | 14 | 0 | 1 | 1 | 0 | 30 |
| | Boys | 8 | 16 | 3 | 0 | 1 | 1 | 29 |
| | Total | 22 | 30 | 3 | 1 | 2 | 1 | 59 |
| Higher Secondary Level | Girls | | 8 | 8 | 6 | 3 | | 25 |
| | Boys | | 3 | 11 | 11 | 1 | | 26 |
| | Total | | 11 | 19 | 17 | 4 | | 51 |

*Source: Field Data*

A decline in the girl's enrolment in government schools as well as private schools was thus observed. Studies have shown that this district has the highest proportion of out-of-school children. Data also show that a majority of the population is engaged in agricultural activities here and that it has a negative impact on educational attainments. It has been said that most of the children remain absent from school during the agricultural season --- while boys join the field work at an early age, girls manage the household chores when the parents are in the field. (Basak & Mukherjee, 2014)

*Overage and Underage Children:* The table 5.47 shows that a small proportion of girls in government schools was overage at the secondary level as well as the higher secondary level. At the secondary level, in private schools, Class IX students were generally 14 years, Class X students were 15 years, Class XI students were 16 years and Class XII students were 17 years old. On the contrary at secondary level girls and boys age extended till 19 years. These were the girls who had earlier dropped out from a particular grade and had later joined the same grade in the school.

### *5.5.4 Availability of Female Teachers in Schools*

The availability and the number of female teachers in a school is one of the indicators of how gender friendly it is. The data collected from government schools showed that the number of female teachers was low. The proportion of female teachers was higher in private schools. It was found that female teachers' availability directly affects the percentage of girls' participation in government schools. Parents do not find it comfortable and safe to send their girls to a school where there are no female teachers. The focussed group discussions with girls revealed that they were feeling hesitant in answering in front of male teachers. However, in private schools, despite the availability of female teachers, girls' enrolment remained lower. It was found that girls' parents often do not send their children to private schools due to their poor economic condition.

**TABLE 5.48**

**Availability of Female Teachers in Schools**

| Schools | Female Teachers | Male Teachers | Total Enrolment | Girls Percentage |
|---|---|---|---|---|
| School 1 | 8 | 30 | 1709 | 52.49 |
| School 2 | 8 | 30 | 2094 | 30.95 |
| School 3 | 26 | 21 | 1116 | 41.13 |
| School 4 | 8 | 2 | 1587 | 32.01 |

*Source: Field Data*

### *5.5.5 In-Service Training of Teachers on Gender Awareness*

A majority of the teachers agreed that gender sensitisation training help teachers to handle the problems faced by the girls more efficiently. One of the teachers mentioned that there were no such programmes to date. In general, too, the teachers' responses revealed that no such training programme were held on gender sensitisation. But a few teachers did attend a workshop on gender sensitisation training. Teachers were categorical that such workshop were not held in the government schools of West Bengal during the last two years. But a private school principal was of the opinion its teachers had had sessions with non-government organisations and social workers. Its students also had orientations sessions where gender awareness was discussed by the teachers.

### *5.5.6 Observation*

A 360-degree observation was conducted in the sampled schools, classes and the activities. The classes were observed from outside in order to understand the real method of teaching and the mode of transactions between the teachers and the students.

*Government Schools:* In the government schools, the boys and girls had separate sections grade-wise. At the higher levels, boys and girls of the same class sat in separate rows.

The students were unaware of the term "activity." It was found that girls and boys maintained a distance inside as well as outside the classroom. It was found that, in the higher grades, girls were not given responsibilities as they remained absent from school. Barring a few, those who attended the classes did not take any responsibilities. There was one-sided communication on the part of teachers; and girl students are often reluctant to participate in the question-answer sessions. Teachers asked questions to a few bright students only to understand their grasping power. There were some teachers who tried to humiliate the students verbally if they are unable to respond, resulting in reluctance of the students to respond to the questions asked. However, there were a few teachers who understood the problems of the girls and encouraged them to answer. Tutorial classes were arranged for weak students. There were no teaching aids used in the class. Few students prepared class notes.

Teachers would ask questions from the chapters given in the books and claim that it was an activity. The same work was given for home assignment. For the purpose of formative evaluation, teacher gave assignments to the students. But they considered these very assignments as an activity. It was found that some government school girls were more studious and more serious about study than boys. Teachers sometimes encouraged girls in classrooms but often they were overlooked. The Bengali language was preferred in classroom. The use of English was rare in the classroom sessions.

Teachers came to the classrooms with a specific frame of mind, i.e., to deliver the topic given in a book. The sessions were based on the lecture method. There was no participation or involvement on the part of the students. Most of the students paid little attention to studies and focussed on various things happening outside the classroom. The frequency of questions asked by students was very small. There were social sciences and science labs with teaching aids in some schools. But these labs remained locked and were rarely opened.

*Private Schools:* In private schools, classrooms were well illuminated and properly ventilated. Desks were arranged in rows. There were separate seating arrangements for boys and girls who maintained a distance but joined together both in academics and extra-curricular activities wherein they participated equally. These extra-curricular activities for boys and girls were meant to ensure a holistic development of the students. In most of the cases, girl students emerged as winners. The school arranged special sessions for the girls to learn self-defence through karate and other fitness programmes, right from the junior sections. Teachers and the principal played an active role to motivate the girls. The girls and boys formed separate groups. Both girls and boys were elected as group leaders for the classrooms, as classroom monitors, and for the school captaincy. For instance, if a boy was selected as the vice-captain, then a girl was selected as the captain, and vice versa. Classroom monitors were selected on the basis of merit. The students who had outshined in the school earlier set examples and were quoted by teachers as the role models for other students. English language was used by teachers during the classroom transactions. The use of the local language in the school campus was rare.

Teachers used the lecture method in the classes and examples were cited for a better understanding of the topic. Teachers asked questions gave the students individual attention. Girls and boys equally responded to the questions asked by teachers and often put their own questioned before the teachers to get their doubts cleared. Teachers arranged the question answer sessions after the classes. Extra classes were arranged for weak students, both boys and girls, for subject-wise improvement. Teaching aids were not brought to the class. A few practical sessions were conducted subject-wise in the labs.

**Picture 5.25 : Class rooms without electricity in Government schools**

**Picture 5.26 : Broken fan inside the class room in Government School**

## 5.6 THE ROLE OF TEACHERS' AND PRINCIPALS IN GENDER FRIENDLY SCHOOLS

The present study also gathered data on the roles being played by teachers and principals. This section deals with the opinions of teachers, principals and students about building gender friendly schools, and how far the schools help them and empower them to continue education. It also discusses the barriers which girls face in schools. Parents' opinion was sought in some instances for triangulation of the data. There are various factors which play a pivotal role in helping in or obstructing the creation of gender friendly schools. These include the presence and number of female teachers, role of teachers and principals in schools, and gender sensitive training.

### *5.6.1 Factors influencing Classroom Environment:*

The role of teachers in encouraging girls in a gender friendly classroom can be classified into various sub-themes. The interview and discussion with the teachers provided a view of the teachers providing motivation and encouragement to the girls in their classrooms.

*1) Providing equal opportunities for participation of students:* The teachers motivate the girls to continue their education. Educated girls receive dignity and respect. They are financially stable. Teachers said they try to erase the demarcation between the boy and girl, insist on both of them to take part in every activity from reading and writing to class management, in order to understand their capacities. One of the private school teachers told us that "*In our school we rarely find any difference between girls and boys. Still, I encourage the girls to come up and lead the activity so that girls should get confidence and courage to improve their position.*" The teachers find out their areas of interest and share information related to education and job prospects for them.

In one of the private schools, the principal told us that teachers do tell the students about equality, and the girls are encouraged to speak and perform. These girls, coming from different religious backgrounds, have restrictions at home. But when they are in the school, girls speak freely and feel more relaxed. The principal also said that "*Girls participate in sports activity and are better than the boys. Girls are given responsibility of house captaincy and vice-captaincy alternatively with boys. The teachers and the management ensure to maintain a proper balance.*" The private schools also organise sports meets and seminars to share information among the students. These seminars augment their awareness about the career opportunities with higher education.

*2) Activities Conducted by Teachers in Classroom:* Teachers of the government and private schools conducted various activities. The classroom activities assigned were drawing, recitation, oral examinations, and projects on various topics. They are also given projects on various topics in holiday homework. They are taught different activities such as handicrafts, drawing and story writing in class. The teachers plan activities for the purpose of formative evaluation. One of the government school teachers told us that "*There should be separate teaching models for assigning of homework to the students as per the level of their understanding.*"

Classroom activities and holiday homework are so assigned as to match the standards so that they do their activities and homework on their own effort. A majority of school teachers discussed that the activities are based on the materials taught in the class. The students were asked to complete the question-answer modules and then it was discussed in the class. Some social science teachers of government and private schools keep the classroom activities creative and interesting. For instance, they hold cultural activities, games, word puzzles, discovering of new things in the surroundings and general knowledge. English teachers plan activities such as sentence matching games, parts of speech competition, peculiar paragraph analyses, grammar building as a fun, links for practice, and sentence formation from the given words.

*3) Cite examples of Role Models:* Some of the teachers cited the examples of possible role models for their children. They told them inspirational and real-life stories of some successful women in order to develop an understanding of the successful and independent women. Government school teachers organise plays on these role models and encourage the girls to participate. They motivate girls to participate in classroom activities in order to build their leadership skills. English teachers share the stories of feminist writers with the students, and also enhance their grammar skills and vocabulary through the stories. It was found that a high proportion of teachers encouraged the girls and had a positive attitude towards girls' education. One of the private school teachers said: "*We set practical examples of the girls who have done excellent in our own school in the past.*" Another teacher mentioned that "*I make them feel the importance of education is their life and give the examples of Sarojini Naidu. Mrs Indira Gandhi, Rani of Jhansi, Saina Nehwal, Malala Yousafzai.*"

*4) Awareness on Financial Independence and Self-Reliance:* It was found that a high proportion of girls from government schools were facing financial problems. For this reason, teachers encourage the girls to continue their study and not to work part time before their age. The principal of government school informed that financial support and counselling are provided for girls from the socially and economically weaker sections of society. The girls are also informed about the government schemes meant to facilitate their education and avoid dropout. The teachers and principals hold discussions with the girls about the hindrances and the measures to overcome them through various government schemes, and to get in touch with the school management committee for the proper implementation of these schemes. It was evident that girls from government schools are facing different sociocultural and economic hindrances. One of the teachers stated that "*We have to motivate the girls in various ways by providing school uniforms, books and several other ways.*" A teacher of a government school told us that "*I encourage the girls and boys to study. I remind them that the socioeconomic backwardness is a curse and they have to fight with it on their own. The most important weapon to combat it is education."*

*5) Providing individualised Attention and Activities in Classroom:* For these purposes, girls are given special attention and help even after school hours. Teachers told us that many students were unable to read in Bengali and English. They identify the weak students and try to understand the reason involved. Teachers acknowledged that girls were keener about studying and achieving higher grades, than boys. In private schools the teachers had to convince the girls to maintain patience and take time while understanding a subject.

### *5.6.2 Motivating and Counselling Girls for Higher Education*

*1) Self-Reliance and Awareness on Higher Education:* The teachers motivated the girls, informally, to go in for higher education so that they could earn high social esteem, be self-reliant, not be treated as a burden to parents, and positively face the challenges of their life. Some of the teachers felt that the educated girls receive respect from society. The decrease in infant mortality rate, decrease in population explosion, decrease in child marriages, decrease in domestic and sexual violence, and an increase involvement in political participation are some of the positive results of education. In an interview with us, a government school teacher shared how the success stories of educated mothers used to motivate the girls. He told us: "*I would encourage the girls to go in for higher education. We have to explain the necessity of education to their mothers. If mothers are made aware of it and agree to this, then children will also receive education. We have seen a few girls who are working and performing well in studies because of the encouragement and motivation they receive from their mothers. When mothers are working, they motivate their daughters to come to fore front.* The teacher further added: "*These girls should attend the schools regularly, learn the subjects heartily and complete homework. They should contact the teachers if they have a problem. They are encouraged to participate in talent search examination and read the autobiographies of some famous female personalities.*"

One of the teachers from a private school stated: "*Our school often calls its ex-students, including the girls who are now established in society as doctors, engineers, bankers. They do come and highlight the pleasure of studying in a university.*" One of the government school teachers told us "*Teachers communicate with parents personally and listen to their problems. The teacher of the government schools counsels the girls about their future security. They spread awareness among the girls and their parents, and make arrangements of special scholarships for those girls who are willing to pursue higher education. At the same time, the teachers forbid the girls to get married at an early age which is a burning social curse in our society. They help them to dream for a highly educated life style full of social respect.*"

The principal of a private school remarked that many of the parents are ambitious and aware. They send their daughters outside West Bengal for higher education. However, some other instances show how parents are conservative and do not send their girls away from home, although these girls could have done much better with bigger opportunities.

*2) Counselling on Higher Education:* Every school has a responsibility to prepare their children for higher education. This process of grooming students for higher education starts after the secondary level of education. Teachers try to understand the girls' interests in one or another subject and counsel them for higher education.

As a government school teacher said: "*Teachers make the girls dream of a new future within the classroom together. They assess their special aptitude in different subjects in which they can build up their future. The parents are encouraged to assist their offspring to make them self-reliant. Different biographies of great women are cited to the girls in order to inspire them.*"

He further added: "*Each and every student is special in terms of their thoughts, principles and obvious interests. Therefore, care is taken for every child to pursue higher education. The girls are guided as per their interests in particular subjects. Sometimes it is not possible for the students/parents to fulfil their ambition due to financial and other obstacles. At such junctures, they are guided as far as possible to get through the proper channel in order to get financial assistance."*

Another government school teacher discussed the financial opportunities which girls can get to enter higher education: "*Everyone should be aware of the benefits of higher education. Students and their parents should imbibe that the Government of West Bengal has taken various steps like Kanyashree Prakalpa to encourage the girls to continue higher education.*" The benefits of higher education need to be discussed with the girls at school counselling sessions. The thought process should be developed towards enrolling girls in higher education. Awareness should be created among parents regarding a better future. The girls should be motivated to get higher education for getting attractive jobs and a higher social status.

A private school teacher claimed: "*Nowadays in our school, girls are equally aware, just like boys, about higher education. There are special counselling sessions arranged for girls. In these sessions, they are made to understand and believe that they are no less than the boys for building up society and have to be an active part of it.*"

He further added: "*Teachers do recognise the girls' talents and encourage them. The girls are encouraged to realise the role of education in their personal life. Counselling sessions are arranged for girls according to their choice of subjects and discussions are held on the career graph, job prospects and financial benefits of that particular subject.*"

In schools under different managements, girls are motivated in different ways to enter higher education after school. The government school teachers focus on the financial aspect that would help the girls to continue higher education. They are motivated to be independent and self-reliant. The teachers of private schools focus on the choice of the subject girls have made and the careers linked to the subjects chosen.

### *5.6.3 Achievement level of Students*

Though a majority of the teachers stated that girls had the capability of achieving higher grades than boys, they also said girls lack interest and motivation due to the burden of household responsibilities. A teacher told us that some girls were capable and could achieve a higher grade than boys. Girls were, on an average, keener to study than boys. It is evident from the fact that girls showed better results than boys. Yet all the girls do not achieve higher grades and some teachers of private and government schools hold remedial classes for them. A majority of the government and private school teachers give individualised attention to the low performing girls in their respective classes. Some teachers provide private tuitions to the girls of private schools. According to the teachers of government schools, a considerable proportion of girls and boys are involved in part time work to help the parents financially. In private schools, the teachers and students are called for additional classes during the holidays.

### *5.6.4 Eradicating Girls Absenteeism*

Absenteeism leads to more dropouts and a lower achievement level of girls than boys. There are instances of girls' absenteeism in schools of rural areas. Teachers then send a message to the students who live nearby. Some teachers of government and private schools go to the girls' homes for inquiry. In government schools, para-teachers are sent to visit the girls' homes. A high proportion of teachers contact the parents through school diaries of respective students. They also try to make the parents aware of maintaining contacts. There are several reasons of absenteeism such as early marriage and domestic work. The absenteeism from school leads to a negative impact on one's educational growth. This raises the question why children miss the school and which children miss the school (Garcia & Weiss, 2018).

As said, there are various factors for girls' absenteeism which gradually led them to drop out. The economic condition of the family largely presses a girl to stay away from school. In rural schools, girls are mainly engaged in agricultural work during the harvesting seasons. One of the teachers revealed: "*Some of the parents go to construction work to break stones. Girls have to stay back at home, do household work and look after their siblings.*"

Some teachers opined that girls are neglected by their family members. They are compelled to work hard within the household. These low-income families prefer to send male children for education and insist on early marriage of girls. Another teacher thus listed the main causes of girl's absenteeism which gradually led to their dropout from the school --- first, poor economic condition and malnutrition; second, child marriage and pregnancy at an early stage; third, deprivation and neglecting attitude of family members towards girls. Poverty is the main reason for this backwardness, dropout or illiteracy. Girls have to assist their parents and then come to school --- only when they get some free time. This increases the girl's absenteeism and dropout. The parents who do not have the basic education are not interested in educating their girls. One of the teachers said: "*Financial crises and long absenteeism are the major reasons for dropout of girls from schools. Moreover, uneducated parents do not have any focus towards getting their children educated. One of the major factors is societal unawareness towards education. Girls have to stay home not only for doing household work but also for taking care of younger members of the family when their parents are out for work.*"

Another teacher said: "*In some of the rural and backward areas girls are ill-treated. They are not given any importance in the family. Some of the parents are also conservative and think that there is a hell-and-heaven difference between girls and boys. Boys are made to go to school whereas girls have no right to go to school and become educated. They are meant to do only household chores and activities.*"

When these teachers were further questioned, they mentioned that many of the parents were not strict about sending their girls to school regularly. Their daughters miss school regularly. The financial crisis coerces the girls to miss school and leads to prolonged absenteeism.

The unavailability of toilet facilities in schools in the village is one of the major reasons behind girls' absenteeism. Girls are not able to attend school at the time of a mensuration cycle. There is a lack of female attendants who can assist girls during mensuration cycle in school. The medical box and sanitary kits are with the teachers who are busy with the classes. Girls do not get immediate resolution and have to wait for the teacher. Sometimes they are even scared to speak to female teachers. Parents do not find it safe and comfortable to send their girls to school. This is a common problem in both government and private schools. It has been found that the lack of proper hygiene and sanitation affects the health of girls. Most of the rural schools, both government and private ones, do not have even the handwash facility. Teachers did claim that their schools have toilets and water facility, but in reality, most of the rural schools do not have functioning toilets, leading to dropouts after the primary level. It was observed that even if some schools had toilets, they were not clean. The recent initiatives of the government in all the states shows that sanitary napkin vending machines are installed in the toilets for immediate access to sanitary napkins at the time of mensuration cycles along with-it insanitary disposal machines have also been installed to dispose the sanitary napkins. These machines have been allotted and installed in all the sample schools of Raiganj to avoid inconvenience caused during mensuration days.

Similarly, absenteeism of boys is mainly during the harvesting seasons. Some of the boys miss school due to poverty. They work in fields and shops to help their parents to earn daily living. These boys are mainly migrating away from West Bengal to work as low skill worker in mobile shops. They learn to repair laptops and mobile and return to Raiganj to work in electronic device repair shops. It has been found in studies that family's low income and poor health face many challenges particularly in disadvantaged areas which reinforces absenteeism and drop out of children from school. Absenteeism among boys is slightly less than girls (Garcia &Weiss, 2018).

### *5.6.5 Non-Completion of Home Assignments*

In many cases, home assignments were not completed by boys as well as girls. Teachers claimed that 20 per cent of the boys and 40 to 50 per cent of the girls do not complete their homework. Many of the boys were lazy, inactive, and showed lack of interest in studies. Some of the boys are unable to study due to household and field work. The girls were more active and gave more importance to home work than boys. It was observed that more than 60 per cent of the students come from economically and culturally backward families. The teachers claimed that girls hesitate to disclose their problems. They are shy and do not reveal their identity in front of the class. Their way of living is different from others. The poor economic condition of some of them compels them to assist their parents in several domestic works. Though the girls do not complain about work, it is known to everybody that most of the girls do household tasks and help their mothers. Some girls were definitely able to focus on their studies. It was disheartening to know that many girls and boys remained absent from school to work in fields to help their parents. It is mainly during the ploughing and harvesting seasons. They need to participate in the farming activities and also in household work. One of the teachers said that "*There are several poor families who are unable to have food for two times. In this condition they have to work with their parents. They arrange for bicycle stand in different weekly markets.*"

Other than household factors and socioeconomic factors, the paucity of space or seats in government school classrooms also prohibits the students from attending a school. One of the teachers revealed that "*The girls do not often complete their homework due to household work, financial crisis, and distance from home to school. The other reasons are space constraints in classrooms for which the school is unable to set up the rule of daily attendance and girls remain absent from school and do not complete their homework."*

Some teachers give little or no homework to avoid this problem. One such teacher said: "*We are teaching in a classroom which is based on pragmatic outlook. The type of homework given are free from burden and grievances. The work given are based on clear sense of activities. As a result, they solve them at ease. They do have burden of household work hence we prefer to give homework which they will do easily.*"

The girls in private schools live in towns and have a sound economic background. Their parents are concerned about them and take initiative to make them complete their homework. It was also found that a majority of girls and boys from government schools work on a part-time basis. The girls engage themselves in farming and household activities. The boys are engaged in field work.

### *5.6.6 Importance of Parent Teacher Associations*

Parent Teacher Associations (PTAs) play a pivotal role in enhancing the participation of girls in school. It is necessary for parents to understand the importance of education and PTAs encourage the parents to send their girls to school.

*1) Awareness about Parent Teacher Associations:* Parent teacher associations are useful in rural schools to raise the parents' awareness about the early marriage issues and to regularise the attendance of the girls. Generally, the parents of lower middle-class families are unaware of the potentialities of their girls. Parent teacher associations make them aware of the progress of their daughters. These meetings also inculcate an awareness of the schemes and rules framed by the government for the education of girls. A teacher of a government school told us that "*Most of the guardians are first generation learners. They should be made aware of the necessity of girls' education. The government and private schools offer scholarships for pursuing education by girl students. This can also motivate the parents in getting their girl children educated, resulting a lesser number of absentees and school dropouts amongst girls.*"

When the same teacher was questioned on the benefits of this, he replied: "*It had an overall good impact and some parents did participate in this kind of meetings.*"

A majority of teachers thought that parent teacher meetings build a positive relationship between the parents and teachers. The parents are convinced by the teachers to send their wards to school regularly. Another government school teacher said: "*Awareness has to be created amongst all the family members and to make them understand the importance of educated girls. In such parent teacher meetings, conscious parents come to the school. Then the weak areas and issues faced by the girls are discussed and both of them can overcome problems.*" The teachers claimed that "*through different associations, parents are made aware about the progress of the girls across all segments. Today's girls are doctors, engineers, pilots, nurses and teachers. They have established themselves in different fields. Parents can in turn make their girl children aware of the same. Some parents are conscious enough to take proper care about the same. The conscious parents do participate in and encourage such associations.*"

In one of the informal discussions with us, a teacher told us that parents are marginal workers and do not attend such meetings as they are involved in field work. They should understand the importance of such associations and take out time for participation as their daughters are often absent.

*2) Performance and Development of the Child*: A parent teacher association is one of the means for a child's development. It helps in positive development of the girls and resolves the issues the child faces. The teachers and parents develop a balanced understanding about bringing up the child. It is achieved through the meetings and discussions with the parents at regular intervals. One of the government school teachers said that parent teacher meetings enable the teachers and parents to take care of the girls better. There are many problems faced by parents as well as teachers which can be sorted through mutual discussions. The parents and teachers discuss the weak areas of girls and these can be overcome through conscious efforts, by participating in and encouraging such associations. Teachers provide guidance to the parents that help in better performance of the students. The teachers perceive that if these parents are conscious, girls attend school regularly and miss the school only occasionally. A teacher from a government school said that "*A parent teacher association acts as a guide to the teachers and parents. The important issues are sorted out through discussion about the child's growth and development. Natural healthy discussions about a child can take place through a parent teacher association.*"

Some of the private school parents have a balanced understanding about the upbringing of their children. In these schools, parents are strict and take initiative in the learning process of the children. The parents and teachers have elaborate discussions on classroom behaviour, career and future decisions. A private school teacher said: "*Parents directly contact the principal and the teachers, which gives a wider scope of communication for both the groups to discuss and understand the difficulties faced by the girls in class, study the environment and relationship between teachers and students for the personal growth and progress of girls.*"

On further probing, the teacher revealed that such meetings help the teachers to know about the strength and weaknesses of the girls. Many parents were not at all aware of the positive side of girls' education. After such a meeting, parents better understand the value of girls' education. In an interview with the principal of a private school on school attendance, he revealed that the "*parents are informed about the children's presence in school through SMS within 45 minutes as the school starts daily. This message shows whether the child has reached the school or not. The school has also borrowed space on the website through agencies to inform the parents about report cards of the students. Parent teacher meetings are held across all the classes and sections individually. All the parents related to the school want their children to be educated. There are many holidays for local festivals and pujas. Sometimes students are keen to join the school due to long holidays during local festivals."*

*Motivation of the Parents*: A majority of teachers in the government schools tried to motivate the parents through the parent teacher associations. When the principal was probed, he told us that "*the teachers and the parents will be benefited by conversing with each other. Parents will be motivated to send their daughters to school. It is necessary as the parents do not take any interest in girls' schooling and they miss school regularly.*"

We did find some instances in which mothers motivates a girl child and sent her to school regularly. Some of them have a second child, but they do not hesitate to send their children to the same school and with the same goal. They believe daughters are no less capable than boys. Parent teacher associations were found to be an important means to understand the mindset of parents as most of the parents are unaware, are first generation learners and allow their children to miss school off and on. However, there were a few parents of government school children who were strict about sending their girls to school. Some parents let their girls miss school on important occasions such as during the harvesting season. In comparison, private school parents are more conscious and do not let girls miss the school. They take interest in their studies on a regular basis and see to it that their children are attending school.

### 5.6.7 Teachers' Initiatives to Improve Girls' Participation in the Community

Community members play an important role to improve the participation of girls in school. These community members can convince the children as well as guardians and thus eradicate the orthodox ideas and notions about education (if any) from their minds. But here a majority of teachers did not participate in community mobilisation and responded vaguely. Some of the teachers made efforts to mobilise the community members. Teachers visited the villages in the school's vicinity to enlighten the villagers. One of the government school teachers claimed: "*I go to the houses located near the school, motivate them to visit the school and send children to receive education. In school children will find a number of friends of the same age group, get mid-day meals, school dress and books. Those girls who belong to the SC and ST categories would receive scholarship. I discuss all the benefits of schooling with them so that they are motivated to study.*"

When he was probed, the teacher told us that "*the para teachers, along with SSA members in our school, visit different villages within the close vicinity and try to bring in the out-of-school children. Sometimes, parents ask their children to hide in the trees and cowsheds. In school, separate classes are arranged for their development. There are bridge courses to prepare them to sit for the class as per their age group.*"

These girls also participate in extra-curricular activities to develop their interest in school. The school has a separate volley ball team for girls. The National Cadet Corps recently started to organise its camps for girls. There are some cultural activities arranged specifically for girls in the school. Some of the female teachers have been deployed specially, and they discuss the problems, both mental and physical, faced by girl students.

Some teachers further brought to our knowledge that bringing the girls to school means to train them for a better life. This included, first, separate classes on the life style pattern --- to maintain cleanliness and hygiene such as to take bath, brush teeth, washing hands and eating properly; second, to train them to use the toilets; third, to arrange special counselling for them to solve their family problems and even physical deformities (if any); fourth, to look after their health. The schools, along with the West Bengal Government, have launched campaign for girl children from time to time to spread awareness and motivation about the learning process and give them social viability. The schools also organise other campaigns, for instance Kalianshree

Prakalpa or Sahaj Sathi. The government schools provide mid-day meals, free tuitions and special classes to improve their level of study. The girls are encouraged to participate in sports and cultural programmes actively. Teachers of government schools emphasised that members of the school management committee and other educated people of the village encourage parents to educate their daughters. Thus, community members help to improve the participation of girls and working children in school. In these visits, the teachers reported that they discussed with guardians about the benefits of schooling; some of these discussions were at a personal level. Girls were encouraged to participate in such discussions. These discussions were done at the individual level and suggestions were provided for a betterment of their life.

The same teacher then added: "Government scholarships are distributed among the girls. Library facilities and free books are provided. Their physical and mental wellbeing are also looked after by their teachers."

Sometimes, local people try to encourage the girls by giving them awards and prizes for their performance in the school. The para-teachers of government schools work on a regular basis to encourage the parents to send their daughters to school. Meetings with guardians are arranged on a regular basis and the school timings are kept flexible. In private schools, captainship charges are given to girls. They are made leaders in group activity and are encouraged by rewards and recognition in different fields. Karate classes are arranged for girls so that they are able to protect themselves physically. These classes are conducted from the VI standard onward. The girls are trained for singing and dancing so that they could flourish in extra-curricular activities. SUPW (Socially Useful Productive Work) classes are conducted to increase the creativity of the girls. Counselling sessions held for girls play an important part in their life and make them feel comfortable. At the secondary and higher secondary levels, classes are arranged on sex education.

Some other classes develop the vocational skills and work experience of the girls.

### *5.6.8 Challenges to Mainstream Girls in School*

The teachers of government and private schools were aware of the challenges faced by the girls. Some of the teachers told us that these girls were not socially motivated, were burdened with responsibilities at home and, were hesitant to disclose their problems.

*1) Nature and Geographical Conditions of Girls:* In our interactions with the teachers, it was found that the girls of rural areas were mostly introvert and some of them faced personal problems which affected their participation in class. A majority of girls in rural areas are timid and shy. It was found that they were hesitant while participating in the class. It was evident that these girls come from diverse backgrounds. Geographic conditions were an important factor in the life of these girls who have to travel from the interior and deserted places. They have to cross the streams, forests and highways, and then they have to take a shared auto rickshaw (*toto* or *chakra*) to reach the school. Thus, these girls have to walk miles for the purpose. It causes a sense of fear and insecurity in their hearts. Their parents are not comfortable either, and insist them to drop out of school. They are not able to settle in the class easily. They are hesitant to face the competition and they harbour an inferiority complex within. It was also revealed that these girls are not socially motivated by their parents. Many of the girls still think that they belong to the weaker sections of the society and must be protected by men. This makes them more vulnerable emotionally.

One of the government school teachers pointed out: "*These girls are meek in voice and shy by nature. So, one should try to interpret the silent language of their hearts or unspoken words which they intend to tell someone.*"

Teachers explained that girls are hesitant to come forward, whereas boys enjoy the opportunity. Hence the teachers motivate the girls so that both boys and girls work together and move forward. For this purpose, extra-curricular activities like debates and discussions are arranged in order to have a better classroom environment. A teacher from a private school told us that the girls were quiet and submissive. Teachers encouraged the girls to participate, by counselling them individually and appreciating their efforts. Once a week a special counselling session is arranged whereby girls may feel comfortable to participate in the class. These girls go through a lot of physical and emotional stress. Government school teachers revealed that most of the girls are first- and second-generation learners and earlier they rarely came out of home. They have to overcome so many superstitions and social barriers. They speak less and hear more --- a habit imbibed in them from their elders. The girls who are first generation learners do not know even their mother tongue well. Teachers give them individualised attention to make them read and understand a text. Some of the students are unable to read and write. Teachers encourage them to express their thoughts and imaginations, so that they get pushed into the activities organised by teachers in the class. A considerable proportion of girls are not able to prepare their lessons regularly due to social backwardness. They lack the courage to dream about their future. In many instances, parents arrange their daughter's marriage early. Those who get married early are not allowed by their in-laws to come to school and continue their study.

*2) Burden of Work:* A majority of girls in government schools come from villages. These girls get lesser opportunities when it comes to education. They are inattentive and have irregular attendance in class. They are not able to complete their daily homework. A majority of them get involved in various household works. This leads to a lack of involvement in the classrooms. The girls are not able to express openly about their physical difficulties. Sometimes their parents are informed to meet the teachers. The strength areas are discussed with the parents. The efforts of the girls are appreciated and parents are advised to take proper care. Although the girls are bright in studies, it was found that they lack motivation. These girls are self-satisfied with their performance and progress. This is due to the uncertainty in their mind about their future. In most cases, an average Indian girl has the intention to get married early and have a family life as comfortable as possible.

*3) Situations of Bullying:* In most of the cases of bullying by boys, a teacher listens to the girls and counsels the concerned boys to avoid such behaviour in future. In most cases, the boys are cautioned while they are counselled about their career. In some instances, a guardian is called and, also, proper steps are taken against the boy to deter or reform him. It depends on the situation. One of the teachers explained: "*At first, I would help the girl to regain her confidence and get out of the trauma. Later I would call the boy to know the reason, talk to him personally and give him advice about good and bad things. Then, if needed, I would talk to the guardians of both, the boy and the girl, and the headmaster.*"

In most instances, teachers are empathetic, listen to the girls' worries and constantly encourage them to face such situations boldly. Teachers motivate the students to handle the situation, on their own as far as possible, and solve the problems themselves. They guide and support the girls. Some of the teachers insisted that the girls must ignore such circumstances as well as the negative aspects of society; that they should not bother and help them concentrate on their studies. Another teacher revealed: "*Such a boy should be called individually, and advised with love and care. I try to find out the root cause of this behaviour and deal accordingly. Later I call the concerned girl and counsel her how to deal with such situations.*"

In such a situation, the concerned teacher speaks to the boy and the girl separately in order to find out the reason for the problem. Then she or he tries to normalise the situation so that the girl and the boy become friends again and concentrate on their studies. The teacher pursues them to behave as equals in every respect, helps them to develop a friendly attitude and makes them understand that they are not in a state of competition with one another. They should help each other to go ahead in their career.

## 5.7 PARENTS' PERCEPTION ON PARENT TEACHER MEETING:

There were a few parents of government school children who admitted that they were unable to meet the concerned teachers to know the progress of their children. They did not attend any parent teacher meeting. These parents work in fields as daily wage labourers and hence cannot come for the meeting. They think that sending their children to school would lead to labour losses. These parents therefore think that a meeting with the parents might not be beneficial. However, in private schools, parents regularly attend the parent teacher meetings. One of the government school parents said: "*One of the teachers stays near our place; if we have any difficulty, we meet her to solve the doubts which our child has after the class.*"

## 5.8 PARENT'S PERCEPTION ON TEACHERS' HOME VISITS:

A majority of the parents from government schools said that teachers do not visit their homes to know the progress of the child. But a high proportion of private school parents was of the opinion that teachers visit students' homes regularly in order to know their progress. There were instances of long absenteeism whereafter the concerned teacher of a government school, along with block level officers, visited a girl's home to find out the reason for her not coming to school.

**TABLE 5.49**

**Teachers' Visits to Students' Homes**

| | Teachers' Visits to Students' Homes | | |
|---|---|---|---|
| **School Type** | **No** | **Yes** | **Total** |
| Government | 10 | 6 | 16 |
| Private | 3 | 13 | 16 |
| Total | 13 | 19 | 32 |

*Source: Field Data*

The father of a government school child stated: "*No, they do not come home to visit the child. We send a leave application to the class teacher in case the child is not able to attend the school. There is no contact over phone.*" Another parent said: "*We discuss the problems with the teacher over phone.*"

## 5.9 PARENTS' PERCEPTION ON CHALLENGES WHICH GIRLS FACE IN SCHOOLS

There was a significant proportion of parents who raised their concerns about the challenges girls were facing in school. Some of the challenges are thematically categorised here.

*1) Problems of Communication*: Some parents raised their concern about the girls studying in co-educational schools. One of the private school parents felt: "*Due to the presence of boys, girls cannot express their opinion and speak freely in the class.*"

Some of the parents of government schools explained how girls were unable to discuss the problems related to studies. They felt girls face problems of communicating with the teacher. One of them stated: "*If they do not understand anything in class, they are not able to communicate it to the male teachers as they are scared. Sometimes they feel shy to discuss in front of the boys of their class who make mockery of them later on.*"

*2) Teasing by Boys in School:* It was said by some parents that girls face problems of eve teasing by boys in both government and private schools. In most cases, parents accompanied the girls back home in government as well as private schools. One of the government school parents stated: "*On the way home from the school, some boys sit idle and gossip outside the school. They create problems for girls.*"

Another parent stated: "*The school is co-educational. My daughter is in the IX standard. She started facing problems when a group of boys chased her after the school. She got frightened and did not go to school for a long time. I behave as a friend with her so that she may share her feelings with me.*"

*3) Lack of Infrastructural Facilities:* A considerable proportion of parents from government and private schools believed that schools lacked some key infrastructural facilities. The parents of the government schools complained that the school was located near the highway which causes problems during the rainy season. One of the parents said: "*The school gets flooded and it becomes difficult to go inside the school. Classes on the ground floor get waterlogged.*"

A private school parent said: "*Girl's face sanitation problems. toilets are not clean and there is no adequate water in toilets. There is no playground in the school and the backyard is used for parking the school buses. So, there is no scope for physical the development of our children.*"

The mothers of a government school girl said: "*The school does not educate the teenage girls about the mensuration cycle. During their mensuration cycles girls have to take help from female attendants in school who are rarely available. Girls hesitate to discuss these problems even with female teachers.*"

These problems lead girls to miss school for a period of time. It is a common factor in government and private schools

*4) Early Marriage:* The parent of a government school child was vocal about the practice of early marriage; he is also a member of the school management committee. He said: "*In case the parents are poor, girls are married at an early age, after completing Class X. Parents want their children to get matured and hence send them to school. The school management committee members and teachers raise funds for the poor girls from the village panchayat and other households. These funds are utilised for girls who elope from their home due to marriage pressure or stay in far-off areas where there is no school. These girls then stay in a hostel to complete their studies.*"

The specific problems which affect the girl's education in the study area.

The government schools lacked infrastructural facilities. Sanitation was poor and it was difficult for girls to maintain cleanliness and hygiene. Tap water was provided for drinking. There were frequent power shortages and insufficient lights in the classrooms. There was no electricity during the rainy seasons. The benches and fans were often broken. Three classrooms were under construction. Schools were without playground and boundary walls.

Another major problem identified in the study region is waterlogging in the government schools which disrupted the classes in rainy seasons. The monsoons started from July to September which included long break in the schools due to festive season. The schools did not function for the minimum number of days (200 days in an academic year) as prescribed in the RTE.

The availability of female teachers is low in government schools. The availability of female teachers' directly affects the percentage of girls' participation in government schools. Parents prefer not to send their girls to a school without any female teachers.

Gender disparity is high at the senior secondary level. Mostly children remain absent from school in the harvesting season. The number of integrated schools is less in this district.

The practice of gender stereotyping within the school was evident. Girls were not given prominent leadership role such as captain in school. This was because girls mainly remained absent from school. Schools did not indulge karate classes and basketball facilities for girls. The girls followed the traditional extracurricular activities painting, music, gardening.

Lecture methods were used in the classrooms. There were no activities conducted within the classrooms or stereotype activities were conducted such as drawings, oral recitation etc. Teachings aids were not used in the classrooms. The social science, science and mathematics laboratory were not maintained properly. The teaching learning material like maps and charts were not used.

Girls' absenteeism is one of the major problems identified in rural schools. Absenteeism leads to more dropouts and a lower achievement level of girls. The parents were not strict about sending their girls to school regularly. The unavailability of clean toilets and water facility is one of the major reasons for absenteeism. Girls did not attend school at the time of a mensuration cycle. Sometimes long absenteeism girls' leads to loss of interest in studies and incomplete home assignments. They preferred to stay at home. The teachers along with block level officers paid home visit but such instances are rare.

***Focussed Group Discussions***

The discussions conducted with a group of girls in a government school showed that students were made to sit together in the class in the primary classes. But, then, separate sections were allotted for boys and girls till the ninth standard. In the tenth standard, sections are combined together but seating arrangements are separate for boys and girls who sit in different rows. The girls stated that since they do not share the same classroom, the concept of equal participation had no meaning. There were instances of opportunities of equal participation in sports activities but, in some instances, boys got more importance than girls. When they were further questioned whether teachers gave equal importance to girls and boys, girls revealed that teachers give more chance to weaker students for participation in the classroom. In private schools, too, girls and boys are seated in different rows. But the activities given to girls and boys were same. The girls were also given captainship roles. There was no case in any of the private schools where similar activities were not given, but girls revealed that bright students were given more chances. The girls felt that participation was equal.

The researcher observed that some students did not even understand the meaning of an activity. There were no activities held in some schools except the periodical tests held in the name of formative and summative evaluations. In some instances, there were group activities in private schools.

A majority of girls were hesitant and reluctant by the presence of boys and teachers in the class. As a girl said: “It happens when we are not sure of the responses and we are afraid that the teacher would scolds us. We feel humiliated in such situations and do not participate in the class. It creates a sense of awkwardness in the presence of peers.” These girls thus felt less confident while responding to the teachers. In private schools, too, some of the girls felt hesitant in class as they were not confident about the responses.

The researcher further probed the students about the behaviour of their teachers. A majority of government and private school students responded that general attitude of the teachers was strict inside the classroom. Hence girls were apprehensive while responding in the class. This shows the autocratic behaviour of their teachers. Yet, some teachers were democratic and flexible, empathetic and helpful outside the class. They tried to resolve the issues faced by girls. The government school teachers make special efforts to understand the problems the children are facing inside the classroom. They motivate the students and encourage them to continue their studies. They motivate the parents in case of serious problems faced by the girls at home. Some government school teachers protected the girls from the custom of early marriage.

Focus group discussion highlighted a significant issue that the girls are bullied by the boys. Girls are harassed by the boys after school hours. The boys follow the girls from school to home. This creates problem in the girl’s life as the parents are reluctant to send their girls to school. It was difficult for the girls to discuss these issues with parents. Some of the parents were aware about the teasing of the girls. In such instances parents accompanied the girls to the schools. In most of the cases the boys are cautioned while they are counselled about their career pros and cons. There were very few instances guardian was called and proper steps were taken against the boy to deter or reform them.

## 5.10 CONCLUSION

The study attempted to explore the life of rural girls and their access to schools, their aspirations for education and the decisions related to the choice of subject, profession, entry into the higher education, their aspirations to express their rights and freedom and to take significant decision in career choices on the basis of their education. The enhanced yet gender-wise unequal progress in education is due to some significant socioeconomic, geographical, mobility-related and household factors. The school related factors --- lack of infrastructural facilities, unequal participation in classroom --- continue to pose obstacles for girls. However, the girls expressed the hope about overcoming these challenge and complexities in the path of empowerment.

CHAPTER 6

# BEYOND THE SCHOOL: A CASE STUDY ON GIRLS IN UTTAR DINAJPUR

## 6.1 INTRODUCTION

This chapter presents a few case studies to understand the life of the girls in Raiganj block of Uttar Dinajpur, their educational status, and how they view the schooling experiences, aspirations, decision-making capabilities within and outside the household, their activities and the major obstacles in the path of education. It seeks to get an insight into the journey of empowerment of girls through education and to understand how some of them became the role models for other girls in society. The girls selected for the case study were from the villages located near the school and belonged to the sampled schools. There are two girls from private schools (case 1 and case 6) and six from government schools (case 2, case 3, case 4, case 5, case 7 and case 8). The background data needed for the case studies were collected from the households.

These case studies have been classified into four categories: (a) the girls who are pursuing college/university education (case 1, case 2, case 3 and case 4), (b) girls who are employed (case 5 and case 6), (c) housewives (case 7) and (d) and dropouts (case 8) from school.

The case studies covered three themes: (a) the background, schooling experiences and societal attitude, (b) economic independence and family decision-making, and (c) patriarchal family norms.

## 6.2 FAMILY BACKGROUND AND SCHOOLING EXPERIENCES

### *Girls Pursuing College/University Education*

CASE 1: Respondent 1 is a college student. She is 23 years old. She passed the senior secondary exam in 2011 from a reputed private school. The subject selected at the senior secondary level was science. She opted for English (Honours) for her Bachelors study, and later did the Masters in English. She is at present trying to enrol herself for a Bachelor of Education (B.Ed.) degree. Her father is working with a private sector bank. She belongs to a nuclear type family, and her mother is working as an officer in a government job. The respondent was of the opinion that women should be educated. For, educated women can well influence other members of the family and it has a good impact on family environment and future generations of the family. She had a pleasant experience in school. She recalled that the teachers in her school were supportive and taught well. She belongs to an affluent family. Her parents motivated her for higher education. She opined that the major support came from her mother as she was educated and holds a significant place in familial decision-making.

*Preference on Choice of Subject:* The respondent did not have her own preference in the selection of a subject. She was interested to study English and selected humanities at the secondary level. She was inspired and developed a keen interest in English because of her English teacher. But her parents forced her to take science at the secondary level for her career. Her parents thought that she could become a doctor or an engineer after studying science. After completing school education, she fought with her parents about her interest and subject preference. Later, she graduated and then mastered with English from the Raiganj University.

CASE 2: Respondent 2 is a graduate student. She is 23 years old. She completed her senior secondary education from a government school in 2012. Then she graduated from Raiganj

University. She has been preparing for various competitive examinations so as to get a suitable government job or to enrol herself in the university for the Masters course in English. She feels a government job is safe as well as secure for girls. Her father is handicapped and owns a small grocery shop in the village. She lives in a nuclear family. After completing her studies and household chores, she sits in her father's shop to look after the family business. She felt that girls should be educated and independent. Education is necessary for the girls so that after marriage you are not dependent on your life partner and you are able to take decisions in the family independently.

Initially, respondent 2 was living in a joint family. But her parents moved out of the joint family as other members were against the education of girls. Her parents fought against their relatives and other family members, and got separated for her education. Her parents motivated her to continue education. Schooling experience was good as both the parents and teachers were supportive. She told us that their family income was not much. Teachers and the nominated party members of the panchayat raised funds to pay for her school fees and sometimes waved it off under special circumstances.

*Preference on Choice of Subject:* Respondent 2 had chosen social sciences as her subject. She had interest in English and opted for English honours at the undergraduate level. This decision was taken in consultation with the parents and teachers in school.

CASE 3: Respondent 3 is a college student. She is 18 years old. She completed senior secondary education in 2016 from a government school near her house. But she hardly got time to study at home. Both father and mother were illiterate. Her father is an agriculturist and they live in a joint family. She cooks food and does the household chores. She has enrolled for admission in Raiganj University for graduation course. She dreams of completing graduation and getting a job to support her family economically. When the researcher asked her opinion on girls' education, she kept quiet for a while as if she were blank about it. But then she started murmuring that girls should be educated like boys, so they could earn and support the family. She informed that before going to school, she used to complete the household chores and she struggled to balance the household responsibilities and study. She told that all her family members motivate her to pursue higher education.

*Personal Preference on Choice of Subject:* She has selected humanities at the senior secondary level with the support of the teachers and parents. She selected history, education and Political Science subjects at the senior secondary level. She is now a college student and got enrolled in the Bachelor of Arts (Pass Course) programme in Raiganj University. She aspires to complete her higher education and lead an independent life.

CASE 4: Respondent 4, a final year college student in Raiganj University, is now studying for a Bachelor of Arts (History Honours) degree. She studied in a government school. Her father is a daily wage labourer. Her parents have completed their school education. Her mother has her own start-up; she took a loan from the government and started her own business. The monthly family income of the family is about five thousand rupees. They lived in a joint family with grandparents. She explained that the aim of education was to fulfil her dreams and be independent. In villages, the parents educate their girls to get married in a cultured family. There are very few parents who aspire that their girls should work after competing their education. It would benefit them by reducing their dependence on their husbands and in-laws.

Respondent 4 struggled to balance her responsibilities at home with her studies. She wakes up in the morning at 5.00 a.m., cleans the room and utensils. She then prepares the meals --- morning breakfast and lunch --- before leaving for college. Her college is far away and she rides a bicycle to reach there. The college is 27 kilometres away from her home. She stays with her parents who are daily wage labours. The bicycle was provided by the Government of West Bengal.

*Personal Preference on Choice of Subject*: Respondent 4 selected humanities for her senior secondary education at the guidance of her teachers. The parents and teachers motivated her to pursue higher education. After completing higher secondary education, she had planned to join a nursing college in Karnataka. But it did not materialise because of her father's illness. He had undergone a major surgery in Vellore. Her parents feared that her career would be wasted and enrolled her in the Bachelor of Arts course in Raiganj. She is a final year student now. This time she had planned to take admission in the nursing course. Her parents have already fixed her marriage and but the boy's parents do not want their daughter in law to stay out of Raiganj.

### *Employed Girls*

Case 5: Respondent 5 is a Hindi teacher in the primary section of a government school. She studied in the government senior secondary school. Her father had a government job. She has a younger brother. She is married in a joint family and she said everyone of that family motivated her to study. Her husband works in a factory. Her family income is Rs 20,000 per month. Her parents and teachers have been supportive which made her schooling experience smooth. She studied science at the senior secondary level. She gives importance to education, and she feels that girls are important members of their families and need to be educated. For the purpose of girls' education, she thinks, government schools are not as good as private schools. In government schools the knowledge base of the students is not very solid. They do not understand the subject clearly and cannot write in the exams. Students in the higher classes do not understand the subject. Yet, poor parents enrol their children in a government school for a secured future and want their children to work. Education has become a must in the view of all the families.

*Preference on the Subject Choice*: This respondent informed that she and her parents had a similar choice of subjects. She had full freedom to study any of the subjects of her choice. She then chose computer science and painting at the senior secondary level.

CASE 6: Respondent 6 works with a non-government organisation which is helping the poor people of North 24 Parganas. She is 23 years of age. She completed her senior secondary education from a private school. Her father, a graduate, a retired jute mill employee in the government sector. Her family income is less than one lakh a year but it does not include her father's pension. Her mother works as a primary school teacher. Respondent 6 was always particular about her studies and made her own choice of an institutions. She said: "*In the background I belong to, I was specific about the institutions which I selected and where I wanted to study. In my experience, there have been a number of factors which matter, like the family background a girl and the location of her school, such as Cooch Behar.*"

She told us that there were only a limited number of higher education institutions and girls had to go to Kolkata or Siliguri for higher studies. But many parents do not allow girls to travel. On the basis of her experiences, she asserted that society does help to educate a girl. But there is also a clash as a girl has to be prepared for marriage and for a heteronormative family where gendered roles are predetermined and girls have to manage the household chores after marriage. But a middle-class family expects its daughters to earn after the completion of her higher education. She therefore had to choose between earning and education while the job market is tough.

Education of a girl is not only class specific but also caste specific. In her school days, she recollects that there were brilliant girls in her class. They scored seventy to eighty per cent in the senior secondary examination. Girls from the socially backward castes or disadvantaged groups were married at an early age and became mere housewives. She, on the contrary, managed to live on her own terms. She moved out of the house to earn and save money for higher education. In higher education institutions, too, there were various barriers. She was, for example, not fluent in spoken English and was looked down by the elite group in the university.

*Preference on Choice of Subject:* Respondent 6 opted for science at the higher secondary level. All the good students in her school opted for science and she was influenced by other students so that she selected science after the secondary level. Later on, she realised that she could not relate to science and could not apply it in life. She could not take it as a career either. At the undergraduate level, she studied comparative literature because she had not scored well at the higher secondary level and the results were pathetic. She had no choice left to get into a good college with a honours course.

***Housewife***

CASE 7: Respondent 7 is a housewife. Her age is 22 years. She completed her schooling from a government high school near her home. At the senior secondary level, she selected humanities. She was married after she completed her Bachelor of Arts course in a college. Her father was in a low-paid government job and her mother was a housewife. After she had completed her graduation in history, her parents fixed her marriage with a person of their choice. Her husband has a diploma in polytechnic and works in a nearby factory. Her family income Rs 4.5 lakh a year. She lives in a nuclear family with her daughter. She gives equal importance to the education of boys and girls. She thinks education enables a girl to become economically independent. While at school, she spent most of the time doing household chores and had lost interest and energy to study. Her parents did not motivate her to study. But the teachers in her school were supportive. Her father was never ambitious and insisted her to marry after the higher secondary examination. However, her mother knew about her aspirations and helped her to get admission in college.

*Preference on Subject Selection*: Respondent 7 chose humanities as her subject of choice. She admitted that she was an average student and did not understand science. Subjects were selected at the higher secondary level in consultation with her parents.

### *The Dropout*

CASE 8: Respondent 8 is a dropout from a government school. She is 22 years old. She did not complete secondary education and dropped out at the secondary level. Her parents are illiterate. Her mother was a housewife and father worked as an agricultural labourer. She belonged to a poor family. She did not have interest in studies. When her parents were in the field, she did the household chores and played in the free time. She did not get time to study at home. Her parents did not pressurise her to study further. She was married at the age of 17 years. Her husband acts as a delivery boy in a bank. She has one child. Her family income is approximately Rs 20,000 per month. She works as an Asha Karmi in a government school and helps in the preparation of mid-day meals. She opined that since she did not study and had suffered a lot in her life, she wanted her children to complete their education and become doctors and lawyers. She agreed that her schooling experience was not good and she did not have regular time to study. Her teachers scolded and punished her for not studying. She was therefore scared of the teacher and did not go to school regularly.

## 6.3 IMPACT OF SOCIETAL ATTITUDE ON EDUCATION OF GIRLS

Societal attitude plays a major role in the education of girls. This theme discusses the opportunities of higher education for girls, parental support, social recognition and societal attitude towards educated girls.

### *College/University Girls*

CASE 1: The role of mother was significant in the education of a girl. Respondent 1's mother was working and took major family decisions. Her parents initiated her to pursue higher education. She felt graduate women enjoyed more social prestige. Through quality education one can inculcate values and skills. She told us that "*The people from northern India do not encourage their girls to study, as compared to West Bengal were parents encourage the girls to study for the purpose of employment and marriage. In Raiganj, the situation can be better explained with the help of my mother who is educated and influences family decisions, compared to my friend's mother who has not completed higher secondary education. She has also been subjected to domestic violence. If only she had been educated, she would not have faced such challenges. Parents encourage the sincere girls for higher education.*"

The society's attitude towards uneducated women remains unchanged to a great extent. Educated women get more respect and preference, compared to uneducated ones. Women can achieve an equal status to men through education. Education has not been able to change the mindset of the people or society towards women.

CASE 2: Respondent 2 realised that higher education has helped her to speak in public places. She has developed self-confidence and can expresses her individual opinion in her family. Her parents thought that education is necessary for a girl to be knowledgeable. They had encouraged her for higher education. However, it is not the same with others. She said: "*Parents did not allow me to go outside Raiganj for higher education. There are two reasons. First, a girl would not be in a position to protect herself in case of unforeseen circumstances. Second, neighbours and people of the wider society had the opinion that she was going out and they did not take mixing-up in free company in a good sense. This led to an adverse impact on my family's thinking. My parents were discouraged to send me outside Raiganj for higher education. They were threatened to be boycotted by the village. However, such restrictions are not applied for the boys going out for job and higher studies.*"

Respondent 2 felt that outlook of the parents is now changing with time. Although society still has to play a vital role in encouraging girls' education, they are not encouraged to work and pursue higher education. Society imposes restrictions on the girls for security purposes, on moving out of the geographical boundaries of their district. All the reputed higher education institutions are in Kolkata, girls of Raiganj are not able to study. Educated girls are acknowledged for being knowledgeable but they are not able to earn respect.

CASE 3: Respondent 3 comes from a socially disadvantaged group. Her parents thought of providing her higher education till she got married. Her parents are not literate and are not aware of the importance of education. They do not give special recognition to her in family on the ground of her higher education.

CASE 4: Respondent 4's parents motivated her to pursue higher education. She knows how to operate a computer. She received a scholarship under Kanyashree scheme after the age of 18 years, which helped her to continue her higher education. Her parents would not be able to support her studies financially. The school and teachers kept her parents aware of the schemes to help her continue the education. She is a bright student and received scholarships from the school and government. She has also availed of the merit scholarships from the government. For enrolling in higher education, she received annual scholarships from the government. Education helped her in seeking a job. Educated girls can earn. There is a lot of competition in the job market. People ask for money to provide a job. The government wants the girls to complete the higher secondary level at least. Free mid-day meal and scholarship attract the villagers and they send the girls to school. Educated girls have no recognition at home though they receive respect and recognition at the workplace.

*Employed Girls*

CASE 5: Respondent 5 has a strong and supportive family. She is from a socially deprived community. Her parents desired that both their children pursue higher education. Respondent 5's mother desired that her daughter become a computer engineer. She had health issues and was not able to get admission. She did her Masters in Hindi and then her B.Ed. Her brother went in for computer engineering. Education has helped her gain confidence and get a job. She gets recognition for her education and job. She told us: "*Society has changed over the years. Parents understand the benefits of schooling. My in-laws including my sister-in-law encourage me to work. She does the household chores. She has never been to school. Even in her childhood days, she used to work. She has immense respect for education and jobs.*"

She mentioned that girls from high income groups send their children to school and encourage them to learn painting, singing and karate. Though parents from low-income groups send their children to school, they cannot spend anything on their hobbies. These girls work as teachers and give home tuitions to complete their higher education. She felt that educated girls receive respect in society.

CASE 6: Respondent 6's mother motivated her to get enrolled in a better school and insisted that she go in for higher education. Education has inculcated values and skills with knowledge. She felt: "*Education helps in getting special recognition in family. The brothers and sisters or young generations understand the importance of education. The other members of the family felt that education is a formality that needs to be inculcated just as ritual to be shown to the larger society.*"

She further added: "*Society educates girls and pays for their schooling. People in villages send their girls to school out of social obligation. But society as a whole is not ready for educated girls. When the educated girls raise their voice and make their choices, people do not like them and they are termed as disobedient. Social prestige depends upon one's class and caste. I belong to a good family and went to good universities so I have those tags with me and received social prestige, but it is not the same for a Dalit girl. Hierarchy is such that people of different castes, classes and genders would not get similar social prestige. There is a huge gap between the girls coming from different social groups. The drawback for girls is not so much because of marriage as the clan from which they come."*

***Housewife***

CASE 7: Respondent 7's mother was more ambitious than her father. She insisted on her to complete graduation before getting married. She believed that education promotes knowledge, skill and values. But social attitude towards women have not changed to any significant extent.

She stated: "*In comparison to uneducated women, educated ones get more preference, respect and social prestige. Education helps women to get the same status as men. The parents encourage both girls and boys to study. Parents support education of girls who score high grades.*"

***Dropout***

CASE 8: Respondent 8 understood the importance of education much later after she got married. Now she is an Asha karmi worker (daily wage labourer) in a school. Her parents insisted on her to do the household chores. They did not plan anything about her education. When she could not attend school for a long time, they discontinued her education. Her parents took the opportunity to marry her at an early age. She knows that educated women get more acknowledgement than uneducated women. She felt let down vis-à-vis the women who are educated and have jobs. These women are not dependent on their husbands. These women have a better work culture and distinguished style of living, of presenting themselves and speaking in public.

It has been observed that the educated women receive more social recognition at workplace. The society's attitude to girls is determined by factors like class and caste. The societal opinion about the on uneducated remains unchanged. The situation for girls from the socially deprived groups is more challenging compared to those from other social groups. Society acknowledges girls who are educated and employed.

## 6.4 ROLE OF EDUCATION AND CAREER IN ECONOMIC EMPOWERMENT

### *College/University Girls*

CASE1: Respondent 1 was pursuing a professional teacher training course as she desired to be a teacher. She agreed that education enables women to be an earning member of the family. Her mother is working and plays a prominent role in family decisions. She stated that "*educated employed women get a chance to influence family decisions. Financial stability is a must to influence the family decisions. There are a few instances where working women take decisions on a shared basis with husband. An employed wife has a share in the decisions taken by her husband. Sometimes the husbands influence the decisions. It is only in a few exceptions that a housewife's opinions are taken into consideration. I am a student and all the decisions in my family are taken by parents.*"

There are reasons why parents are apprehensive about the girls' employment. These include marriage and sexual harassment of young girls at the workplace.

CASE 2: Respondent 2 runs her father's grocery shop and sells household items. She regularly sits in the shop from 7 am to 12 noon and in the evening from 5 pm to 8 pm. Her father is specially abled. She desires to work and was preparing for the competitive exams. Her parents had given her permission for to take up a government job which they thought is better than a private job. She said: "*Educated women can be an earning member of the family. Parents and society do not allow the girls to work. Parents are concerned about the safety and security of the girls. The neighbours and relatives may have varied opinions about the work and workplace of the girls.*"

It was exceptional in her case. She decides all the monetary expenses in her household. She believed: "*If my father was not a specially abled person, then probably, as in the case of other girls, their family would have been controlled by the father.*"

The daily expenditure of the household and monthly savings is planned and decided by her. It is decided on the basis of items sold in the shop daily. She fixes the monthly budget and savings of the household. Her mother gets involved whenever she needs help. However, decisions such as marriage are to be decided by the parents. She is a qualified girl but her family does not allow her to access mobile phones and social networking sites as it is not considered good in the village. People in the village think girls should not use a mobile phone and the social networking sites. They may be trapped in a bad company and misuse their freedom. It is not the same for the boys. They have enough freedom to use phones and social networking sites.

CASE 3: Respondent 3 told that girls and boys should be equally educated. However, her behaviour showed her disbelief in the ideology of equality. The girls can work but after marriage their responsibility should be of taking care of the family members. The researcher noticed that she was not interested in attending a college. She had no intention to work either. The decisions in her family were taken by her father. She indicated that there were certain restrictions on her mobility. She had to ask for permission from parents while going out and she went out only if they granted her permission to go out.

CASE 4: Respondent 4 felt that education had helped her immensely through the scholarship received from the government. She is a graduate student and will pursue her career after completion of the professional degree. She desires to go in for a nursing job. She has no contribution to the family income. Job will help her in decision-making and there will be no dependence on family. Her parent- in-laws was not in favour of letting girl's to go for work. Any information about family expenditure is not shared with her. Girls participate only in small decisions such as arrangement for the pujas. Such a responsibility is given on the basis of capability.

***Employed Girls***

CASE 5: Respondent 5 demonstrated the education and employment plays a pivotal role to reach the goals of life. She felt that a job gives a girl immense opportunity to meet people, to discuss and share their problem with others. She said: "*I feel a job gives mental satisfaction. When you discuss your problems with others, you find people facing more serious problems. Thus, sharing your problems with them helps you to find a solution. While sitting at home people become frustrated, but going outside and meeting people make you feel relaxed.*"

A job provides a better life for a girl's family. Parents educate their children to be independent and earning member of the family. She said: "*I work as a teacher in a government school on temporary (ad hoc) basis. I have been working for nine months now.*"

She is an earning member of the family though there is no pressure on her to contribute to the household income. "*I do not contribute any fixed percentage. In case of medical emergencies, my contribution is higher.*"

While male members of the family contribute to the family's expenses, family decisions are taken in consultation with all the family members. She stated: "*We have equal rights to share our opinion. If my opinion is found suitable, it is applied. All decisions in household are taken by my husband and brother-in-law.*"

There are various social barriers regarding the security of a girl. Her family members feel that all people in society are not same. Hence girls have to take precautions. When girls work during day time, family feels more relaxed.

CASE 6: Respondent 6 desires a better life. She worked in a non-government organisation and plans to teach in future. She has a contribution in the family. She stated: "*When I started contributing, my parents asked for my opinion which they had never done before.*" She regularly participates in decision-making and guides her father to invest in property and health. She helps her father to pay his hospital bills.

She clearly explained the factors which influence a girl's life, like the barriers like her location and background. She said, "*If a girl coming from a poor family pursues higher education outside Uttar Dinajpur, her social integrity is questioned. Firstly, the people feel the girls staying outside home misuse their freedom. They may fall in the trap of a wrong kind of companion. The family support is necessary to overcome these barriers. Secondly, the employers have their own unacceptable demands while hiring women from the labour market. The employment market is not very favourable for women. Simply attaining education does not enable a girl to get employment. Women have to take care of households and children which men find as hindrances to employment. Thirdly, migration for work from the place of education is a problem. The parents prefer to stay with their children. It is not possible to pursue a career in Raiganj. The parents are not supportive for girls staying alone in a city. There can be safety issues while renting in a house. I have shifted to Bombay where there are less safety issues and a majority of the people are working ones.*"

***Housewife***

CASE 7: Respondent 7 believed that women should be involved in income generating activities. It is possible when family supports a girl to pursue a job and this enhances her position in the household. Respondent 7 said: "*I never desired to pursue a job. I was interested in household activities. Now I feel it is important to become a working member of the family. It enhances the ability to take economic decisions and support my husband. The expenditure of the household is borne by my husband. Sometimes I do not purchase things of my choice due to shortage of money. My desires and wishes remain unfulfilled. I realised that working women do not have the binding to do the household chores. A woman's contribution to family income raises her position in family. I have participated in shared decision-making about the expenditures on*

*Durga Puja which is our major festival. We have taken decisions pertaining to the buying of new clothes. The expenditure on purchases was fixed by my husband."*

She too had something to say about the barriers for girls who are restricted about the travelling distance and working hours. Girls do not get the same freedom as boys do. Boys are appreciated if they work for long hours. But girls are questioned if they staying out of home for long hours, at their workplace. Sometimes they are even forbidden to work.

***Dropout***

CASE 8: Respondent 8 decided to work in a parlour after her marriage, as her husband was not able to meet all the financial responsibilities. She spends eighty per cent of her income on family and twenty per cent on herself. She has no role in family decisions. She gives suggestions and her husband decides what to listen. She agreed that women should be involved in income generating activities outside home. Education is not a significant factor for earning. The actual difference lies in the type of job. Educated people gets respectable jobs. It is not true that educated women get a chance to regulate the decisions.

Respondent 8 said: "*My family member was concerned with the safety and security of the girls. The scope for the girls is less. In villages, girls from the disadvantaged groups work in fields. Good jobs are there in cities. But parents do not allow girls to work there, for security purpose. They stay at home and later on get married."*

The girls and women did not have personal assets. If some of them have their own bank accounts, these are mostly operated by husbands and parents. The educated and educated girls cannot decide about their own bank accounts.

The main barriers for education and employment of girls are socioeconomic and cultural. Girls from the remote areas or socially deprived groups face more barriers, while educated girls with working parents face them less. Similarly, a girl's family background, and her social and economic status are important factors about overcoming these barriers. There is an intrinsic link between education, employment and workforce participation. It has been observed that the educated girls who are not employed does not participate in the decision-making process within or outside family. Nor do uneducated girls participating in the workforce play any role in family decision-making. It is worth mentioning that the workforce participation and economic independence are necessary, along with education, for participation in decision-making. But the dominance of hierarchy in decision-making within family is also noteworthy. Even employed girls had to reach a decision in consultation with their husbands who were the household heads and made a majority of the family decisions. The decision about marriage is taken by the parents. It is a constant factor for the educated, employed or uneducated girls.

IHDS data from NCEAR suggests that decision on marriage is based on mutual understanding between parents and children. Girls are able to understand the correct motives of their parents. Hence decision taken on marriage are in consultation between the girls and her parents based on mutual understanding and respect. These cases can be for a specific group of educated girls above 18 years age. It has been noted that there are many cases of early marriages and discontinuance of education of the girls in West Bengal. These girls are married at an early age. There are various parameters which comes to foreplay in decisions regarding marriages of girls. These are location, religion, social and economic background, attitude of parents and preference of son over daughters.

## 6.5 DOMINANCE OF PATRIARCHY

The family environment has been changing in the recent times. A majority of the respondents now have their dinner together, though there are some girls who do not have food with family. These girls are mainly from the socially deprived groups. Employed girls have food whenever they need. There are a majority of girls staying in a joint family. They have food mostly after their family members have eaten. Some of the college students have food together.

CASE 6: Respondent 6 believed though men and women are equal but still they do not share equal rights. The researcher could see the glare in her eyes as she protested in favour of women. She said: "*Unfair treatment of women is common.*"

## 6.6 OVERALL VIEW

### *College/University Girls*

CASE1: Respondent 1 belonged to a nuclear middle-class family where education of girls is considered important. She completed her Masters in English and worked as a consultant in Kolkata. Her parents have planned her marriage with a boy of their choice. They have brought her to Raiganj to settle her with a qualified boy. Her parents have asked her to take up the teaching profession which is safe and non-transferable. They did not want her to stay outside Raiganj independently. Her parents got her enrolled for a B.Ed. programme. She felt that her freedom was restricted. She could go outside Raiganj on her own. She has to take permission of her parents when she goes out.

CASE 2: Respondent 2 told us that her family was supportive about she pursuing a career. However, freedom was restricted and it had no relations with education. The freedom to work and find a job is not supported by family. Education is considered the means for a better marriage. She said: "*Though I am trying hard to pass the competitive exams and get a job, my parents feel that government jobs are safer and securer than other jobs.*" Boys, on the other hand, can study and go outside their geographical area and has no mobility restrictions. Girls have to take permission while going out of the house. The researcher could observe the pain in the eyes of this respondent while disclosing her views. She had the courage to speak the truth. She aspired to work outside Raiganj and earn more money for herself and her family members, especially for her father's treatment. But there were restrictions on social mobility and on wearing western clothes. Education is one of the factors that leads to empowerment of females but girls cannot succeed without the support of the family members.

CASE 3: The social mobility of the girls is restricted. Girls have to take permission from parents to go out. Her mobility is restricted. She does not attend her college regularly. She has to take permission from her father before going out.

CASE 4: Respondent 4's parents planned her marriage after she completed her graduation. She would then have been twenty years of age. Her parents had applied for the *Rupashree Scheme*. Under this scheme, the state government provides twenty-five thousand rupees for a girl's marriage. This scheme was introduced by the Government of West Bengal to eradicate the custom of early marriages, before the age of 18. The gram panchayat provides a form for the scheme. The recipient's family has to provide original documents such as age proof and address proof. On the day of the marriage, the concerned Block Development Officer (BDO) gives a cheque on the basis of the receipt given by the Registrar of Marriages. Respondent 6 felt that girls should be empowered, and that education and employment help girls to be independent. The freedom of the girls tends to be curbed after marriage. She said: "*Girls should work after marriage and no one should curtail their freedom.*"

Respondent 6 also mentioned about the self-help groups launched by the government to empower the girls. There are schemes such as *Amanda Dhan* which gives money to woman to start their own businesses. They take loans from the small micro finance banks. For instance, if a woman purchases four cows and sells 20 litres of milk daily to the market, her daily income would be sixteen hundred rupees. Then they can pay the loan back to the State Bank of India. This can help women to maintain equal rights as men.

### *Employed Girls*

CASE 5: Respondent 5's overall view about life was that she was struggling hard to maintain her married life as well as her job.

She wakes up early in the morning, at 4:00 am, to prepare food and breakfast for the family and husband. She gets ready and leaves the house around 6.30 am to reach the school. She has to travel for one and a half or two hours every day to reach the school. After reaching there, she takes a little rest and then starts the school work. The school timings are from 10.30 am to 4.20 pm. She reaches home back at 7.30 pm. At night she helps her sister-in-law with the household chores. At 9.00 pm, she goes to bed. She said: "*In villages girls are married at an early age of 15 to 16 years. There is a provision of test and retest method till the eighth grade in government schools. The girls start to drop out from the ninth grade. Those girls who go in for higher education and job, marry at a later age.*"

CASE 6: Respondent 6's mother was a teacher. She was supportive in all her ventures and helped her move from Raiganj to Bombay. Her father had a low paying job and people looked down on them. Her parents supported her to pursue a career.

***Housewife***

CASE 7: Respondent 7 stays in a nuclear family and can go out with her female friends anytime. But she had to take permission from her in-laws when she lived in a joint family.

## 6.7 SUMMARY

The objective of the case studies was to get the real-life experiences of girls, to understand the significance of school education in their life, and how far they have benefitted from schooling. The role of school is crucial in the empowerment of girls. Their schools empowered them to be independent and make their own choices of a career. Schools also empowered them to overcome the diverse social and economic challenges. Though education has helped these girls to be independent but they had to compromise with their freedom, choices and decision to some extent.

CHAPTER 7

# CONCLUSION AND RECOMMENDATION

## 7.1 INTRODUCTION

Education is globally acknowledged as a powerful means to empowering girls and protecting them from the violation of human rights. Investing in girls' education can transform and save lives. It is a way to develop positive and sustainable change. Girls' education goes beyond getting them to school. It is not only about ensuring what they learn in school but to provide equal opportunities to complete the various levels of education. The girls need adequate knowledge and skills to compete in labour market and earn higher incomes to make their own decisions and contribute to society (Mondal. A, 2022)

Education is a critical indicator of status. In India raising the status of women must be a goal to be achieved through education on a priority basis (Chanana, 2006). The educational statistics since Independence show that while gender gap has indeed decreased, it is still nowhere near closing. In other words, enrolments of girls have been lower than that of the boys. A majority of the out-of-school children are from the Scheduled Castes and Tribes, minorities and from rural inaccessible areas. But there are enough data to show that girls from a sizeable proportion of these are out-of-school drop-outs, working children, non-enrolled children, children of migrants and the poor, and the disabled children too. It is also true that while caste, tribe, socio-cultural and economic factors keep more girls belonging to specific social groups out of schools than boys. (Chanana 2001). The dropout rate is higher from upper primary to secondary and higher secondary. It is more common among the girls belonging from Socially-Economically Disadvantaged Group (SEDG) in rural areas. The story becomes more pronounced when other factors – location, identity, economic status, school type and gender (Ramchandran, V. 2018). It is in this context this research study has been taken up to explore the education and empowerment of girls in rural areas.

Empowerment is a radical approach which was articulated in the 1980s and 1990s concerned with changing power relations in favour of women and better equality between men and women. Empowerment is defined as the 'process of challenging the existing power relations and gaining control over the sources of power' (Bandkar, 2012).

In India the central and state government has been working on universalization of elementary education. Education has been made a fundamental right in the 86$^{th}$ constitutional amendment for the age group of six to fourteen years (Singh, 2018). The major initiatives taken by the central government are direct involvement of the central government with the state government at the ground level. Secondly, decentralization of governance through Panchayati Raj Institutions. Thirdly promoting community mobilization drive. The interventions taken by the central and state governments promotes enrolment, retention and learning achievements to bridge the gender gap (Govinda and Bandyopadhyay, 2011). The Sarva Shiksha Abhiyan flagship programme focusses on interventions to encourage girls to maintain pace with the boys. The special interventions were adopted to include gender equality goals-infrastructure, academic inputs, governance and incentives (Sudarshan, 2018).

In this context the study has three objectives highlighting the factors determining the girl's education, the influence of education on different components of empowerment (decision-making, right awareness and aspirations) of girls and to explore how the school education has helped the girls in their lives. It unravels their perceptions, present status and experiences of schooling and beyond. It focuses on their path after schooling and its benefits drawn from education. The study was conducted in Uttar Dinajpur district of West Bengal. The study is descriptive in nature, based on mixed method approach to understand the impact of higher secondary level of schooling on girls' lives. Purposive sampling was used to select the schools and participants of the study.

Primary and secondary sources were used to collect data about the selected schools. The method used to collect data from primary sources are school information schedule, questionnaires for the students enrolled in secondary and higher secondary school, observation schedule, in-depth interview with parents and teachers, and case studies of students through in-depth interviews. The secondary data were culled from the U Dise reports and Human Development reports of Uttar Dinajpur. There were various other books, articles and reports on girl's education used for secondary data.

The study depicts a picture of the present status of the state of West Bengal through secondary data. The state has 32nd ranking in accordance to the Educational Development Index constructed by NIEPA in 2006. The Census of India 2011 stated that West Bengal had the sex ratio (ratio of females to males in a population) of 950 females per 1000 males. This sex ratio shows an inequality between the male and female segments of our society. The district of Uttar Dinajpur and subdivision Raiganj show that the sex ratio here is lower than the already skewed state average. The Net Enrolment Ratio was less than 50 per cent at both state and district level. There is a sharp decline in the Gross Enrolment Ratio and Net Enrolment Ratio from the secondary to the higher secondary level in West Bengal during 2019-20. The enrolment of girls increased from 2016-17 to 2019-20 at the state level and also at the district level. The gender parity index in higher secondary classes has improved at the state level in the year 2019-20. The repetition rate is higher among girls at the secondary and higher secondary levels in the state. At the district and block levels, the repetition rate is low. The transition rate of girls is higher in the secondary level of the state in comparison to the district and block levels.

## 7.2 MAJOR FINDINGS

The major findings of the study are:

***Profile of the Students, Parents and Teachers***

- The profile of the students shows that a large proportion of students belongs to the Scheduled Castes, Muslims, Other Backward castes and Scheduled Tribes. It is evident from the data that most of the girls belonging to these categories goes to government schools. It has been observed that, in the case of these categories, there is a wide gap in the proportion of girls attending government schools and those attending private schools. A high proportion of general category girls attends private schools. In some case, it has been noted that the proportion of boys belonging to the deprived social categories (Other Backward Caste and Muslims) are higher than girls in private schools.
- There is a high proportion of government school students who are first generation learners. From the data it is obvious that there are more fathers with no formal schooling in the socially disadvantaged groups. This is due to the educational backwardness of the district. The proportion of fathers with primary education is significantly high in government schools. The children of private schools have more qualified fathers --- graduates and postgraduates.
- The data shows that an overwhelming proportion of mothers had no formal schooling. Most of the mothers with no formal schooling hailed from the socially disadvantaged categories. It was seen that most of the first-generation learners among the girls had uneducated mothers. This too is responsible for the fact that literacy level is low in most of the blocks of Uttar Dinajpur. Girls' mothers belonging to the general category are graduates, post-graduates or have other higher educational qualifications.

- Mother's education plays an important role in a girl's years of schooling. It was found that mothers with no formal education or only a minimal level of education were sending their daughters to government schools. Educated or non-educated, mothers always want their girls to be educated. Similarly, a large proportion of mothers have primary and secondary education in government schools. A majority of qualified mothers with graduate and postgraduate degrees send their children to private schools. The proportion of such girls in private schools is low. The data indicate that the parents of 15 per cent children enrolled in secondary and senior secondary classes had no formal education and the parents of more than 60 per cent children had had higher education (secondary, senior secondary, graduate and above).

Parental education matters not in school enrolment and average years of schooling. It is evident that a higher proportion of children enrolled had had fathers and mothers with higher education (secondary and higher secondary levels). This shows the intergeneration transmission of education from parents to children (Thangjam and Ladusingh, 2018). Multiple studies have shown that mother's education has positive and significant relation on daughters' enrolment and average years of schooling more than fathers. It was found that additional years of mother's education increases daughters' average years of schooling. Similarly, mother's cognitive skills and education impacts the schooling of children (Sperling, Winthrop and Kwauk, 2015).

- As for the occupational patterns, a majority of fathers are involved in agricultural activities since it is predominantly an agricultural region. Parents are from diverse backgrounds. Most of the parents are graduates and run their own small-scale businesses, like grocery shops and bicycle business. Some own huge tracts of land from which they sell vegetables in the market. A few of the villagers are in the lower rank government jobs. A majority of the mothers managed the household chores.

Some of the mothers of government school girls are employed are daily wage labour in agriculture or are self-employed. Some of the private and government school children have working mothers.

The social and economic inequalities and the gender relationships lead to the formation of a complex web that helps or hinders the girls to complete their school education. The social, economic and educational inequalities depend upon the status of the girls (Ramachandran, 2018). Recent research on the parental gradients and educational attainment by M. Thangjam and L Laduisingh (2018) revealed that the economic wellbeing of a household is an insignificant factor of educational outcome in the regions, where mothers' literacy is limited.

- The number of male teachers is more in government schools than private schools.
- According to the data from DISE (District Information System for Education), the school profile of the sampled schools revealed that government school teachers were more professionally qualified (had a B. Ed. degree). In private schools, a majority of teachers did not have a B. Ed. degree or any equivalent degree.
- It is evident from data that teachers in government schools had more experience in teaching than private schools. The majority of male teachers in government schools had accumulated more experience than female teachers.

### *Decision Making Process in Choice of school*

The choice of school depends largely on who has access to what kind of school. The study tried to understand the girls' and boys' access to different kind of schools. Girls from diverse backgrounds had different preferences for school. Similarly, parents from diverse social and class backgrounds had differential preference about the choice of school. The choice of school depended on school location, availability of incentives and quality of education provided in schools.

*School location*: The proportion of private schools are less. The girls have to travel by foot to far flung, deserted areas. Government schools are located within 1 km radius from the habitation. It was found that majority of girls and few boys of government schools favoured schools in nearby locality.

*Availability of Incentives*: Field data revealed that a majority of the girls belonging to the low-income groups thought that financial conditions and the availability of incentives in government schools play an important role in schooling. Fees in the government schools were much less in comparison to the private schools while a number of facilities were available there.

*Quality of Education Provided in Schools*: A small proportion of girls from government schools said that private schools were better than the government schools. There was a girl who had earlier studied in a government school and then shifted to a private school. She shared her views and experiences: "*I have been studying in a government school earlier from class one to five and then in a private school, and according to my experience private schools have better educational facilities. Teachers, rules and everything else is very strict and students are brought up in a proper and disciplined and organised manner.*"

It is evident from our data that there is a positive relationship between mothers' educational qualifications and girls' education on the one hand and the selection of choice of school, irrespective of gender, on the other hand. The girls and boys had preferences for a school on the basis of their understanding and experiences. It was found that government school students preferred private schools which have better educational facilities and a better environment, where teachers are strict and disciplined and children are nurtured in an organised manner. Many girls were in favour of a government schools due to the family's economic condition. They opted for the benefits provided by the government schools. They valued the quality of education less compared to money. Some of the girls listed the financial benefits provided by the school. The time to travel from home to private school is long and it has kept many girls away from private schools as parents do not find it safe for the girls to go there. In India, the access to schooling has enhanced significantly. But the access to and choice of a school depends on a number of factors. Their location involves the region --- rural or urban, mountainous or marshy. The identity revolves around the caste, religion and community affiliations of parents. The economic status means how many people belong to which strata (the poor, rich, below poverty line and migrants). The school type tells us about the school children enrolled in government, private and private aided schools. The disability factor is about the disabilities faced by different types of pupils. But in all the above instances, gender plays a significant role (Ramachandran, 2018). The data reflect an inequality in their choice of schools for the girls and boys. Govinda & Bandyopadhyay (2019) make a reference to the rising inequalities in in school education, pointing out that the disparities have not yet come down to acceptable levels.

### *Decision Making Process in Choice of Subjects*

The subject choices made by girls were based on the decision about career and future aspirations. In government schools a lesser proportion of girls chose science for study. There was a higher proportion of boys choosing science or commerce as a subject. In comparison, a higher proportion of girls and boys in private schools chose science as a subject. Some of the girls selected humanities, followed by commerce, at the senior secondary level. In most cases, it was seen that adolescents internalise the roles played in daily life, which impacts their choice of subject (Vleuten & Jaspers, 2015).

The choice of subjects was influenced by various factors.

- First, some girls were unable to make their own choices and mostly depended on their friends or peers for the purpose. But those unclear about their choice also had low aspirational levels and were indecisive about their career. It is seen that girls mostly opt for subjects like humanities while boys opt for science under peer pressure.

- Second, it was observed in the case of many girls that parents made the choice of a subject. In government schools, a majority of the girls select humanities while a considerable number of boys select science as a subject. Many of these boys were pressurised by their parents to opt for science.
- Third, in several cases the choice was based on interest. Such choices made by girls were based on their interest and understanding of the subject. The proportion of girls who made such choices was higher than the boys in private schools.
- Fourth, there is a small proportion of girls who selected a subject on the basis of their ideas about higher education. Girls selecting science mostly fell under this category.
- Fifth, it was found that girls studying in private schools selected science as a subject on the basis of the career prospects. A small proportion of girls in government schools selected humanities on the basis of career aspirations.

It was critical to understand whether the subject choices made by girls and boys were under the guidance of their parents or purely on their own. It was clear from the data that a considerable proportion of students did not have any personal preference while selecting a subject in school. Academic achievements tend to be greater higher for the students who had a personal preference on the issue. The findings show that there were five categories of responses.

CATEGORY I: Decisions are taken by parents, and students are convinced. These students do not have their own personal preferences and follow the decisions taken by their parents.

A majority of them selected the subjects preferred by their parents.

CATEGORY II: Decisions are taken by parents, and students are partially convinced. The proportion of such students was higher in government schools than in private schools. Though these students had their personal choices, they agreed with their parents' choice of subjects. The factors behind such preferences were similar --- choice of profession by parents and their children, ideas about entering higher education, interest in the subject, and better learning environment in schools.

CATEGORY III: Decisions are taken by parents but students are not convinced. These students did not choose a subject on their own but were forced by their parents to select a particular subject. The proportion of such students was higher in government schools.

CATEGORY IV: Decisions are taken by students and parents supported their choice. In this category, students selected a subject in consultation with their parents. The proportion of boys outnumbered that of girls in this category. It was found that government school girls opting for humanities and private school girls opting for science fell in this category. It is evident that all such students had their own personal preferences.

CATEGORY V: Decisions were taken by students without the guidance and support of parents. These students had their own personal preference in the selection of a subject. In government schools, the first-generation learners came under this category. In private schools the girls with high aspirational levels made their subject choices independently. Decision-making in choice of subjects reflects the aspirational level of these girls.

CATEGORY VI: Decisions were taken by students with the guidance of teachers and peers.

It was found from the study that boys were underrepresented in the "feminine tracks" (humanities, arts and education) and girls were also underrepresented in "masculine tracks" (science and mathematics). The choice of subjects was often influenced by the surrounding social environment in which children grow and the social behaviour patterns which they adapt. Thus, gender ideology affects boys' and girls' choice of subjects and occupational values (Vleuten & Jaspers, 2015).

The decisions made on the choice of a subject were also based on the preference for a profession. Teaching profession was more liked by girls of government schools as it was considered safe. The girls in private schools selected the profession of doctors or engineers. These choices were based on their career goals. The boys in private schools too chose these professions. In government schools, only a small proportion of girls aimed to become doctors or engineers or join other professions. On the contrary, in private schools, a larger proportion of girls aspire to become doctors, engineers, lawyers, forensic researchers, journalists and police officers. It was observed that boys chose the subjects and occupations which are traditionally considered "masculine" but it was not always the same in case of girls. Some of the girls did select the "masculine tracks" and occupations. Surprisingly, such girls had a higher level of verbal and mathematical competency (Vleuten & Jaspers, 2015).

It is evident from the data regarding the government schools that a higher proportion of girls had aspirations to continue their education after the senior secondary level. It was observed that the proportion of such girls who opted for higher education remained low compared to the boys. Some girls had aspirations to work after completing school education as the economic condition of their families do not permit to go in for higher education, though these girls had high opinions about higher education. The girls who were not able to convince their parents for higher education confined themselves to the household chores or opted for a job after passing the school. The perception of the parents revealed that they were supportive in sending their girls for higher education, except a few who were restrained due to financial problems. They proclaimed that higher education would give their daughters special recognition and that girls should work after completing their education. Yet some parents talked about the financial and labour losses. R. Anderson's (2016) study on girls' education and empowerment relates to freedom through education and their aspirations for a better life. Education helps one to develop a positive self-image, active learning and self-confidence. Thus, it enables the girls to stand proudly and make a mark in family and society (Ramachandran, 2018).

There was a positive attitude about girls' education among the parents and teachers. They thought education would give raise their aspirations and make them independent and fearless. The whole idea of giving them education was to help them get into higher education, then get a good job, and thus achieve special recognition. Similarly, parents who were uneducated and daily wage earners want their children to be educated but did not know how they would be able to support them financially.

Martha Nussbaum's question on human capability approach --- "What are people able to do and to be?" --- reflects the aspirational goals of girls to continue higher education. The theory supports the fact that girls can achieve their aspirations through education. One of the most important items in Nussbaum list is women's control over the environment and the right way to it is to augment women's literacy. Women who are literate can find jobs outside home. These women can protect themselves from assault and bodily integrity. This can enhance their decision-making power and they can make various choices in life. The findings related to the choice of a school, choice of a subject, career goals and aspirations. The school provides space for the development of the child. The choices made by the girls would have been impossible without education. The various components of empowerment are aspirations, achievements, decision-making, expressing of an opinion, mobility. The study encapsulates empowerment through the aspirations or decision-making ability. The girls are now making their choices of career and achievements in life, which the out-of-school children cannot make. It was observed that while making a choice of subject, girls had to use a combination of capabilities. It means that the choice of a subject is not decided by a girl alone; it can be influenced and guided by the other family members. M. Nussbaum elaborates the internal capability which is present in a child but the combined capabilities are non-existent. She explains that internal capabilities are drawn from the external surroundings, but it may not function when it is influenced by the surrounding conditions. A child learns to play in a natural environment, love, sing and exercise her choice. Similarly, a woman who has never been supressed can exercise her own choice and exercise the freedom of speech. The girls in our study elucidated the importance of education and achievements. They thought higher education would enable them to get jobs which would free them from poverty and financial constraints. The study illustrates their will to achieve wellbeing, freedom from poverty, and be able to live life freely. It has been argued that many women are keen to work but are unable to do so because of the family restrictions. Thus, Nussbaum focusses on an unbiased equality of opportunities for all women rather than a kind of ritualistic equality. Stromquist (2015) links empowerment with the process of social change. She elucidates that education is a path for economic empowerment. Education helps a person to be independent and take decisions in family. She stresses on the market demand for wage labour and on the economic gains that can be achieved through employment.

### *Other Factors Influencing Education*

*Household Chores*: The factors behind the intra-household decision-making include the household chores. Many of the government school girls and boys were found doing the household chores but their proportion was lesser in private schools. The common household activities which the girls are performing are looking after siblings, sweeping the floor, helping in kitchen, fetching water and helping parents in the fields. The boys are involved in activities such as sweeping the floor, fetching water, feeding the animals and washing clothes. It was found that a majority of boys are involved in activities outside home --- helping parents in the fields and in their small-scale family business (grocery shops, cycle business) after the school hours.

*Time for Study and Completion of Home Assignments*: After performing the household chores, evidently, a majority of the girls did not have enough time for studies. A significant proportion of girls had less than one hour time to study. Boys had more time to study in comparison. The perceptions of the teachers were not different --- about fifty per cent girls did not complete their homework in time. Similarly, some of the boys did not get time to complete their homework. But their proportion was smaller compared to girls. During the ploughing and harvesting seasons, girls and boys remained absent from school and did not complete their homework either.

Thus, the theoretical framework of the study suggests that there is a huge difference between the roles assigned to boys and those assigned to girls. Boys who have opportunities to play, can spare time for other extra-curricular activities and also have more time to study. But those who are already burdened with household responsibilities do not have enough time for studies and extra-curricular activities. This may be referred to as double-duty day that makes women unable to work for non-household tasks. Girls are unable to study through the day due to household pressure. It seems that games and extra-curricular activities are as important for them as literacy and skills.

*Experience in School*: When the sampled children were asked about their experiences in school, it was found that a significant proportion of government school girls had to struggle with responsibilities at home and studies. A considerable proportion of girls viewed their schooling experience as very good with helpful teachers and supportive parents. The proportion of girls in this category was higher in the private schools. A majority of girls in government schools felt that education enabled them to inculcate societal values. But the proportion was higher for girls in private schools. Girls in government schools opined that they gained confidence through education and can speak to people confidently. It was observed from the data that the family environment was patriarchal.

*Patriarchal Family Environment*: A significant proportion of girls was not able to express their opinion at home or in school. It is worth mentioning that the percentage of girls and boys who were able to voice their opinion was higher in government schools than in the private ones. At home the girls are generally scared of their fathers and hardly speak to them. Some girls opined they were close to their mothers and could share their problems with the latter, whenever needed. But in most of the cases they could not share their problems and opinion with their parents. They therefore shared their views with friends. Girls of the private schools were of the opinion they could express their opinions before their parents and friends. Girls who are able to attend school develop greater analytical skills and are able to navigate the surroundings in better ways. From this comes a sense of control and ability to exercise their voice. Women with higher levels of education are less likely to accept domestic violence and have control over the household decisions, along with the freedom of movement (Sperling, Winthrop and Kwauk, 2015).

It was evident from our data that the decisions on marriage largely depended on parents. It was found that 50 per cent of the girls had awareness of the marriageable age. But boys had greater awareness on the legal age of marriage. The sampled girls and boys informed about the prevalent practice of early marriage.

*Mobility*: It may be summarised from data that girls' mobility is limited. The proportion of girls who only sometimes go out is higher compared to those who go out frequently. The proportion of boys who go out frequently is higher than the girls. The proportion of girls going out with family members and friends is high. There are rare instances of girls travelling alone. There are safety issues related to the girls travelling alone.

The theoretical framework of the study suggests that combined capabilities prevent a child to speak in a mixed company. For instance, when a child's environment does not permit to practise the freedom of speech or of religion, the child does not learn to safeguard these liberties.

***Educational Factors***

*Availability of Physical and Academic Facilities in Government Schools*: In most cases, the school building was spacious and spread over a large area, in a circular shape. One of the schools did not have a playground and boundary wall. There was no room for the Head Teacher; the single room designated as the staff room for the teachers was shared by the Head Teacher in one of the schools.

*Availability of Physical and Academic Facilities in Private Schools*: The school has a pucca boundary wall. It also maintained a good security service. It was found that a record register was maintained at the gate for the visitors. No playground was found in most of these schools. Drinking water was provided in the school through the filters. The classrooms were well ventilated and in good condition.

*The Availability of Female Teachers in Schools*: The number of female teachers in government schools showed that the number of female teachers is quite low. The proportion of female teachers is higher in private schools. It was found that female teachers' availability directly affects the share of girls' participation in government schools. It was also seen that government school teacher are more qualified than private school teachers. They are also more supportive and help to eradicate the social problems faced by their girl students.

*In-Service Training on Gender Awareness:* A majority of the teachers agreed that gender sensitisation training helped them to handle the problems faced by the girls more efficiently. One of the teachers mentioned that there were no such programmes to date. In general, the teacher's responses revealed that no such training programmes were held on gender sensitisation.

*Class Environment*: It was evident from the focussed group discussions that boys and girls had separate sections in government schools; this was so in one of the private schools as well. The concept of equal participation thus becomes a mockery. In private schools, girls are given prominent roles. Though in private schools too, girls and boys are seated in different rows, they are given the same activities. The girls were also given captaincy roles. Yet, all the private schools where similar activities were given, girls revealed that bright students were given more chances. The girls felt that the participation was not equal. In government schools, teachers were empathetic to their students. Government school teachers made special efforts to understand the problems the children are facing inside the classrooms. They motivate and encourage them to continue their studies.

***Teachers' and Principals' Role in Gender Friendly School and Classrooms:***

- The teachers claimed that they provide equal opportunities for children in the school setting. They encourage the boys and girls to participate on the basis of equality, which improves the class environment.
- Teachers in government as well as private schools discussed the possible role models in classrooms.
- The schools and their teachers counsel and guide each and every student for higher education. The teachers motivated the girls, informally, to pursue higher education so that they could achieve a higher-level social self-esteem, be self-reliant, not be treated as a burden to their parents, and positively face the challenges of their life. The government school girls had more of the financial difficulties. But they were informed about the various government schemes to facilitate their education

and avoid dropout. The benefits of higher education were discussed with the girls at the school counselling sessions. This thought process should be developed so as to get more girls enrolled in higher education. Awareness should be created among parents about a better future for their daughters. Girls were motivated to get higher education in order to get attractive jobs and social status.

- Girls' absenteeism has been seen as one of the major reasons for girls discontinuing education. Teachers contact the parents through school diaries of the respective students. Some teachers of government as well as private schools go to the girls' homes for inquiry. There are several reasons of absenteeism such as early marriage and domestic work. Such absenteeism eventually leads to drop out from school.
- Teachers' perceptions on the parent teacher associations are that they create awareness among the parents on various issues. These meetings encourage the parents to educate the girls, and the potentialities of the girls are discussed. But it was found that a majority of the parents from government schools do not regularly attend such meetings. These meetings provide insight to the parents on the girls' career choices, discuss the financial issues and inform the parents about the government schemes. Though parents are not compelled to attend such meetings, they need to be motivated about it. As parents become more aware, they constantly participate in such meetings.
- It helps in a positive development of their children. In PTAs, parents and teachers discuss the weak areas of the girls; these can be overcome through conscious efforts, by participating in and encouraging such associations. The teachers provide guidance to the parents that help in a better performance of the students. It develops a positive relationship between the teachers, parents and students.

- Teachers claimed that girls face challenges in schools. The girls from rural areas are shy and hesitant while participating in the class. Those girls who are first generation learners do not even know their mother tongue well. They are unable to read and write. The teacher encourages them to express their own thoughts and imaginations. These girls get lesser opportunities when it comes to education. They are inattentive and have irregular attendance in class. They are not able to complete their daily homework.

***Parents perception on Schools and Girls Education***

- Some parents of government school children admitted that they were unable to meet the teachers to know the progress of their children. They did not attend any parent teacher meeting. Several of these parents work in farms as daily wage labourers and hence cannot come for a meeting. They perceive that sending their children to school leads to labour losses.
- A majority of the parents in the context of the government schools said that teachers did not visit their homes to know the progress of their children. A high proportion of private-school parents, on the contrary, informed that teachers visited students' homes regularly to know their progress.
- Parents raised their voice against the lack of infrastructural facilities in school. Most of the toilets are not clean and girls face problems during their mensuration cycles.
- There were problems of early marriage for girls in government schools. It was found from the responses of boys and girls that the correct age of marriage was not being followed in Raiganj, in Uttar Dinajpur district. Many girls were married at an early age. A disheartening feature is that a majority (65 per cent) of the girls and boys informed about the practice of early marriage in the

villages. Several girls were married before attaining the stipulated age of 18 years.

Nussbaum (2001) have pointed out how education reduces human insecurity and widens the capabilities of women, thus having a powerful effect on them. This can be linked to the aspiration of the girls and their parents who want their girls to complete their education and take a job for their better future. Similar evidences have been found from studies where the mothers voiced their opinion in favour of educating their girls and attaining their dreams for a secure and happy life (R. Anderson, 2016).

## 7.3 ROLE OF FAMILY IN EDUCATION OF GIRLS

Family plays an important role in the education of the girls. The size of investment in female education and sending their girl to school determine current cost on and future benefits of education. The process of decision making in household are less gender biased when mothers participate equally with the fathers, daughters receive preference over their sons. It was found that mothers with no formal education or only a minimal level of education were sending their daughters to government schools. Educated or non-educated, mothers always want their girls to be educated.

Families from diverse social and class backgrounds had differential preference about the choice of school and subject. Parents' guide and counsel their girls to select subjects. Parents often selected subjects of their own choice without consulting the girls. Parents selected traditional subjects for girls and boys. Parents guided their children in selection of subjects after secondary level. Few girls did not receive any kind of guidance from parents in choice of subject. The socio-economic inequalities and gender inequalities hinders the girls from obtaining education. Mobility of girls in the villages are restricted. Parents accompany the girls to school and tuitions. Parents in the villages are concerned with their safety. Some parents guided and motivated their daughters for higher education. However, some parents from socially and economically disadvantaged groups felt that marriage was a better option. They thought that girls can study after marriage. The parents of first-generation learners and socially disadvantaged groups (migrant landless labourers) do not have sufficient earnings to run the family and educate their daughter. They prefer their daughters to drop out after elementary school (if the school is not integrated) and get them married. The system of early marriage is still prevalent in West Bengal. Sometimes the girls reach out to the teachers of the schools or local police station to stop the rituals of marriage. The schools along with SMC members and gram panchayat actively participates in enrolling the girls in schools to eradicate early marriages. They also mainstream them in schools through the bridging courses and life style skills.

## 7.4 LINKAGES BETWEEN EDUCATION AND EMPOWERMENT

Education is one of the essential links to empower girls to make their decisions in regard to the choices of school, subject, profession and higher education. Education enables girls to understand and evaluate their socio-economic conditions through a process of live and learn. It enables the girls to justify and participate in the decision-making process to achieve their future aspirations. Educated girls can voice their opinion in family and household decisions. Educated and employed men and women can share their opinions and take decisions mutually within households. Even uneducated working women get an opportunity to share their opinion in the decisions regarding savings and expenditure. It is linked with economical aspect of empowerment. Another aspect of empowerment is educated women has the chance of making decisions related to the wellbeing of themselves and their family. It can be related to attitudinal changes and outlook changes. There is a strong positive link between education of mothers and their daughters. It was found that educated mothers have educated daughters and their average years of schooling increases. A considerable percentage of educated parents support their daughters to complete schooling and opt for higher education. Thus, inter-generational transmission of education from parents to their children.

There were certain issues which the researcher came across at the time of field visit.

Firstly, the prevalent culture of early marriages in West Bengal. The parents from socially and economically disadvantaged sections of society were forcing their girls to enter the institutions of marriage. The researcher identified many married girls from different districts of Uttar Dinajpur when they participated in an inter-district sports meet.

Secondly, gender stereotyping of the girls within the family. The higher education of the sons was preferred over their daughters. These parents wanted their daughters to marry after completing school. Some of the parents were sending their daughters to government schools and son to private schools. They also thought that educating their daughters were loss of labour and finance as they could help their parents at home and fields.

## 7.5 POLICY RECOMMENDATIONS

In regard to girls' education in Uttar Dinajpur district, we venture to make some policy recommendations on the basis of our study. The issues that are negatively impacting girl's education can be addressed through the following:

1. School infrastructure to be improved with proper playground and boundary walls. Lights and fans should be repaired and new lights to be installed in the classroom with poor lighting. Furniture to be replaced with new ones. There is a need to install water filters. Female attendants to be kept for maintaining cleanliness and hygiene of the toilets. They can help the girls during the mensuration cycle.
2. Water logging in schools can be prevented through proper drainage system in and around the school areas.

The schools can use water suction pumps to dry the excess water in the classrooms. Extra classes need to be arranged for elementary and higher secondary level. These classes can be conducted during the summer and autumn vacations.

3. To reduce gender disparity in schools at higher grades, long absenteeism of students should be prevented through proper monitoring by the teachers and state level officers. Parents should be made aware of not indulging the students in farming activities during the harvesting seasons. This leads to non-completion of homework, loss of interest in studies, feeling shy and timid and non-participation in classroom settings and in long run can lead to drop out. Teachers should visit the children's home once a month to eradicate prolong absenteeism. Awareness can be spread among the parents about the impact of absenteeism in the PTA meetings.

4. The integrated schools with pre-primary should be promoted. This would enable the girls to complete the schooling till higher secondary level. It was found that the girls discontinue schooling after primary and elementary level. This is due to various reasons - lack of proper facilities in schools, distance of high schools, and insufficient number of elementary and higher secondary schools in rural areas. Sometimes parents do not enrol the girls after elementary level and prefer to involve them in low paid jobs, farming activities and often get married.

5. NEP 2020 emphasizes on activity based learning and applicative learning to be encouraged in schools. The teaching learning material should be used in classrooms. New teaching learning materials to be arranged for the students. Students with the help of teachers can prepare teaching learning materials with the available resources. ICT resources can be made available in schools with

computer labs. The English lesson can be shown as movies in these labs. The teachers can prepare lessons and videos for teaching students as well. The schools can arrange excursions to botanical gardens and zoological parks to give the students better understanding about various types of plants and animals.

6. Gender stereotyping should be totally eradicated to engage girls in leadership roles. School should evolve strategies to address gender stereotyping with the help of SMC members and parents. To avoid gender stereotyping equal opportunities to be given to boys and girls within and outside classroom. Since girls from remote areas are shy, timid and naïve. They should be treated with dignity inside the classroom and not humiliated in front of others. The weak students should be given opportunity to take responsibility and participate in activities that can build their confidence like sports, karate, playing basketball. Girls should be given leadership role such as house captains and school captains. They should be given opportunities to conduct theme-based assemblies in schools and also volunteer in school events such as exhibitions, annual functions and sports day celebration. This must be ensured through regular monitoring of the schools by head teachers, block and state level officers.

7. There is a dearth of female teachers in government schools. There is a need to appoint more female teachers in the rural area on a permanent basis. In the remotest areas female teachers do not join as there are safety and security issues. If teachers are selected from the local areas with the same background as the students it will be easier for the teachers to sustain. A healthy and positive relationship would develop with the students and teachers. The teachers would be able to understand the problems faced by the girls.

8. Gender sensitive training to teacher so that they can empathy with the children. There should be workshops for teachers and students to maintain personal hygiene. The doctors, nurses or medical students from nearby medical institution should be hired to educate the girls on mensuration cycle. The female teachers and female attendants to be trained so that girls can freely discuss any problem related to mensuration cycle or any other physical ailment.
9. There is a need of pre-service and in-service training of the teachers to understand gender sensitivity in a better way. Teachers should be trained not to give unbiased statement, instructions and follow professional norms. School related violence can be related to humiliation, harassment and bullying by the other students. In the study it was found that bullying of girls made them more sensitive as they could not discuss issues with parents in the fear of discontinuance of school. These should be addressed by the teachers through mutual discussions between student and teachers. Parents to be informed about the child's behavioural issues. Appropriate measures to be taken to counsel the child and issue warning by the school principal. Thus, under the child protection act, the children should be made aware of the anti-bullying policies in schools. To conduct workshop with parents and teachers to create awareness about anti-bullying policies. To teach parents and teachers to listen and communicate with their child. To encourage them to express their problems.
10. The government schools need separate guidance and counselling department for students especially the first-generation learners. This can help the student select a subject conveniently after secondary level. There is a need of formal discussion of the parents, students and teachers on their choice of subject. It will enable the

students to select a subject of their own choice based on their interest and understanding.

## 7.6 POLICY IMPLICATIONS OF THE STUDY

The three major policy implications are

- Infrastructural deficiencies have a greater impact on the quality of education of children, lack of clean and proper toilets is one of the major reasons that leads to girls' absenteeism.
- There is a need to appoint more female teachers in the rural area on a permanent basis. Teachers to be selected from the local areas for better understanding and positive relationship between the students and teachers.
- In-service training of teachers at regular intervals is needed. In particular, there is the need to train the teachers in gender sensitisation programmes. There should be workshops, seminars and discussions for teachers and students to maintain personal hygiene. The doctors, nurses or medical students from nearby medical institution should be hired to educate the girls on mensuration cycle.

## 7.7 SCOPE FOR FURTHER RESEARCH

- To understand the perception and beliefs, and to draw general conclusions on complex matters, one has to pierce through the surface of the people's living, social norms and behaviours, their agreeing and disagreeing on their practices. Hence ethnographic research can be conducted to develop a better understanding of this region.
- A comparative study can be conducted on the rural and urban regions of the states to understand the difference in the context of girls schooling and empowerment

- An exploratory study can be undertaken on the different states of India and different blocks of West Bengal to understand the perspectives in better way
- A study can be conducted on girls aspiring to enter and actually entering higher education in Uttar Dinajpur district
- A study can be conducted on vocational subjects available in schools and higher education institutions and their impact on career aspiration of girls and boys

**Picture 7.1 : School Going Girls of Uttar Dinajpur District**

# NOTES

1) UNESCO (2012): *From Access to Equality: Empowering Girls and Women through Literacy and Secondary Education*, Paris: United Nations Educational, Scientific and Cultural Organisation

2) Md Shahidul Sarker (2013): Mothers' Participation in Household Decision-Making Process: Its Effect on School Dropout Behaviour for Girls in Bangladesh, *International Education Studies*, 6 (1): 132-141, ICHGE

3) Lloyd, C.; Mensch, B. & Clark, W. (2000): The Effects of Primary School Quality on School Dropout among Kenyan Girls and Boys, *Comparative Education Review*, 44: 113-147

4) Khandker, S. (1996): *Educational Achievements and School Efficiency in Rural Bangladesh*, Washington: World Bank Publications

5) Stromquist, N. P. (2015). Women's Empowerment and Education: Linking Knowledge to Transformative Action, *European Journal of Education*, 50 (3): 307-324.

6) Sex ratio is the ratio of females to males in a population. It is viewed as the number of females against every 1,000 male population.

7) U-DISE stands for Unified District Information System for Education.

   The DHDR (2010) showed that there is a gap of 38 per cent population between rural and urban literacy and it was found to be the highest among all the districts of West Bengal.

# REFERENCES


1. Acharya, Susan (2006): *The Functioning of Effectiveness of Scholarship and Incentive Schemes in Nepal*, Bangkok: UNESCO

2. Alam, M. S. (2011): Unequal They Stand: Decision-Making and Gendered Spaces within Family. In Raju, S.; Lahiri, K. & Dull (Ed): *Doing Gender and Doing Geography: Emerging Research in India*, pp 230-247

3. Anderson, R. (2016): *Freedom, Agency and Optimism: A Feminist Case Study on Girls' education in South Eastern Turkey*, Unpublished Doctoral Dissertation, Kent State University College of Education, Health and Human Services, USA

4. Anupama,K & Chaudhary, P., (2022): Understanding Mixed Methodology in Research. Int JEth Trauma Victimology. IJETV Vol 8 issue 2, Pg 18-21

5. Arnot, M. (2012) Reproducing Gender? Essays on Educational Theory and Feminist Politics, Routledge Falmer, New York

6. Arnot, M., and Reay (2007): A Sociology of Pedagogic Voice: Power, Inequality and Pupil Consultation, *Discourse Studies in the Cultural Politics of Education* 28 (3) pp-311-325

7. Awasthi, D. (2016): Gender Bias in Textbooks: Obstacle in Appropriate Conceptualisation of Gender. In Awasthi, D. (Ed): *Girl Education in India. Still Miles to Cover*. Vol.1: *Understanding the Status and Gender Issues*

8. Bailey, K. D. (1982): *Methods of Social Research*, London: The Free Press, Collier Macmillan Publishers

9. Bandkar, M. (2012): Viable Measures to be Adopted for Women Empowerment on the Basis of Pragmatic

Consideration for Metamorphosis of the System, Delhi: Deep& Deep Publication Pvt Ltd.

10. Bandyopadhyay, M., Kandary, M. et.al (2022): Women Education and Development in Indian Context. In A. Mondol & N. Snehi (eds) Dynamics of Women Education in India.

11. Bandyopadhyay, M. (2018a): Gender, Educational Deprivation and Exclusion: A Case Study of Madhya Pradesh and Chhattisgarh. In Sudarshan, Ratna M & Tilak, J.B.G (Ed): *Gender in Contemporary Education Research*, Delhi: Gyan Publishing House and National Institute of Educational Planning and Administration

12. Bandyopadhyay, M. (2018b): Gender Equality in School Education in India: Where Do We Stand? In Mete, J.; Borah, R. & Manna, R. (Ed): *Women Empowerment for Girls' education in 21st Century*, New Delhi Publishers

13. Bandyopadhyay, M. (2012) Gender and School Participation. Evidences from Empirical Research in Madhya Pradesh and Chhattisgarh, NUEPA Occasional Paper 41

14. Bandyopadhayay, M. & Subrahmanian, R. (2008a): *Gender Equity in Education: A Review of Trends and Factors*, New Delhi: CREATE, NUEPA

15. Bandyopadhayay, M. & Subrahmanian, R. (2011b): *Gender Equity in Education: A Review of Trends and Factors*. In R. Govinda (Ed) Who Goes to School? Exploring Exclusion in Indian Education, Oxford University Press, New Delhi.

16. Basak, P. & Roy Mukherjee, S. (2014): *Differential Literacy Attainments of the Blocks of Uttar Dinajpur District, JIEPA, New Delhi*

17. Batliwala,S. (1994): *The Meaning of Empowerment: New Concepts from Action, In Population Policies Reconsidered: Health, Empowerment and Rights*, Eds G.Sen, A. Germain and L.C. Chen. Cambridge, MA: Harvard University Press

18. Bilkis,S. (2005): Girls Education and Empowerment: Impact of Secondary Level Schooling on Women's Lives in Bangladesh, Ph.D. Study. University of Dhaka

19. Borg & Gall (2003): Educational Research: An Introduction (7th Edition), British Journal of Educational Studies.

20. Bryan, A (2004): *Social Research Methods*, New York: Oxford University Press.

21. Carvey, M. (2012): *Qualitative Research Skills for Social Work: Theory and Practice*, Ashgate Publishing Limited

22. Chanana, K. (2001): *Interrogating Women's Education: Bounded Visions, Expanding Horizons*, Rawat Publications

23. Chanana, K. (2006): *Educate Girls, Prepare Them for Life? The Crisis of Elementary Education in India*

24. Chaudhary, P. (1995): *Women's Education in India: Myth and Reality*, New Delhi: Har-Anand Publications

25. Cohen, Louis & Manion, Lawrence (2007): *Research Methods in Education*, Routledge Publication

26. Department For International Development (2005): Girls' education: Towards a Better Future for All. Secretary of State for International Development. OHCHR (Office of the United Nations High Commissioner for Human Rights).

27. Dreze, J. & Kingdon, G. (1999): *School Participation in Rural India*, The Development Economics Discussion Paper Series, London: London School of Economics

28. Dutta, N. (2022): Universalization of Secondary Education (USE) for Girls. In A. Mondal & N. Snehi (Ed) Dynamics of Women Education in India.

29. Elliot, R. & Timulak, L. (2005): Descriptive and Interpretive Approaches to Qualitative Research, *A Handbook of Research Methods for Clinical and Health Psychology*, pp 147-159

30. Falkowska, M. (2013): *Girls' education in Bangladesh: Lessons from NGOs*, Budrich Uni Press Ltd.

31. Francis, B. (2000): The Gendered Subject: Students' Subject Preference and Discussions of Gender and Subject Ability, *Oxford Review of Education*, 26 (1): 35-48, Taylor & Francis Ltd.

32. Garcia, E. & Weiss, E. (2018): *Who Misses School and How Missing School Matters for Performance*, Washington DC: Economic Policy Institute

33. Ghara, T.K & Roy, K. (2017): Impact of Kanya Shree Prakalpa-District-Wise Analysis. IOSR Journal of Humanities and Social Sciences, 22(7), 27-35

34. Ghosh, R, et .al (2015): Women's Empowerment and education: Panchayats and Women's Self-Help Groups in India. Policy Future in Education, Sage Journal,13(3)

35. Ghosh, B. (2010): Persistence of the Practice of Dowry in Rural Bengal. Journal of Social Work and Social Development, 1(1):1-17

36. Government of India (2007d): Eleventh Five Year Plan (2007-12) Social Sector, Vol-II, New Delhi: Planning Commission.

37. Government of India (2011): *Census Report*, New Delhi: Ministry of Home Affairs

38. Government of India (2018a): Minority Concentration District Project, Uttar Dinajpur, West Bengal, Ministry of Minority Affairs, Calcutta: Centre for Studies in Social Sciences

39. Government of India (2018b): *Educational Statistics at a Glance*, New Delhi: Ministry of Human Resource Development, Department of School Education and Literacy

40. Government of India (2005): CABE Committee Report on Girl's Education and Common School System, New Delhi, Ministry of Human Resource and Development

41. Government of India (2018): Draft for the Implementation of the Samagra Shiksha Abhiyan- An Integrated Scheme for School Education, New Delhi, Ministry of Human Resource and Development

42. Government of India (2019): Draft National Policy on Education, New Delhi, Ministry of Human Resource and Development

43. Government of West Bengal (2010): *District Human Development Report: Uttar Dinajpur*, Kolkata: Government of West Bengal, Development and Planning Department, Saraswati Press Ltd

44. Government of West Bengal (2011): *District Census Handbook of Uttar Dinajpur, Village and Town Directory*, Series-20, Kolkata: Directorate of Census Operations West Bengal

45. Government of West Bengal (2012): *Inventory of Soil Resources of North Dinajpur District, West Bengal Using Remote Sensing and GIS Technique*, Kolkata: Soil Survey Department Report

46. Govinda, R. & Bandyopadhyay, M. (2011): Access to Elementary Education: Analytical Overview. In R. Govinda (Ed) Who Goes to School? Exploring Exclusion in Indian Education, Oxford University Press, New Delhi.

47. Govinda, R. & Bandyopadhyay, M. (2019): Exclusion and Inequality in Education. In Haque, T. & Reddy, N. (Ed): *India Social Development Report 2018: Rising Inequalities in India*, New Delhi: Oxford University Press

48. http://en.wikipedia.org/wiki/Socioeconomic_impact_of_female_education

49. Govinda, R & Bandyopadhyay, M (2021) Literacy and Elementary Education in India: Emerging Issues and Policy Paradigms, JIEPA, October, pp 269-295, New Delhi

50. Hasan, Z. &Menon R (2005): Educating Muslim Girls: A Comparison of Five Indian Cities, Women Unlimited

51. Hill, A.M & King, E.M (1993): Women's Education in Developing Countries. Barriers, Benefits, and Policies. A World Bank Book. The Johns and Hopkins University Press, Baltimore and London.

52. Hira, P. & Das, A. (2018): Disparity in the Level of Literacy and Factors Affecting Female Literacy: A Case Study of Uttar Dinajpur District, West Bengal, *International Journal of Research and Analytical Reviews*, 5 (3): 96-103. Retrieved from ijrar.com

53. Hunte, P. (2005): *Household Decision-Making and School Enrolment in Afghanistan, Case Study 1: Chahar Asyab District, Kabul Province*, Kabul: Afghanistan Research and Evaluation Unit

54. Ishak, N. & Bakar, A. (2014): Developing Sampling Frame for Case Study: Challenges and Conditions, *World Journal of Education*, 4 (3): 29-35

55. Islam, Md. N (2022): Universalisation of Elementary Education (UEE)for Girls. In A. Mondol& N. Snehi (eds) Dynamics of Women Education in India.

56. Indiradevi, M. (1987): *Women Education and Family Living: A Study of Emerging Hindu Wives in Urban India*, Delhi: Gian Publishing House

57. Johnson, R. B., Onwuegbuzie, A. J., & Turner, L. A. (2007). Toward a definition of mixed methods research. Journal of Mixed Methods Research, 1(2), 112-133

58. Kabeer, N. (1994): *Reversed Realities: Gender Hierarchies in Development Thought*, Verso, Crescent Printing Works Pvt Ltd

59. Kabeer, N. (2011): *Gender Schooling and Social Justice, Comparative Education*, Taylor & Francis Publication

60. Kabeer, N. (2012): *Women's Economic Empowerment and Inclusive Growth: Labour Market and Enterprise Development*, Department for International Development and International Development Research Centre

61. Kumar, K. & Gupta, L. (2008): *What is Missing in Girls Empowerment? The Economic and Political Weekly*

62. Kumar, A., Upadhyay, P., Adeeb, S., Chaturvedi, S. (2007): Status of Girls' Education (6-14 Years) in Delhi's Slums. Promoting Right to Education. The India Sponsor Foundation.

63. Kingdon, G. (1996): The Quality and Efficiency of Private and Public School: A Case Study of Urban India. Oxford Bulletin of Economics and Statistics-Oxford: Wiley-Blackwell

64. Lockheed, M. (2010): Gender and Social Exclusion, IIEP, Paris.

65. Majumdar, M. & Mooji, J. (2011): *Education and Inequality in India: A Classroom View*, Taylor & Francis Publications

66. MHRD (2005): *CABE Committee Report on Girls' education and Common School System*, New Delhi: Ministry of Human Resource Development

67. Miles, B. M.; Huberman, A. M. & Saldana, J. (2014): *Qualitative Data Analysis: A Method Sourcebook*, Sage Publications

68. Mollah, K. (2018): Present Status of Secondary Education in West Bengal: District-Wise Analysis, *International Journal of Basic and Advanced Research*, 4 (4): 220-223

69. Mondal, A (2022): Women Education. In A. Mondol & N. Snehi (eds) Dynamics of Women Education in India.

70. Morgan, D. L. (2007). Paradigms lost and pragmatism regained: Methodological implications of combining

qualitative and quantitative methods. Journal of Mixed Methods Research, 1(1), 48-76

71. Moser, C (1989): Gender Planning in the Third World: Meeting Practical and Strategic Gender Needs, *World Development*, Great Britain, 17 (11): 1799-1825

72. Nawani, Disha (2013): Corporal Punishments in Schools, *Economic and Political Weekly*, XLVIII (24): 23-26

73. Nambissan, G. (2005) *Integrating Gender Concerns, Changing English: Studies in Culture and Education*12 (2) pp-191-199

74. National Report of Second Evaluation of KGBV Programme of GOI, November-December 2013

75. NFHS-4 (2015-16): *National Family Health Survey, State Fact Sheet: West Bengal*, Mumbai: International Institute of Population Sciences

76. NFHS-4 (2015-16): *National Family Health Survey: India Fact Sheet,* Mumbai: International Institute of Population Sciences

77. NFHS-5 (2019-20): *National Family Health Survey, Compendium of Fact Sheets: KEY INDICATORS, India and 14 States UTs (Phase-II),* Mumbai: International Institute of Population Sciences

78. NSSO (National Sample Survey Organisation) (2010): NSS 64th Round, Department of Statistics, New Delhi: Government of India

79. Nuna, A. (2003): *Education of Muslim Girls: An Area Intensive Programme*, NCERT: Department of Women's Studies

80. Nussbaum, M.C. (2001): Women and Human Development. *The Capabilities Approach.* Cambridge University Press.

81. NCAER (2011-12): Indian Human Development Survey I & II

82. NCERT (1998), Sixth All India Educational Survey 1993-94, New Delhi, NCERT

83. Paul, S (2018): Government Projects for Women Empowerment: The Impetus for Sabla and Kanya Shree for Empowering Adolescent Girls in West Bengal. In Mete, J., Borah, R., Manna. R., (Eds) Women Empowerment for Girls Education in 21st century. New Delhi Publishers: Kolkata

84. Paul, A (2018): Dropout Rate of Girls Students and it's Problems in Elementary Education in Uttar Dinajpur. In Mete, J.; Borah, R. & Manna, R. (Ed): *Women Empowerment for Girls' education in 21st Century*, New Delhi Publishers

85. Rani, M. &Goel, M.M (2008): Women Empowerment in Haryana: A Study of Decision Making in Household Economy

86. Rajagopal (2009): A Gendered Analysis of Secondary Schooling Process in India. In E. Page and J. Jha (eds): In Exploring the Bias: Gender and Stereotyping in Secondary Schools. London: Commonwealth Secretariat

87. Ramachandran, B (2016): Educational Constraints among the Mukkuva Community in Kerala: Anthropological Insights and Empirical Realities. Indian Journal of Educational Research, Volume-V, March 2016, Pp. 86-97

88. Ramachandran, V. (1998): *Girls and Women's Education: Policies and Implementation Mechanism, Case Study: India*, Bangkok: UNESCO

89. Ramachandran, V. (2018): Heterogeneous Gendered Realities and Multiple Disadvantages: Issues That Frame Women and Girls' education in India. In Sudarshan, Ratna M and Tilak, J. B. G. (Ed): *Gender in Contemporary Education Research, op. cit.*

90. Ramachandran, V. (2017): Education and the Status of Women. In (Eds) R. Govinda India Education Report, New Delhi, NIEPA

91. Rawat, S. (2011): Status and Functioning of Kasturba Gandhi Balika Vidyalaya Uttarakhand, *VSRD Technical and Non-Technical International Journal*

92. Reena, R. (2007): Factors Affecting the Enrolment and Retention of Students at Primary Education in Andhra Pradesh: A Village Level Study, *Essays in Education*, Vol 22

93. Reinharz, S.& Davidman, L. (1992): Feminist Methods in Social Research. Oxford University Press

94. Rose, P. & Subrahmanian, R. (2005): *Girls' Education: Towards a Better Future for All*

95. Rowland, J (1995): Empowerment Examined. In Mary B. Andersons (Ed): Development and Social Diversity, Oxfam Publications.

96. Saha, S and Debnath, G.C. (2016): Status of Literacy in West Bengal: A Geographical Appraisal. International Journal of Applied Research

97. Sandhya Rani, G. (2010): Women's Education in India: An Analysis, *Asia Pacific Journal of Social Sciences.......*

98. Sarker, M. S. (2013): Mothers' Participation in Household Decision-Making Process: Its Effect on School Dropout Behaviour for Girls in Bangladesh, Third International Conference on Humanities, Geography and Economics, Bali (Indonesia), pp 153-158

99. Sarva Shiksha Abhiyan Report (2009): *A Glimpse of Kasturba Gandhi Balika Vidyalaya, South 24 Parganas*

100. Sedwal, M., &Kamat, S., (2011) Education and Social Equity in Elementary Education. In R. Govinda (eds) Who Goes to School? *Exploring Exclusion in Indian Education*, Oxford University Press.

101. Sekhar, T. V. (2010): *Special Financial Incentive Schemes for Girl Child in India: Selected Schemes*, International Institute for Population Sciences

102. Shahidul, S. M. (2013): Household Decision-Making Process: Its Effect on School Dropout Behaviour for Girls in the Secondary School Level in Bangladesh, *International Education Studies*, 6 (1): 132-141

103. Shah, P. (2015) Spaces to Speak: Photovoice and the Reimagination of Girls' Education in India. Comparative Education Review, The University of Chicago Press, Vol-59, No-1, pp-50-73

104. Siddiqui, M.S. (2016) Educational Empowerment of Muslim Girls: Some Reflections in the Context of West Bengal. Indian Journal of Educational Research, Volume-V, March 2016, Pp. 98-118

105. Sinha, K. A. & Pankaj, Prabhat (2008): *New Dimensions of Women Empowerment*, Delhi: Deep and Deep Publications

106. Singh, G. (2018): Elementary Education for Girls in India. In R. Sudarshan & J.B.G Tilak (Eds)Gender in Contemporary Education Research.

107. Sperling, G. Winthrop, R and Kwauk, C. (2015): What Works in Girls Education. Evidence for the World's Best Investment, Brookings Institution Press, Washington, D.C.

108. Stromquist, N. P. (2015). Women's Empowerment and Education: linking knowledge to Transformative Action. European Journal of Education, 50(3), 307-324

109. Srivastava, A. K., (2022): Gender Equality through Curriculum and Transaction. In A. Mondol & N. Snehi (eds) Dynamics of Women Education in India

110. Sujatha, K. (1987): *Education of Forgotten Children of Forests: A Case Study of Yenadi Tribe*, New Delhi: Konarak Publishing House

111. Sudarshan, R.M. (2018): Gender Equality Outcomes of SSA: A Case Study. In R. Sudarshan & J.B.G Tilak (Eds) Gender in Contemporary Education Research.

112. Thangjam, M. & Ladusingh, L. (2018): Socio-Economic and Parental Gradients on Educational Attainment of Children in Northeast India, *Journal of Educational Planning and Administration (JEPA)*, New Delhi: NIEPA, XXXII (3) (July): 183-203

113. UNESCO (2012): *From Access to Equality: Empowering girls and Women through Literacy and Secondary Education*, Paris: UNESCO

114. UNESCO (2004): The State of the World's Children, UNICEF, New York

115. UNESCO (2020): Global Education Monitoring Report: Gender Report, A new generation:25 years of effort for gender equality in education, ISBN :978-92-3-100411-7

116. UNESCO (2020): Global Education Monitoring Report: Inclusion and Education – All means All.

117. UNICEF (2005): Strategies for Girls' education: For Every Child Health, Education, Equality, Protection, Advanced Humanity

118. UNGEI (2008): Making Education Work: The Gender Dimension of the School to Work Transition. Case Studies in East Asia. East Asia and Pacific Regional UNGEI.

119. Unterhalter, E. (2007): Gender, Schooling and Global and Social Justice. Routledge: London New York

120. Verma, N. & Roy, A. (2019): The Study of the Literacy Pattern and Its Differentials in Uttar Dinajpur District, West Bengal, *NGJI, An International Peer Reviewed Journal*, 65 (3): 257- 271

121. Venkatanarayan, M., (2004): Educational Deprivation of Children in Andhra Pradesh: Levels and Trends, Disparities and Association Factors, Working Paper no.362, Thiruvananthapuram: Centre for Development Studies.

122. Vleuten, M. & Jaspers, E. (2015): Boys' and Girls' Educational Choices in Secondary Education: The Role of Gender Ideology, *Educational Studies*, 42 (2): 181-200, Routledge, Taylor and Francis Group, U.K.

123. Velaskar, P. (2018): Education, Caste, Gender: Dalit Girl's Access to Schooling in Maharashtra. In R. Sudarshan & J.B.G Tilak (Eds)Gender in Contemporary Education Research.

124. Wantabe, M. (2009): *Interpretive Policy Analysis on Enhancing Education: Equity and Empowerment of Girls in Rural India*

125. Warner, A. & Malhotra, A. (2012): *Girls' education, Empowerment and Transitions to Adulthood: Adolescent Girls, Adolescents and Youth*, Washington: International Centre for Research on Women

126. Xaxa, V. (2004): Women and Gender in the Study of Tribes in India, *Indian Journal of Gender Studies*, 11 (3), New Delhi: Sage Publications

127. https://www.udkvk.in/about-kvk html (1.17.2021) Krishi Vigyan Kendra Report

128. Yin, R.K (2011): Qualitative Research from Start to Finish. New York: Guilford

129. ttps://dashboard.udiseplus.gov.in/#/reportDashboard/sReport

www.ingramcontent.com/pod-product-compliance
Ingram Content Group UK Ltd.
Pitfield, Milton Keynes, MK11 3LW, UK
UKHW040242300726
14061UKWH00002BD/106

9 798894 981284